Encyclopedia of
AIRCRAFT

Edited by

Michael J. H. Taylor
& John W. R. Taylor

G. P. Putnam's Sons New York

Designed by Charles Elton

Library of Congress Catalog Card Number: 78-53408
SBN: 399-12217-6

Filmset by Keyspools Limited, Golborne, Lancashire
Printed in Great Britain

Contents

Introduction

More than 35 000 different types of aircraft have been built. They range from the famous, such as the Supermarine Spitfire, to the almost forgotten prototypes that never went into production. Obviously in any aviation encyclopedia a selection has to be made and in the present volume a thorough coverage of the major aircraft from all periods is considered to be more worthwhile than brief mention of a vast number of less important types.

This book, therefore, covers the most important aircraft. Many are instantly recognizable but others – not so familiar – are worthy of mention because of their historical significance. Such an aircraft is the Sikorsky VS-300 – for although only one was ever built it was the forerunner of the modern helicopter.

The earliest aircraft listed is the Wright Flyer – because it is officially recognized as the first heavier-than-air machine to have achieved a piloted, powered, controlled and sustained flight. Historians sometimes suggest that a host of pioneers preceded the Wright brothers: Carl Jatho, Alexander Mozhaisky and Sir Hiram Maxim, for example. All of these flew before the Wright brothers but failed to satisfy the strict criteria laid down for an officially recognized flight. It is certainly true that aviation's history goes back a long way. A carved wooden bird in the Cairo Museum, dating back to the time of the ancient Egyptians, has aerodynamic features not found among birds but resembling rather those of a modern glider. Similarly, Leonardo da Vinci designed all manner of flying machines (in the fifteenth and sixteenth centuries) which show that, at the very least, man was by then considering flight with the aid of mechanical devices.

The first manned flights were achieved with hot air and hydrogen balloons. Nevertheless, the true father of aerial navigation is generally recognized to be Sir George Cayley. He not only set out the principles of heavier-than-air flight, but designed and built a man-carrying glider which is said to have carried a man in sustained flight in 1853.

This present encyclopedia is designed to tell the story of powered, manned flight – a truly formidable task. To do this, it relies more on easily understood narrative than on highly technical data, to build up a complete picture of aircraft and events. So rapid has the development of aviation been that, stimulated by two world wars, aircraft today have the ability to destroy whole cities or carry civilian passengers between continents at twice the speed of sound. To illustrate this explosive growth, particular emphasis has been placed on the technological or historical importance of each of the 244 aircraft described. The entries are listed alphabetically for ease of reference, and are supported by technical details tabulated at the back of the book. Details of a great many other aircraft can be found among the pages.

An encyclopedia is not the place for speculation about the future. However, events in aviation occur so rapidly, and sometimes so unpredictably, that several major changes had to be made to this book while in production to ensure that it was kept up to date. For example, prior to the time of writing, most people expected the Rockwell International B-1 supersonic bomber to replace the ageing Boeing B-52s of the United States Air Force. Nevertheless, the project was cancelled in the summer of 1977. The entry on the B-1 remains because it is significant enough to warrant inclusion but it has been modified to record the change in status. Similarly, the future of the Concorde was until recently very doubtful despite its success as the pioneer supersonic transport. This uncertainty too has been reflected in the relevant entry.

In other than the technological aspects it is proper to ask how far aviation has really progressed. Certainly, in the event of a nuclear holocaust, aircraft would be responsible for the delivery of nuclear weapons. In this respect the words of Orville Wright spoken at the time of the First World War are still only too true: 'What a dream it was – what a nightmare it has become!' Nevertheless, it is possible to argue that peace has been born out of deterrent air power; that nations have been brought closer together by commercial aviation; and that aircraft have given speedy relief to the sick, and help when all else has failed in times of the world's worst natural disasters.

Acknowledgments

The editors would like to thank the many individuals, companies and organizations who helped in the preparation of this Encyclopedia, especially Malcolm Passingham who worked on several of the French and Japanese entries, Pilot Press for their excellent artwork, Gordon Bain, the Imperial War Museum, de Havilland Canada, British Aerospace and Rockwell International.

Photographs and illustrations are included by kind permission of the following:

The Aeroplane: 23 (above), 84, 97
The Age: 101
Air B.P.: 163 (above)
Air Portraits: 217
Anglia Aeropics: 106 (above)
M.J.Axe: 145 (below)
Robert D.Archer: 150 (below)
BAC: 30 (below)
Gordon Bain: endpapers, 6–7, 15 (above), 18 (above and below), 26, 27, 51 (above), 67 (below), 94 (above and below), 107 (centre), 130 (below), 131 (above), 134 (below), 159 (below), 175 (above), 190 (above), 206 (below), 210 (above and below), 223 (above)
Peter J.Bish: 22 (below)
Charles E.Brown: 24, 28–9, 52 (below), 59 (below), 89, 199 (above), 220 (above)
R.A.Cole: 161
J.B.Cynk: 187 (below)
L.E.Deal: 78 (above)
Downie and Associates: 181
E.C.P.Armées: 15 (below), 19 (above and below)
Flight: 90 (centre)
Richard Gardner: 107 (below)

James Gilbert: 62–3, 183
Denis Hughes: 178 (below)
Imperial War Museum: 20 (above), 72, 93, 109 (below), 133 (left), 142 (centre), 186 (below), 189 (top and centre), 228 (below)
Italian Air Ministry: 36–7 (below), 55
Laker/Guardian Publishing Consultants: 30 (above)
J.Leggett: 99
Howard Levy: 98 (above)
Karel Masojidek: 164–5
T.Matsuzaki: 145 (above)
Ministry of Defence: 121 (above), 131 (below), 216 (below)
Harry McDougall: 103 (below)
NASA: 154 (above)
Novosti: 168 (top), 208 (above)
Stephen Peltz: 176
Marius Prieur: 21
Pilot Press: 23 (below), 50 (top and centre), 59 (top and centre), 67 (above), 78 (below), 82 (above), 95 (below), 107 (above), 115 (above), 118, 119, 123 (below), 124–5, 126 (above), 127 (below), 130 (above), 135 (bottom), 138 (top), 139, 140–1, 142 (top and bottom), 144, 162, (top and centre), 166 (above), 171, 174, 184–5, 187 (above), 191 (above), 206 (above), 207 (below), 212–13, 222 (above), 227 (above)
Royal Australian Air Force: 88 (below), 172
Schliephake Archiv: 133 (right)
Smithsonian Institution, Washington D.C.: 169, 173
Swiss Transport Museum, Lucerne: 38 (below)
TASS: 171 (above), 216 (above)
US Air Force: 177
Gordon S.Williams: 114

Aeritalia G91 *Italy:* One of the main problems confronting any group of countries that form a military alliance is that the diversity of equipment operated by the armed forces of the various partners makes the provision of supplies and support equipment very difficult. It would clearly be much more sensible if all allied air forces flew similar aircraft, to make logistics easier.

It was such thinking that inspired the development of the G91, which won a 1957 international competition for a single-engined, light strike fighter to equip NATO air forces. First flown on 9 August 1956, powered by an 1837 kg (4050 lb)st Orpheus B. Or. 1 turbojet engine, the G91 proved to be a sturdy and adaptable aircraft, capable of carrying large weights of bombs, rockets and missiles on underwing attachment points, in addition to standard fuselage-mounted cannon. However, although the G91 has been the subject of large production contracts, it has entered service only with the Italian, German, Portuguese and Angolan air forces. So the diversity of types continues, to the detriment of NATO's combat efficiency.

The basic G91s were produced in Italy and Germany as tactical strike-reconnaissance fighters and two-seat trainers. They have been followed in Italy by the G91Y, which differs from earlier versions in having two General Electric J85-GE-13A turbojet engines, giving it much improved take-off performance, better load-carrying capability, and the ability to extend its flying time by switching off one of the engines in cruising flight. Take-off distance can be further improved by the use of JATO rockets, and landing distance can be reduced in forward battle areas by using an underfuselage arrester hook to stop the aircraft once on the ground.

Most popular models with the public are probably the G91PANs and G91Rs of the Italian aerobatic team (the Frecce Tricolori-Tricolor Arrows) who fly their ten blue and silver aircraft at air displays throughout Europe.

Aermacchi MB326 *Italy:* With the high cost of aircraft and tight defence budgets, it is no wonder that most basic and advanced jet trainers are also designed for light attack duties. These dual-purpose aircraft – like the Aermacchi MB326 – are ideal for small air forces that do not envisage a major air-to-air confrontation with purpose-built fighters, but see their role mainly as the suppression of ground forces.

Designed in the mid-1950s and first flown as a tandem two-seat jet trainer on 10 December 1957, the MB326 is powered by a Rolls-Royce Bristol Viper turbojet engine. The first hundred production examples were all for the Italian Air Force, these and subsequent versions forming the major equipment of Italian training units. Since then, constant development has led to many refined versions in two-seat and single-seat configurations, with more powerful engines, additional fuel capacity for increased range, more advanced electronics, higher weapon-load-carrying capability and armour protection for the crew.

The MB326, like other dual-purpose trainer/attack aircraft, has customers in the developing countries of Africa and South America – including Dubai, Zaïre, Zambia, Tunisia, Ghana, the Congo, Argentina and Bolivia. Others are licence-built in South Africa and Brazil as the Impala and Xavante respectively. Although a successor has been built – the MB339 – the MB326 will be flown in many countries for a long time to come.

Aero L-39 *Czechoslovakia:* The Czechoslovakian-built Aero L-39 is the Eastern bloc equivalent of Western types like the Hawker Siddeley Hawk and Dassault Breguet-Dornier Alpha Jet. Intended as a jet trainer with which to introduce new pilots to the techniques of flying jet aircraft, and as an advanced trainer to enhance flying skills prior to progressing on to fully operational types, the L-39 can also be operated on light attack missions armed with air-to-air missiles, rocket pods or bombs.

Production began in 1972, and L-39s have since become operational with the air forces of the Warsaw Pact, except for Poland which continues to fly its own Iskra trainers. In the other countries, including the Soviet Union, L-39s are superseding the earlier Aero L-29 Delfin as the main jet trainers, although the latter are still widely operated in Eastern Europe and by several African and Middle Eastern nations.

Powered by a turbofan engine nearly twice as powerful as the M-701 VC-150 or S-50 engine in the Delfin, the L-39 has improved performance and a cleaner configuration, although it retains straight wings. It also appears to give the rear pilot a better forward view, by virtue of the fact that the nose slopes down at a greater angle. An important point is that the aircraft can be flown from unprepared runways, if required.

The L-39 itself forms only part of a complete training system, the pupil pilot having first been introduced to the aircraft via a flight simulator, a pilot ejection ground training simulator, and other special equipment.

Aero Spacelines Guppy *USA:* Perhaps the ugliest aircraft flying today, although highly successful in their role as transporters of outsized aerospace components, the Guppy family comprised only about seven aircraft in five versions – the original Pregnant Guppy, Super Guppy, Mini Guppy, Super Guppy-201

Aero L-39

and Guppy-101. Development began in the early 1960s, with a need for an aircraft capable of transporting sections of US space rockets. Using an airline surplus Boeing Stratocruiser as the starting point, the fuselage was lengthened by over 5 m (16 ft) and the upper fuselage was removed and replaced with a huge bulbous extension with an inside height of 6.20 m (20 ft 4 in). The modified aircraft was named Pregnant Guppy and first flew on 19 September 1962.

To carry even larger missile sections, the next version was converted from a Stratofreighter, lengthened by 9.40 m (nearly 31 ft), given an increased wing span and powered by four 7000 hp turboprop engines. It first flew in August 1965 as the Super Guppy and was the biggest of the series. From this version was derived the Super Guppy-201, which was basically a production version, although still using an old Stratofreighter as the basic airframe. Three were built, of which two are based in Europe to carry Airbus A300 airliner sections, and have been used to carry Concorde components between France and Britain.

Two other one-offs have been produced – the Mini Guppy and Guppy-101, which first flew in 1967 and 1970 respectively. The Guppies based in the US have now been withdrawn from service.

Aérospatiale Alouette II and III *France:* This is France's most renowned family of helicop-

ters, whose members are used throughout the world in about 70 countries. The series began in the mid-1950s with two prototype SE 3120 Alouettes, which were equipped eventually for use as agricultural sprayers. Production helicopters, originally designated SE 3130s and later SE 313 B Alouette IIs, were used by the French military services from 1957. A total of 923 aircraft were eventually built.

With basic accommodation for a pilot and four passengers, Alouette IIs were supplied to the armed forces of 21 other countries in Europe, Africa, South America and Asia. They are still operated as personnel transports and air ambulances (two stretchers and an attendant), as well as for freight carrying, liaison, observation, rescue, training and as armed close support aircraft. In addition, many countries use the Alouette II as a civil helicopter. Developed versions have appeared as the Alouette II Astazou and Lama, the latter holding the world height record for helicopters, at 12442 m (40820 ft). Demonstration flights in the Himalayas in 1969 enabled it to establish the highest-ever recorded landing and take-off of a helicopter, at 7500 m (24 600 ft).

The Alouette III was evolved in the late fifties as a larger development of the Alouette II. It has basic accommodation for two extra passengers and has improved performance. In all, 1356 Alouette IIIs and re-engined Alouette III Astazous had been produced by 1976, and operation is world-wide. Army versions can carry a machine-gun or cannon, air-to-surface missiles or rocket pods for operations against armoured vehicles and other targets. Naval versions can be equipped with detection equipment and torpedoes for attacks on submarines and surface vessels.

The Alouettes have seen much wartime service during their years of operation, in the Arab-Israeli War, the India-Pakistan conflict in 1971 and in Cambodia.

Aérospatiale SE 210 Caravelle *France:* The very successful Caravelle medium-range airliner was the brainchild of the French company Sud-Est, which subsequently became part of the present state-owned Aérospatiale group. It was France's first jet-powered airliner to go into service when Air France began operations between Paris, Rome and Istanbul in May 1959,

Opposite above Aeritalia G91Y

Opposite below Aero Spacelines Super Guppy-201

Right Aermacchi MB326 in the insignia of the Italian Air Force

Below Aérospatiale Alouette II of the French Army, carrying AS.11 missiles

and the first airliner to have rear-mounted engines.

The prototype had first flown at Toulouse on 27 May 1955, and the first of the 280 production Caravelles and Super Caravelles followed suit three years later. Since then, more than 30 airlines all over the world have flown the type.

Throughout production, which ended in 1972, variants of the Caravelle appeared to improve general performance, increase the maximum take-off weight, lower noise levels, accommodate extra passengers by a stretching of the fuselage, and improve freight carrying ability. The major variant was the 64/80-seat Caravelle III; the final variant was the Caravelle 12, first flown in October 1970, seating up to 139 passengers in a lengthened fuselage.

Aérospatiale Super Frelon *France:* The Super Frelon is the largest helicopter so far built in France, and is a heavy load-carrying, yet very fast, assault, civil and military transport or anti-submarine aircraft, with a boat hull.

Its general resemblance to American Sikorsky helicopters is understandable, as engineers from that company collaborated in its design. In particular, the design and testing of the rotor system was carried out by Sikorsky.

The prototype, based on the design of the earlier and smaller Frelon helicopter, first flew in December 1962 and soon afterwards set a world speed record for helicopters of more than 350 km/h (217 mph) over a 15/25 km straight course. This was a land version, but the second prototype was configured as a naval variant. The first production Super Frelons were delivered in 1966 as anti-submarine helicopters, to provide aerial patrol support for the French Navy's *Redoutable* class of nuclear submarines while entering and leaving their home base at Île Longue. They can also be operated from the French Navy's helicopter carrier *Jeanne d'Arc*. In operation, three or four Super Frelons normally patrol together, each carrying submarine detecting and tracking equipment and attack weapons, including homing torpedoes.

Other versions of the Super Frelon are military transports, having accommodation for internal or external freight, up to 30 troops, 15 stretchers and attendants, or rescue equipment. Civil airliner versions seat up to 37 passengers.

Super Frelons are flown in France and eight other countries including the People's Republic of China.

Aérospatiale/Westland Gazelle *France/Great Britain:* Designed as a modern successor to the Aérospatiale Alouette II helicopter, the Gazelle is a small but high-speed five-seater which is produced in both military and civil forms. The design originated in France, but, under an agreement with Westland Helicopters signed in 1967, Gazelles are also assembled in England. Well over 700 have been sold to military and civil operators in some 26 countries around the world, although the main operators of the military versions are the French Army and all of the British services. Kuwait is a major operator of the export military model, as is Yugoslavia, which builds its own Gazelles under licence.

Although the Gazelle has five seats, or can carry freight or stretchers, it is also a highly effective armed attack helicopter, and can carry a wide range of anti-tank missiles, rockets, and guns in electrically operated turrets. It also holds several speed records for its class of helicopter, including one of 312 km/h (nearly 194 mph) achieved over a 15/25 km straight course.

Aérospatiale/Westland Puma *France/Great Britain:* Developed initially by Aérospatiale as a medium-size tactical assault helicopter for the French Army, the Puma is, however, in widespread military and civil service throughout the world.

Its design originated in the early 1960s, and by April 1965 the first of the prototypes had taken to the air. Production in France began in 1968, a year after an agreement had been signed with Westland Helicopters of England which allowed them to produce some components and to assemble the 40 helicopters ordered for the Royal Air Force.

In operation, the Puma can carry up to 20 armed troops in the main cabin, or can accommodate freight or six stretchers and four sitting casualties. Various combinations of missiles and guns can also be installed. It first became active with the French Army in mid-1970, and a year later with No 33 Squadron of the RAF. The French Air Force also has a few in service. Others have been exported to countries in Europe, South America and Africa.

The civil version followed later, the first examples not flying until September 1969. It offers several alternative interiors – 17 seats are normally provided, although a 20-passenger high-density arrangement is available, plus 8/12-seat VIP layouts.

High performance of the Puma has been achieved by a combination of streamlined fuselage design, the installation of two powerful turboshaft engines, and the use of a semi-retractable undercarriage. All these factors, plus the advanced technology that has been incorporated throughout the design, ensure that Puma sales can match the French production schedule of eight aircraft per month.

The current production versions of the Puma are the SA 330J and SA 330L, civil and military versions respectively. By mid-1977 a total of 531 Pumas of all versions had been sold.

Aichi D3A *Japan:* On 5 April 1942, 80 Aichi D3A1 dive-bombers, launched from five aircraft carriers of the Japanese Fleet in the Indian Ocean, sank two British cruisers, HMS *Cornwall* and HMS *Dorsetshire,* in under 20 minutes. On 9 April, off Ceylon, these

Aichi D3A1 carrier-based
torpedo bomber

same bombers, led by Lt. Commander Egusa, sent the carrier HMS *Hermes* to the bottom in even shorter time!

The original flight trials of the Aichi D3A, distinguished by its elliptical wing shape, had taken place in January 1938. The production D3A1 (known to the Allies as 'Val') went into service in 1939 and fought in all the major Japanese fleet actions. At Pearl Harbor, D3A1s had as their main targets American aerodromes. Next came attacks on Wake Island, and then the Coral Sea battle, where D3A1s participated in the destruction of the US carrier *Lexington*. At Midway, in June 1942, they were instrumental in sinking the USS *Yorktown*, but all 81 D3A1s engaged in that battle were lost when the Japanese carrier force was totally destroyed. At Santa Cruz, in October 1942, D3A1s crippled the USS *Hornet*. The more powerful D3A2 version participated in the Philippine Sea and Leyte Gulf battles, while land-based Vals were operational throughout the Pacific, ending as suicide bombers in defence of the Japanese home islands.

The D3A, designated Type 99 carrier-based dive-bomber by the Japanese Navy, was a robust and workmanlike design, powered by a large radial engine and fitted with a fixed, spatted undercarriage. The two crew members were housed under a glazed canopy, where lack of protection for them and the fuel tanks caused heavy losses as the war progressed.

For its specialized dive-bombing role, Val had underwing dive-brakes and a special mechanism which lowered the 250 kg (550 lb) bomb forward and down to clear the propeller for release.

Deliveries totalled 478 D3A1s and 816 D3A2s by the time manufacture ended in 1944.

Airbus Industrie A300 *France/West Germany/ Great Britain/the Netherlands/Spain:* The 220 /336-seat Airbus A300 was the first truly multinational airliner to be produced in the world

– with companies from five countries participating in its design, development and manufacture.

Originally Britain and France, with the Concorde programme well under way, set up the Airbus Industrie company to manage development of the short-to-medium-range A300 widebodied airliner. Soon Germany entered the consortium but, because by 1969 no firm orders had been received, Britain withdrew. This left the French company Aérospatiale and Deutsche Airbus (a German company made up of MBB and VFW-Fokker) to continue with the project. Although the British government had opted out, Hawker Siddeley decided to participate privately and was made responsible for the wings and wing-attached structures. Meanwhile, Fokker-VFW of the Netherlands and CASA of Spain had joined Airbus Industrie.

Powered by two General Electric engines (although any similar advanced turbofan engines can be installed in production models), the first prototype made its maiden flight on 28 October 1972. Since then three production versions have been built – the A300B2-100 which began scheduled services with Air France on 23 May 1974, the A300B2-200 for operations to and from airports in hot climates or at high altitudes, and the A300B4 long-range development of the B2. A freighter version, the A300C4 is also available.

By the summer of 1977, A300 orders stood at 50 aircraft (with options held on 23 more) and 33 had been delivered to various airlines including Air Inter, Lufthansa, Korean Air Lines, Air France, and South African Airways. Despite these relatively small totals, the A300 remains one of the world's most promising airliners.

Albatros D.I-D.V *Germany:* From the autumn of 1915 Germany began the virtual elimination of the Allied air forces from the skies over the Western Front. The 'Fokker scourge' persisted until the early months of 1916, when British D.H.2s and other Allied fighters began to prove superior to the German machines. In a bid to regain air superiority, Germany soon fielded a new and very neat biplane fighter known as the Albatros D.I. This and the later D.II/III improved models had far higher speeds and better manoeuvrability than the British D.H.2s, F.E.2s and B.E.2cs, and demonstrated marked superiority over early French Nieuports.

The Albatros fighters had streamlined semimonocoque fuselages of wood, and a large spinner on the propeller. These design features, together with a powerful and smoothly-cowled engine of at least 150 hp, gave the Albatros good enough performance to regain air supremacy. Many top German 'aces' flew Albatros fighters, including the Red Baron himself, Manfred von Richthofen. Soon, British B.E.2cs were again falling like flies, and gaudily-painted squadrons of German fighters were the terror of the Allies.

Confident of their re-established superiority, the German authorities sat back and devoted

Aérospatiale Super
Caravelle of Finnair

Aérospatiale Super Frelon
of the French Navy

Aérospatiale/Westland SA 341F Gazelle of the French Army

Aérospatiale/Westland SA 330 Puma of the French Army

near-massacre and begun to take control of the air-space with new fighters like the S.E.5, Sopwith Camel and SPAD VII. The Albatros was clearly a fighter of the past; and even when German units began operating Fokker Triplanes, it proved impossible to redress the balance.

Amiot 143M *France:* Against a background of blue sky, a small group of 13 old and lumbering shoulder-wing monoplanes made slowly for the town of Sedan in north-east France. The date was 14 May 1940, and the future of France was in doubt. The aircraft were Amiot 143 heavy bombers of the Armée de l'Air, a type developed from an earlier Amiot design of 1928. Although they were well and truly obsolete, this was no training flight. The CO of Groupe GB.I/34, Commandant de Laubier, knowing the nature of the mission, had taken his place as a crew member.

The formation turned sharply for its run-in. The Amiot 143s of Groupement 9 made for the northern approaches of the town, while the other six machines, of Groupement 10, flew on to the bridges over the River Meuse. Suddenly, German Messerschmitt Bf 109E and Bf 110 fighters attacked. Next, the fighters gave way to the flak of the German anti-aircraft batteries. In the final tally the targets had suffered little, but few of the French bombers returned safely. Of Groupement 9's aircraft only one got back; but

most of their continuing war effort to other aspects of the struggle. The Albatros D.III gave way to the Albatros D.V in the summer of 1917, but this fighter was only marginally faster and a little more manoeuvrable than the one it was replacing. Also, its construction was weak, and several D.Vs broke up in the air. Despite this, many D.Vs were built and at their peak in May 1918 more than 1050 were in service at the Western Front, in Palestine and Italy.

In the meantime the Allies had survived the

miraculously only one crew – five men – were lost.

Lack of suitable modern aircraft, and the crisis that France faced a mere four days after the German *Blitzkrieg* breakthrough, led to this last ditch attack on Sedan. It was the Amiot 143 or nothing, to try to hold up the advancing German armies as they pushed deeper into the country.

The 143 was a twin-engined all-metal bomber with a deep balcony under the forward fuselage, housing a bomb-aimer, bomb-bay for up to 900 kg (1984 lb) of bombs, and a ventral gun position. For additional defence, gun turrets were placed in the nose and mid-upper fuselage. A large fixed and spatted undercarriage was fitted.

A total of 153 Amiot 143s were built up to March 1938. The type first entered service in 1935, and at the outbreak of war five bomber groupes still flew 143s. After dropping leaflets over Germany in a vain attempt to deter German forces from attacking France, Amiot 143s went into action immediately when the Battle of France began, the raid on Sedan being their most famous action. After the French collapse, many survived in Vichy France and in North Africa, most of them serving as transports. The last was withdrawn from flying duties in February 1944.

Antoinette *France:* In the period of aviation which most historians call the 'Pioneering Age', most aircraft were biplanes. Of the few monoplanes produced during that time, two spring readily to mind as exceptional – the Blériot and the large Antoinette, both built in France.

The Antoinette was named after the daughter of the man for whom Léon Levavasseur first designed the aircraft. The Models IV and V established the basic configuration from 1908 onwards; during the following years many minor refinements were added to improve handling (notably changing from wing warping to aileron lateral control) and performance. The engines that powered the aircraft were also named Antoinette and were used widely throughout Europe.

The best-known pilot of an Antoinette was the Englishman Hubert Latham who, had his engine not failed, might have over-shadowed Louis Blériot by becoming the first to fly the English Channel in a heavier-than-air machine. On 19 July 1909, six days before Blériot's successful crossing, Latham took off in his Antoinette VII from Sangatte, near Calais, France, in an attempt to cross the Channel and win a £1000 prize offered by the *Daily Mail* newspaper. Unfortunately, after only six or eight miles had been covered, his engine stopped and Latham went down into the water. The French naval ship *Harpon* was nearby to pick him up, but the Antoinette was found to be heavily damaged.

Undeterred by Blériot's successful crossing on the 25th, Latham tried again to cross the Channel two days later, but again made a watery landing, this time only one mile from the Dover coast.

Antonov An-2 *USSR:* 'Don't judge the book by its cover' is a worthwhile reminder when sighting an An-2 for the first time. Antiquated it may look – a biplane it is – yet, as a big, powerful, general-purpose and utility transport aircraft it can fly into outback villages where runways have never been thought of, and then take off again after a run of only 170 m (560 ft).

Above Arado Ar 234 Blitz

Opposite above Airbus Industrie A300 of Lufthansa

Opposite below Antonov An-2

The An-2 has been in continuous production since making its first flight in August 1947, with only slight alterations. More than 5000 were built in the Soviet Union up to 1960, for both the civil and military authorities. Main roles are those of passenger transport for 12 adults and two children, and as an agricultural aircraft for spraying crops and hillsides with liquid or dry chemicals.

Other tasks for which the An-2 has been adapted include water-bombing forest fires, ambulance work (carrying six stretchers), freight carrying, geophysical survey and photogrammetry work, paratroop training, and executive transport for VIPs. Versions have also appeared with twin floats for seaplane operations.

Since 1960, over 6500 An-2s have been built almost exclusively in Poland by the WSK-PZL-Mielec company. As well as exporting many An-2s to other communist countries, a few have been sold to France and the Netherlands, supplementing earlier Soviet-built An-2s which also went abroad – some to Greece, Nepal and India. China has licence-built An-2s since 1957, as Fong Shou No 2s. Polish operators have carried out agricultural operations in several Middle Eastern and North African countries with these Antonov aircraft.

Arado Ar 234 Blitz *Germany:* Before and during the Second World War the Arado Company built several different types of military aircraft, including the Ar 96B trainer, Ar 196 twin-float reconnaissance seaplane, Ar 232 heavy transport (with a 25-wheeled undercarriage) and the Ar 240 heavy interceptor – none of which had the war-winning potential of the Ar 234.

Having developed experimental turbojet engines, Germany was quick to see their potential for powering combat aircraft. With work already started on the Messerschmitt Me 262 and the Heinkel He 280 fighters, Arado began, in 1940, to design a twin-jet reconnaissance aircraft. Because of the intended service ceiling of the aircraft, the Ar 234 was given a pressurized cockpit for the pilot. Another unusual feature of the aircraft was its single central and small outrigger landing skids, take-off being performed from a jettisonable wheeled trolley.

Slow development of the Junkers Jumo 004 engines held up flight testing of the Ar 234. The first flight did not take place until 15 June 1943. It soon became obvious that the skid landing gear was unsatisfactory, as once landed the aircraft was helpless until ground crew remounted it on another trolley. It was therefore

Armstrong Whitworth Whitley Mk V

redesigned with a retractable tricycle under-carriage, under the designation Ar 234B.

The first B-series prototype flew in March 1944, and entered production as the Ar 234B-1 reconnaissance aircraft and the Ar 234B-2 bomber. Development had taken so long that it was not until the autumn of 1944 that Ar 234s began successful, high-altitude reconnaissance flights over the British coast and elsewhere in the West. Within a short time Ar 234B-2s began making highly accurate bombing attacks, the Arado's ceiling of 11 500 m (37 750 ft) and speed of 692–742 km/h (430–461 mph) proving too great to permit interception by Allied piston-engined fighters. With the war nearing its end, only 210 B-series aircraft were built, and many of these were non-operable or grounded because of lack of fuel.

Nevertheless, the Ar 234 will be remembered as the world's first turbojet-powered bomber. When the war ended a C-series bomber, powered by four smaller BMW 003A-1 engines, was just coming off the production line – capable of flying at over 869 km/h (540 mph).

Armstrong Whitworth Argosy biplane
Great Britain: After the First World War, interest in private flying and commercial aviation became enormous. This was partly because a huge number of qualified pilots who had served with the Royal Flying Corps/Royal Air Force were now back in civilian life and partly because the Air Ministry was selling off vast numbers of new and used aircraft cheaply.

The first scheduled daily international airline service was started in August 1919 by the British operator Aircraft Transport and Travel with a de Havilland D.H.16. Although AT and T's fleet consisted mainly of converted military aircraft, the D.H.16 was the first civil aircraft designed by its manufacturer, Airco. Within four years, civil air transport had grown to such an extent that the Air Ministry was able to lay down a requirement for a three-engined airliner to fly in the Middle East, but also capable of later pioneering services to India, Australia and South Africa. One of the aircraft designed to this specification was the Argosy; three were ordered initially, and the first of these made its

Imperial Airways Armstrong Whitworth Argosy *City of Edinburgh* at Croydon Aerodrome

Armstrong Whitworth
Whitley Mk V bomber

maiden flight on 16 March 1926. It had accommodation for the then remarkable total of 20 passengers, who sat in two rows of wicker seats in an enclosed but ventilated cabin. Even so, the pilot and co-pilot still sat in an open cockpit, high in the nose of the aircraft.

Argosy services began on 16 June 1926, on the London-to-Paris route, in the colours of Imperial Airways. All of the first three Argosies and the later four Mk II versions, were given *'City of ...'* names and soon built a reputation as economical and reliable airliners. In the following year, the Silver Wing service was inaugurated on the London-Paris route, the reduced load of 18 passengers receiving a buffet meal served by a steward.

The Mk II Argosies incorporated several changes over the Mk I version, having 410 hp Jaguar IVA engines, increased range and passenger lifejackets. The Mk Is were given similar engines and redesignated Mk IAs.

On 30 March 1929, an Argosy flew the first leg of the new England-to-India air-mail service; two years later, examples were sent to the

Middle East to fly a section of the England-to-Africa route. Imperial Airways finally ceased operating the Argosy in the mid-1930s, although examples were still used by other airlines for a short time.

Armstrong Whitworth Whitley *Great Britain:* When, in 1936, the British government announced its intention of increasing the strength of the Royal Air Force to keep pace with the German Luftwaffe, several new British aircraft were already at the prototype stage. They included the superb Hawker Hurricane fighter and the Armstrong Whitworth Whitley, a twin-engined bomber of low-wing monoplane configuration. Designed to replace biplane bombers like the Handley Page Heyford which, with a maximum speed of only 229 km/h (142 mph), was obsolete, the Whitley first flew in prototype form in March 1936. The Mk 1 entered service with RAF Bomber Command during the following year.

The Whitley Mk V became the major production version and between 1939 and 1943 a

25

total of 1476 were built. Some were delivered to Coastal Command for anti-submarine and maritime reconnaissance missions, joining earlier versions. A number of Whitley Mk VIIs, with ASV Mk II long-range search radar, later supplemented them. However, it is as a bomber that the Whitley is best remembered – although its achievements tend to be overshadowed by the later, more spectacular work of the Lancaster and other four-engined types.

When war broke out in September 1939, Whitleys immediately went into action. They became the first British bombers to fly over Berlin, on the night of 1/2 October 1939, when they released propaganda leaflets as part of a vain campaign to turn the German people against their leaders. They were also the first British bombers to attack the German and Italian mainlands, in May and June 1940 respectively. With Wellingtons, they remained the standard night bombers of the RAF until superseded by larger types. By 1944 the last Whitleys had been withdrawn as bombers, although some continued flying as paratroop trainers and glider tugs. A small number had also been handed over to British Airways in 1942 for use as freighters.

Avro 504 *Great Britain:* The Avro 504 served longer with the Royal Air Force than any other aircraft of First World War vintage. Designed originally as a reconnaissance type, and possessing a maximum speed of a little over 95 km/h (60 mph) in its earliest form, the prototype made its initial flight in mid-1913. By the outbreak of war, both the Royal Flying Corps and the Royal Naval Air Service had 504s on strength and these were used for both recon-

naissance and light bombing duties.

With the beginning of reconnaissance flying by the RFC over the front lines in Belgium and France, it was not long before the first RFC aircraft was shot down in action by ground fire – on this occasion an Avro 504 of No 5 Squadron. The type soon had its revenge. Following successful raids by Sopwith Tabloids of the RNAS on German airship sheds and other military targets from late September 1914, 504s proved themselves equally suitable for this more aggressive role on 21 November 1914, when three of them attacked the Zeppelin airship sheds at Friedrichshafen.

The second variant to be produced was a trainer, a role for which it was to become immortalized. Of the 8340 Avro 504s eventually built during the war and those built after, most were used as trainers, serving with the RAF until 1933. The penultimate and most famous variant of the design was the 504K, which had a maximum speed of over 145 km/h (90 mph) as a trainer. As with some of the earlier production versions which had found a new role as anti-Zeppelin fighters, so a number of 504Ks were converted for night-fighter duties, with their front seats faired over to allow extra fuel to be carried. 504s also carried out trials in connection with aircraft carrier operations.

The final variant was the 504N, powered by an Armstrong Siddeley Lynx radial engine. Between 1927 and 1933, 570 were built and some were used as communications aircraft and for instrument-flying training.

Avro Lancaster *Great Britain:* Under the cover of darkness, on 17 May 1943, 19 Lancaster heavy bombers of Royal Air Force

Avro Lancaster I bomber of the RAF

26

Avro Vulcan B Mk 2

Bomber Command flew over the coast of occupied Europe on a most secret mission. The crews had been specially trained and the aircraft specially prepared to carry barrel-shaped bombs designed by Barnes Wallis. As the targets loomed closer, the designated aircraft initiated their attack runs at very low altitude. The first Lancaster released its bomb, followed by the other aircraft in its group, and as each pulled away the crew could see the bomb bouncing along the surface of the lake towards its concrete target, striking it and finally sinking and exploding.

Back at base the news broke – Lancasters of 617 Squadron had breached the Moehne, Eder and Sorpe dams in north-west Germany and had caused major flooding of the vital Ruhr valley industrial area. The floods had drowned some 1200 German workers and had cost the RAF eight Lancaster bombers and their crews.

This spectacular venture, and the sinking of the German battleship *Tirpitz* in a Norwegian fjord in 1944, are the best known of all the exploits of the Lancaster, yet it was as the ceaseless night-time destroyer of German industrial centres and cities that it did most to bring the war to a close.

The Lancaster flew for the first time on 9 January 1941 as a four-engined development of the Avro Manchester. The RAF began to equip with Mk Is in early 1942 and used them first on 10 March against targets in Essen. Altogether, more than 7300 Lancasters were produced in Britain as Mks I to VII and Canada as Mk Xs, and they dropped more than 608000 tons of bombs on 156000 wartime missions. Some Lancasters were still flying with the RAF in the early 1950s as maritime-reconnaissance, photo-reconnaissance and rescue aircraft.

Avro Vulcan *Great Britain:* The mighty Vulcan was the second of three V-bombers designed and built in Britain to provide the Royal Air Force with a nuclear deterrent. Unmistakable because of its huge delta wings, which housed four Olympus engines internally, the first production examples were delivered to Bomber Command of the RAF in August 1956. These replaced outdated piston-engined aircraft like the Avro Lincoln, which was itself a development of the wartime Lancaster. Vulcans went initially to an operational conversion unit of the RAF. The first squadron proper to operate the type was No 83. Those which followed included the famous 617 'Dam Busters' Squadron, whose improved Vulcan Mk 2s were the last to carry the Blue Steel nuclear stand-off bomb which had been built especially to arm RAF V-bombers.

When Britain's fast-reaction nuclear deterrent capability was transferred to the Navy, in the form of Polaris submarines, the Vulcan turned its hand to other roles, including tactical low-level bombing and strategic reconnaissance duties. While awaiting replacement by the Panavia Tornado, the Vulcan continues to be a major weapon of the RAF, relying on electronic countermeasures equipment to prevent enemy anti-aircraft radar from detecting it. Of approximately 120 Vulcans built, about 50 remain operational, those deployed offensively being armed normally with 21 1000 lb high-explosive bombs carried in the internal weapons bay. No defensive armament has ever been carried by the aircraft.

Overleaf Avro 504Ns photographed in 1933

B

BAC One-Eleven *Great Britain:* Not particularly remarkable in any way, other than the most important – that it works well in its appointed task – the One-Eleven is Britain's short-to-medium-range airliner: counterpart to the American Boeing 737.

The One-Eleven's ancestry can be traced to the almost forgotten Hunting Aircraft company, which produced the original drawings. Later, the design was adapted by the British Aircraft Corporation and the prototype first flew on 20 August 1963. British United Airways had already ordered ten, as far back as 1961, and it was with this airline that One-Eleven services were inaugurated in April 1965. In the same year, Aer Lingus and two US airlines also began to operate One-Elevens on passenger routes.

By the spring of 1977 no fewer than 227 One-Elevens had been ordered by 27 airlines from all over the world. There have been five commercial versions of the aircraft to date, of which the Series 475 and 500 are currently available. The former has a standard-size fuselage and accommodates up to 89 single-class passengers, although first-class and tourist arrangements can be provided by means of a movable bulkhead; the lengthened Series 500 can carry between 97 and 119 passengers.

Alternative configurations can be provided – the three Series 475s operated by the Sultan of

Oman's Air Force can be converted rapidly from passenger to cargo-carrying interiors.

BAC Strikemaster *Great Britain:* Developed from the earlier Jet Provost (the largest user of which is the Royal Air Force), the Strikemaster retains the two-seat basic and advanced training capabilities of its predecessor, but has a more powerful engine, increased range resulting from the use of permanent wingtip tanks, and a heavier weapon load. These changes enhance its potential as a tactical support aircraft, making it particularly suited to counter-insurgency operations.

The Strikemaster flew for the first time on 26 October 1967, and was an immediate export success. Orders came in quickly from countries with small air forces. Saudi Arabia flies the largest number of Strikemasters – 46 having been delivered since 1968. Other users include the air forces of Sudan, South Yemen, Oman, Kuwait, Singapore, Kenya, New Zealand and Ecuador.

BAC/Aérospatiale Concorde *France/Great Britain:* Few would disagree that Concorde is the most controversial civil airliner built in modern times; yet it also represents one of the finest technological achievements in airliner history. The first agreement covering the development and eventual production of a revolutionary supersonic transport was signed by the British and French governments in 1962. Thereafter the project was dogged by high cost, scepticism and opposition.

It was not easy to design an airliner that would carry over 100 passengers at the speed of a military fighter, and the first prototype

Above BAC/Aérospatiale Concorde of British Airways

Opposite above Laker Airways BAC One-Eleven 320

Opposite below BAC Strikemaster of the Sultan of Oman's Air Force

31

Concorde did not fly until 2 March 1969. This aircraft, known as Concorde 001, was assembled in France; the British 002 flew in the following month. Reaching 'first flight' status was an achievement in itself, for the American contender in the supersonic airliner field, the Boeing 2707-300, was abandoned well before this stage, despite huge financial outlay.

Although completed Concordes have been produced in both France and England, each aircraft is built from sections produced in both countries. The British Aircraft Corporation has responsibility for four of the five aluminium-alloy semi-monocoque fuselage sections, the vertical tail, engine nacelles and ducting, and several major systems (including the electrical and thermal). Aérospatiale of France produces the rear cabin section, ogival delta wings and associated control surfaces, flying controls, and the hydraulic and navigational systems, among others. However, much of Concorde's success lies in the excellence of the four Rolls-Royce/SNECMA Olympus 593 Mk 602 turbojet engines which power it. One of the most interesting features of the aircraft is the nose, which can be drooped hydraulically during take-off and landing to improve forward view, while a retractable visor is hydraulically-lifted during cruising flight to fair the windscreen to the raised nose.

Following the two prototypes, two pre-production Concordes and two static and fatigue test airframes were built, the static airframe being tested to destruction to gauge the strength of the aircraft. Then, from the French Toulouse factory, came the first production aircraft, which flew on 6 December 1973. This and the next three Concordes were flown in Arctic and tropical climates to assess their handling characteristics and performance. One of them made two return journeys across the North Atlantic in a single day, on 1 September 1975.

All was now ready for the world's first regular air services by supersonic airliners. For these, the fifth and sixth production aircraft had been delivered to British Airways and Air France. Both airlines started their Concorde services simultaneously on 21 January 1976, the British company flying from London to Bahrain, and the French from Paris to Rio de Janeiro.

Despite objections from anti-pollution factions on both sides of the Atlantic, the two airlines began flights to Dulles International Airport in Washington, USA, on 24 May 1976. Vast crowds cheered the sleek deltas, which arrived in under half the time of a more conventional airliner. But the future of Concorde remained doubtful. Initially, 74 Concordes were reserved by 16 of the world's airlines; however, after the option system was withdrawn, in March 1973, they cancelled their orders. This reluctance to buy stemmed partly from Concorde's high operating costs, and partly from the controversial nature of the aircraft. Anti-pollution lobbies objected to what they considered to be its high noise and smoke emissions, and Concorde was refused landing rights at many of the world's major airports, on the world's busiest routes. Consequently, the British and French governments decided to produce no more Concordes after the sixteenth.

Nevertheless, on 17 October 1977, the US Supreme Court overruled the New York Port Authority's ban on Concorde, thus resolving many of these difficulties. Commercial services between New York and London started at the end of 1977, with daily services beginning in January 1978. In December 1977, British Airways and Singapore Airlines operated a shared Concorde service between London and Singapore.

Bede BD-5 Micro *USA:* One of the smallest and most sophisticated aircraft yet designed for construction by amateurs is the Bede Micro, a single-seat all-metal monoplane of unmistakable styling. The prototype first flew in 1971 and from that time interest in the aircraft has been world-wide.

Would-be constructors have the choice of three versions – the piston-engined BD-5B and improved BD-5G, and the BD-5J – in addition to the BD-5D and BD-5JP ready-to-fly production models.

The BD-5J is the jet-powered version of the Micro, and has a maximum speed of 444 km/h (276 mph). The small Microturbo jet engine is rear-fuselage-mounted and the constructor has the opportunity of fitting a comprehensive instrument panel. As with the other models, it can be built from plans or from finished components.

A sailplane version of the Micro has flown as the BD-5S. This model was unpowered and had extended wings.

Bell HueyCobra *USA:* The HueyCobra is one of the few modern military aircraft which was designed for immediate use in a specific combat role.

The country of Vietnam in south-east Asia was locked in war almost continuously from the 1940s to 1975. When the French withdrew from the area in the 1950s, they left behind the nucleus of a South Vietnamese air force which was subsequently expanded with ex-American aircraft. In the north of the country a separate air force was formed with the help of the Chinese and later the Russians.

From the mid-1950s the two factions entered into hostilities against each other, with the south spending most of its energy trying to stop the flow of northern land forces. While aiding the south as advisors, the Americans did not become personally involved in the war until 1965, when they found that their sophisticated aircraft were unsuited to jungle warfare.

After mounting machine-guns, grenade launchers and rocket pods experimentally on troop-carrying helicopters in an attempt to suppress

Opposite Bede BD-5B Micro

Opposite Bell UH-1E Iroquois of the US Marine Corps

Bell AH-1J of the Imperial Iranian Army Aviation service

enemy ground fire, it was soon seen that a specially designed helicopter would be needed for attacking enemy positions and armoured vehicles, as well as acting as an escort to troop-carrying and rescue helicopters. Anticipating such a requirement, Bell had begun the development of a gunship helicopter, designed to have a speed of over 320 km/h (200 mph) and to be so slim that it would offer a difficult target from the ground. One other special feature of the design was its undernose machine-gun turret.

As the HueyCobra, it first flew in September 1965, and production AH-1Gs began to reach South Vietnam in 1967. They proved a complete success, and a vast number were subsequently built. As production continued, new and improved versions were produced, such as the AH-1Q and AH-1S anti-armour models, equipped to fire TOW anti-tank missiles and other advanced weapons.

The American military services still have many HueyCobras and twin-engined AH-1J and AH-1T SeaCobras (for the US Marine Corps) on strength; others have been supplied to Iran and Spain.

Bell Iroquois *USA:* One of the most important and widely produced helicopters in the world, the Iroquois made its mark during the war in Vietnam. Huge numbers were operated by the US, South Vietnamese and Cambodian forces for troop and cargo transport, rescue and casualty evacuation, as well as in assault, psychological warfare and gunship roles. The latter led to the development of the Bell AH-1 HueyCobra, which uses some Iroquois components.

Deliveries of the Iroquois began in June 1959, as the HU-1A, the first three versions being built under the Model 204 designation. These provided basic accommodation for six to eight

passengers or two to three stretchers. Many were shipped to Vietnam with the US Army in 1965, and others were exported. When the Model 205 Iroquois appeared a few years after the 204, it had accommodation for up to 14 passengers. Early deliveries of UH-1Ds (the first Model 205 version) began in the autumn of 1963 and these too were shipped to Vietnam. The seven-hundredth Model 205 was built in 1973, and production still continues. Iroquois helicopters have also been licence-built in Italy, Japan and Taiwan.

Commercially operated Model 204s and 205s are also flying all over the world, although the civil versions have not been built in such great numbers as the military ones.

Two other helicopters have been derived from the Iroquois, the twin-engined Bell Model 212 (built originally for the Canadian Armed Forces) and the Bell Model 214, powered by one Lycoming engine of 2250–2930 shp.

Bell JetRanger *USA:* Few aircraft bring to mind the idea of top company executives travelling between business appointments by air better than the JetRanger. For here is a luxury helicopter of fairly high speed, which seats four passengers in a style that is unusual for small aircraft of any type.

The JetRanger was designed in the early 1960s to satisfy a growing demand for a small commercial helicopter, which neither the Bell 47 nor a passenger version of the larger Iroquois could properly fulfil. In general design it owed something to the Iroquois, yet was more refined, for a less rugged market. The prototype was first flown on 8 December 1962, as the Model 206, and production quickly got underway as the Model 206A, powered by a 317 hp Allison 250-C18A engine.

Opposite Bell 206B JetRanger II operating as a flying crane

The original JetRanger was superseded in 1971 by the more powerful Model 206B JetRanger II, which provided increased performance at high altitude and temperature. These versions are now in world-wide operation – by the beginning of 1977 sales of the Model 206 had gone over the 5000 mark, including those built by Agusta of Italy under licence. However, under half of the sales were for civil use; a version built specifically as a military light observation helicopter has been produced as the Kiowa, serving with the US Army and Canadian armed forces.

Bell has also produced a new and more powerful JetRanger III, and continues production of the seven-seat LongRanger. Performance of the latter is similar to that of the JetRanger, despite the LongRanger's increased length, because of the installation of a slightly more powerful engine.

Bell Model 47 *USA:* Disregarding the handful of experimental helicopters that appeared in the late 1930s and early 1940s, and which pioneered the basic tenets of helicopter design and configuration, the Bell Model 47 is perhaps the most important small helicopter ever to be produced. It remained in continuous production by Bell Helicopters until 1974, being modified and updated throughout its production span, and continued to be built under licence by Agusta of Italy until 1976.

The story of the Bell Model 47 began on 8 December 1945 when the prototype first flew, although this helicopter was the outcome of experiments carried out two years earlier with the Model 30. Its place in aviation history was secured early in its career, when it was awarded the first Type Approval Certificate for a commercial helicopter and the first commercial licence (NC-1H) by the United States CAA on 8 March 1946.

Although the first 30 Model 47s were built for the US Army and Navy, and many Model 47s of later versions remain in widespread military service in the US and abroad, it is as a civil helicopter that the type is best known. Civil production began with the Model 47B, which was available in two configurations. The first had an enclosed car type of body and a covered tailboom, while the other had an open cockpit for its two occupants and an uncovered tailboom. Neither configuration remained standard. Instead the Model 47D introduced the famous 'goldfish bowl' cabin that became the trademark of the Model 47.

Able to carry between two and four people, according to the version, the Model 47 can also be flown as an air ambulance (with stretcher panniers attached to the landing gear), freight carrier for internal or external cargo, flying crane, survey and aerial photography helicopter, and in many other roles, including agricultural work. This last role is among the most important both to the Western countries and developing nations. For this task, the helicopter can be fitted with special dust spreaders or wide spraybooms, as well as large tanks to carry the dry or liquid chemicals.

Bell X-1 *USA:* Either Britain or the United States might have had the honour of recording the first flight at the speed of sound – but Britain's hopes were dashed when the Miles M.52 programme was cancelled by the government in 1946, as it was thought 'too dangerous' for a man to fly at such a speed.

The US had no such qualms and went ahead with its Bell X-1 programme. Unlike the M.52 which would have been jet-powered, the X-1 (originally XS-1) was rocket-powered, which meant that it had to be carried into the air by a 'mother-plane' and released at altitude to conserve sufficient fuel for its research flight. During the first flight of an X-1, on 19 January 1946, the engine was not started. A first powered flight was made on 9 December of the same year. Eventually, on 14 October 1947, Captain

Capitano Piazza standing by his Blériot monoplane, in which he made the first airplane reconnaissance flight during a war, viewing Turkish positions at Azizia on 22 October 1911

Charles 'Chuck' Yeager of the United States Air Force became the first man to fly faster than the speed of sound, when he achieved Mach 1.015, equivalent to 1078 km/h (670 mph), at an altitude of 12 800 m (42 000 ft).

Altogether, six X-1s were built, and during subsequent flights a speed of Mach 2.435 was recorded and a height of over 27 430 m (90 000 ft). The X-1 programme had shown that once the Mach 1 'barrier' had been broken, there was nothing to prevent much higher speeds from being achieved. Later American research aircraft flew at up to Mach 6.72 (*see* North American X-15).

Louis Blériot

Blériot XI monoplane *France:* The Blériot monoplane was one of the finest aircraft of its time, and is best remembered in its No XI configuration as the first airplane to cross the English Channel, on 25 July 1909, piloted by Louis Blériot himself.

Blériot's crossing was made during the early hours of that Sunday morning, and it took him 36½ minutes to fly the 37.8 km (23½ miles) from Les Baraques in France to Northfall Meadow near Dover Castle, where he landed heavily at 5.17½ a.m. His route had not been direct – for ten minutes he had been lost when the wind carried him off course – but on sighting the English coast he headed west and arrived to a great welcome. The spot where he landed is marked by a concrete silhouette of his monoplane embedded in the grass of the meadow. For completing the epic flight, Blériot received a cheque for £1000 from the *Daily Mail* newspaper, a prize which Hubert Latham had unsuccessfully tried to win six days earlier in an Antoinette monoplane.

In subsequent years, Blériot XIs were purchased by many individuals and by the embryo air forces then forming. A Blériot became the first airplane to be used in war, when Capitano Piazza of the Italian Air Force made a reconnaissance flight to Azizia on 22 October 1911 to

Above Bell Model 47G

Above right Bell X-1 after its first supersonic flight

observe the Turkish enemy ground forces. Britain's Royal Flying Corps purchased several, which were among the first airplanes to be sent over to France on the outbreak of the First World War. As the first four British squadrons were forming up at Dover for the crossing, a Blériot of No 3 Squadron crashed and the pilot, 2nd Lt. R.B. Skene, and his mechanic, were the first British airmen to be killed on active service. Seven days later, on 19 August 1914 a Blériot, accompanied by a B.E.2b, made the first British reconnaissance flight over enemy territory. However, only a short time was to elapse before more suitable aircraft entered service to replace the Blériots, which were transferred to training duties.

Boeing 707 *USA:* The Boeing 707 was the United States' first production jet airliner, and the aircraft with which that country first gained the lead in commercial jet manufacture.

It has remained in continuous production since the mid-1950s. It was not the first US transport aircraft to be jet-powered; that distinction belonged to the experimental military XC-123A powered assault glider.

From the start the 707 had accommodation for approximately four times as many passengers as the original British de Havilland Comet 1, as well as a considerably higher maximum speed. This, combined with a temporary setback to the British aircraft, helped establish the 707 in world-wide service. The developed Comet 4 was first to open a transatlantic passenger jet service, on 4 October 1958, but 707s of Pan American followed from 26 October and went on to inaugurate the first round-the-world jet passenger service from 10 October 1959.

The prototype 707 (Boeing Model 367-80) first flew on 15 July 1954, and the initial aircraft off the production line were military KC-135A

Opposite Blériot XI exhibited in the Swiss Transport Museum at Lucerne

Right Iraqi Airways Boeing 707-370C

flight refuelling tanker/transports.

Only a short time elapsed before commercial versions were built, a flood of orders from airlines all over the world being sparked off by a large contract placed by Pan American. Production centred around two major series, the 707–120 medium-range versions for up to 181 passengers, and 707–320 long-range versions for 189 to more than 200 passengers. By the spring of 1977 total sales of the 707 stood at 920, operating in every continent of the world.

Boeing 727 *USA:* The triple-jet short/medium-range 727 was the first jet airliner to exceed the 1000 sales mark.

Design of the 727 began in 1959, development costs being reduced by the use of a few components similar to those of the earlier 707 airliner, including the upper fuselage section. However, it broke away from previous Boeing designs by having rear-mounted engines and a high-set tailplane. Basic accommodation is for 134 to 189 passengers, although freight-carrying or mixed cargo versions have been produced, the most important being the 727QC which has its seats mounted on movable pallets for a 'quick change' from passenger to cargo configurations, or mixed layout.

Current versions are the lengthened 727–200, first flown in 1966, and the Advanced 727–200, which is quieter than earlier models and has the 'superjet-look' interior.

Deliveries of the original 727-100 began in late 1963 to United Air Lines, which now operates more 727s than any other airline, although Eastern Air Lines initiated the first passenger service with a 727 on 1 February 1964. Sales stood at over 1300 in 1977, with more than 60 airlines operating the type, in nearly every continent of the world.

Boeing 747 *USA:* The famous 'Jumbo Jet' was the first ever airliner capable of carrying up to 500 passengers. Yet, despite its giant proportions, the 747 has a remarkably fine safety record.

First details of the 747 were released in the spring of 1966, together with the announcement that 25 had been ordered by Pan American World Airways. No prototype was built by Boeing, and the first 747 took to the air on 9 February 1969. Deliveries began at the end of the same year, and Pan Am started services with the 747 on 22 January 1970, from New York to London.

By the autumn of 1977 no fewer than 336 had been ordered by 40 airlines in every continent of the world. Flown as long, medium and short-range airliners, they can carry between 385 and 500 passengers, mixed cargo, or up to 101 970 kg (224 800 lb) of freight. They can be fitted with many different engines, the latest for British Airways consisting of four Rolls-Royce RB.211 turbofans. Perhaps the most modified version is the 747SP, or Special Performance model. Announced in 1973, it has a shortened fuselage (up to 360 passengers) to exchange some payload for extra fuel and so allow longer ranges to be flown. However, it can retain the upper deck lounge and bar of standard 747s.

Perhaps the last word should go to the 747 that has been specially prepared for NASA to carry the Space Shuttle Orbiter during its initial test programme. At first, this involved simply carrying the orbiter during flight, but later flights entailed air-launching the spacecraft, so it could carry out its free flight trials.

Boeing B-17 Flying Fortress *USA:* One of the United States' two standard heavy bombers until the introduction of the B-29 Superfortress, the B-17 was flown by the United States Army Air Force throughout the American participation in the Second World War. Wing to wing with B-24 Liberators, B-17s were used by the US Eighth Air Force based in the UK, to bombard German targets in Europe during daylight hours – a method which resulted initially in very heavy losses.

The Flying Fortress was designed for a competition, announced in 1934, to find a modern replacement for the assorted Keystone biplane bombers then in service. The prototype first flew on 28 July 1935, and went on to win the competition. Boeing then built a few pre-production Y1B-17s (later redesignated B-17As), followed by 39 B-17Bs which entered service in the late thirties. Money was short, and by the autumn of 1939 only 30 Flying Fortresses were fully operational. As the US was not then fighting in Europe it did not seem to matter although, as it became clearer that involvement was inevitable, orders were increased. Furthermore, a small number of B-17Cs delivered to the RAF as Fortress Is quickly showed that defensive armament was inadequate.

The Pearl Harbor attack of 7 December 1941 finally brought the United States into the war and production of the B-17 rapidly increased. By July 1942 the US began forming the Eighth Air Force in Britain, equipped with B-17Es. The 'E' represented an important improvement over the earlier B-17s, in that it had a tail turret, so eliminating a previous defensive blind spot. On 17 August 1942 United States B-17s carried out a bombing raid on the railway yards at Rouen in France. The real offensive, however, started on 27 January 1943, when B-17s of the USAAF made their first attack on Germany. Initially, casualties were very high because they attacked during daylight hours to achieve greater accuracy and because proper formation flying (to enable a group of airplanes to defend each other with cross-fire) had not yet been formulated. Delivery of the B-17G (the major production version) helped. The 'G' was the first variant to have a gun turret under the nose, so increasing the armament to 13 guns.

On 19 July 1943 US B-17s and B-24 Liberators carried out the first bombing raid on Rome; and US bombing in Europe reached its high point in

February 1945 with a 1000-bomber raid on Berlin, escorted by 400 fighters, and the Dresden raid (alongside the Royal Air Force) which caused a massive fire storm to sweep the city.

Meanwhile, B-17s were also helping to win the war against Japan, although by mid-1943 the larger B-29 had begun to take over the major strategic bombing missions. By the end of production, more than 12 700 B-17s had been built, of which a few served with Royal Air Force Coastal Command and the United States Navy for patrol, air-sea rescue, anti-submarine and other duties.

Boeing B-29 Superfortress *USA:* The Superfortress is best remembered as the aircraft which dropped two atomic bombs on Japan – one on Hiroshima on 6 August 1945, and one on Nagasaki two days later. It may thus be seen as instrumental in bringing the Second World War to an end. Apart from that, the B-29 has been largely forgotten in favour of the Flying Fortress and the Stratofortress.

The Superfortress was designed to a United States' requirement issued in 1940 for a 'hemisphere defense weapon'. It was a very streamlined bomber and had for its defence two gun turrets above the fuselage, two below, and one in the tail, all remotely controlled. Compared with the earlier Flying Fortress, it offered significant improvement in speed and range, although neither service ceiling nor bomb load was increased.

Deliveries to the United States Air Force started in mid-1943, and within a year Superfortresses were engaged in bombing Japanese targets from US bases in China and India. Over 4200 were built, and huge numbers were deployed to bring about the defeat of Japan. Nevertheless, it became apparent to the Allies that the Japanese would surrender only after the very last battle had been lost and the last of their fighting forces destroyed. This would have necessitated a massive attack on Japan itself, at the cost of enormous loss of life. Faced with this prospect, and the fact that Allied scientists had produced the first atomic bombs, the decision was taken to drop two bombs on Japanese cities. Japan surrendered within a week. The total of people killed by the two bombs was about 100 000, not including subsequent deaths from radiation sickness. What the casualty figures would have been if an air and sea attack had been mounted instead is an open question.

After the war, Superfortresses were flown for some years by the US, becoming the first heavy bombers of the newly-formed 'Strategic Air Command'. They saw widespread action during the Korean War of the 1950s. Others had, by then, been converted for other tasks including photographic reconnaissance, weather reconnaissance and air-sea rescue, and as refuelling tankers and early-warning aircraft.

Probably the strangest guise under which B-29s flew was as heavy bombers of the Soviet Air Force after the war. Under the designation Tupolev Tu-4, there appeared a Soviet-built copy of the US bomber, of which a very large number were built and operated.

Meanwhile, back in 1944, a Superfortress had been given Pratt and Whitney Wasp Major engines. Improvement in performance was such that, with other changes, the Superfortress entered a second phase of production as the B-50.

Boeing B-52 Stratofortress *USA:* The B-52 is the only heavy bomber of NATO air forces, and will remain so for many years following the cancellation of the Rockwell B-1 bomber. The prototype flew as long ago as April 1952, yet, correctly or incorrectly, a few regard the aircraft as being suitable for operation right up to the end of the century, thus saving money through cancellation of the B-1.

The B-52 was designed in the mid-1940s as a bigger stablemate of the Boeing B-47 Stratojet bomber, which first flew in 1947. Between 1954 and 1962, no fewer than 744 eight-engined B-52s were built for the United States Air Force, of which about one-half remain operational. Later versions have a remotely-controlled rear gun turret, and until recently carried Hound Dog nuclear stand-off bombs, which were their primary armament until the introduction of nuclear SRAMs (Short Range Attack Missiles). Twenty SRAMs are carried by each B-52 – internally on a rotary launcher and under the wings – in addition to H-bombs.

The first B-52s became operational with Strategic Air Command, USAF, in 1955, and examples were soon put on 'air alert'. This involved keeping a number of armed and fuelled aircraft airborne at all times in case of a surprise attack by an enemy, in which case sealed orders would give each aircraft a target to attack. This idea was not only to give a fast response to a nuclear attack, but to ensure that a bomber force would be able to retaliate, even if airfields and other home areas were totally destroyed by the enemy.

During the Vietnam War, conventional bombs were carried by the B-52 and used against targets in the North. Here they eventually proved that strategic bombing was capable of bringing the war to an end for the loss of 17 B-52s, and many lives on both sides. Since that time, B-52s have been modified yet again to improve their low-level capabilities.

Boeing E-3A AWACS and Tupolev Tu-126 *USA and USSR:* The Boeing E-3A and Tupolev Tu-126 (known to NATO as 'Moss') both operate as airborne warning and control systems. First to fly was the Tu-126, designed and built in the Soviet Union. Based on the Tu-114 four-turbo-prop commercial airliner, it carries an above-the-fuselage radar in a huge rotating 'saucer' radome, with the associated electronics inside the very large cabin. About 12 are in service

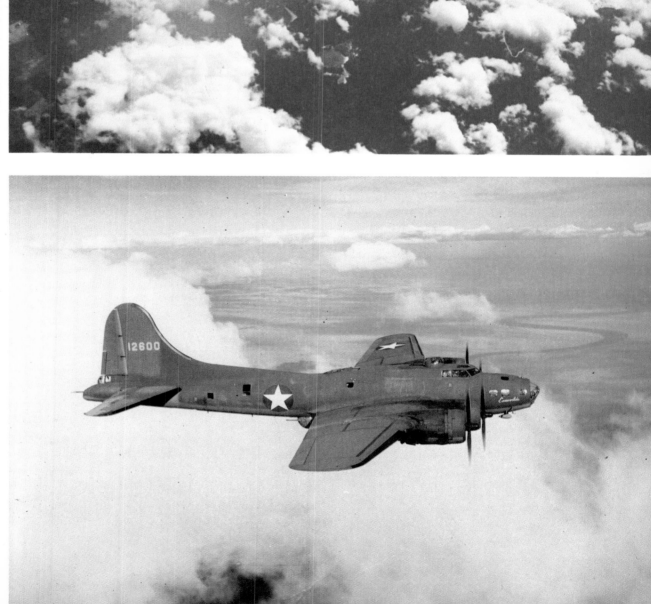

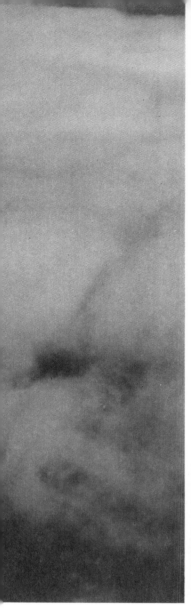

Above Libyan Arab Airlines
Boeing 727-2L5

Left Boeing 747-1D1
of Wardair

Above right Boeing E-3A
AWACS of the USAF

Right Boeing B-17 Flying
Fortress of the USAAF

with the Soviet air defence forces to detect and track from a great height any low-level strike aircraft that fly into their area, and to direct interceptors towards the intruders. Alternatively, the Tu-126 can be used to guide Soviet strike aircraft past enemy fighters sent up to intercept them. However, although the Tu-126 has been operational longer and in greater numbers than its US counterpart, its radar and electronics are thought to be less efficient. In particular they are not considered to be capable of picking out aircraft from the 'clutter' signals reflected back from objects on the ground while flying over land areas. They are more effective over water.

The US E-3A AWACS is based on the commercial Boeing 707, again fitted with a huge rotating radome and associated electronics. The first flight was made in 1972 and the first production examples are now in service. The total USAF requirement is for about 34 E-3As, but it seems unlikely that so many will be built at a time when the US government is trying to reduce defence expenditure.

Boeing Model 247 *USA:* The year 1933 was extremely important in the history of air transport – for it was then that the two original ancestors of the modern airliner appeared. One was the Douglas DC-1, which first flew in July, and the other was the Boeing Model 247, which first flew as a prototype on 8 February 1933.

Although later developments of the Douglas aircraft were to become the most widely used of the early modern airliners, it was the Boeing 247 that pioneered the whole new generation of transports. Around 75 Model 247s were built for customers in the US and abroad, including Luft Hansa of Germany – a creditable total for any aircraft of the thirties.

Early route flying after the First World War convinced airline operators that multi-engined aircraft were preferable for flying long distances and across water, in terms of both economy and safety. However, while huge lumbering biplanes were still the vogue, the Boeing company designed the Model 247 as a new ten-passenger aircraft of revolutionary concept. The all-metal airframe was well streamlined, with low monoplane wings, a smooth oval semi-monocoque fuselage, neatly-cowled twin engines, and an enclosed cockpit for the pilots. The undercarriage was retractable, giving the aircraft a maximum speed of over 290 km/h (180 mph). This was far higher than the speed of contemporary biplane airliners, rivalling the performance of military fighters of the day.

The 247 was an immediate success and the first production aircraft were quickly followed by the refined Model 247D. But destiny still held further success for the airliner. Many great aircraft built between the wars were evolved to take part in air races; such contests were also excellent proving grounds for new or established production types. So, when the Mac-

Robertson Race from England to Australia was organized in 1934, a Boeing Model 247D was entered. Flown by Col. Roscoe Turner and Clyde Pangbourne, it gained second place in the transport section, behind its great rival the DC-2.

Boeing P-12 *USA:* Known as the P-12 by the United States Army Air Corps and as the F4B by the United States Navy, this little fighter was produced in large numbers – despite being active in a time of peace. It also had the distinction of being one of the few aircraft that have ever been fully successful as both an air force and a naval fighter, the requirements usually being so diverse as to make a common design impracticable.

Originally, the US Navy flight tested two Boeing prototype fighters, differing from each other only in that one had an arrester hook for carrier operations while the other had a divided undercarriage so that a 500lb bomb could be carried under the fuselage. Having flown these in mid-1928, the Navy ordered production F4Bs embodying both the arrester hook and the bomb-carrying ability of the two prototypes.

Meanwhile, the US Army had been enthused by the Navy report and, after flying a prototype, ordered its first examples as P-12s. In all, production ran to 586 aircraft in several Army and Navy variants. In a manner that cannot be imagined today, examples of the aircraft – which was clearly the hottest and best US fighter then in service – were sold to private fliers like Milo Burcham, the stunt pilot, who flew a gaily-painted example at air shows.

US P-12s and F4Bs were never used in combat, becoming obsolete well before the outbreak of the Second World War. However, of those exported, one sold to China did see action. This aircraft, called Model 218, was flown by a US volunteer pilot named Robert Short during the war between Japan and China, which began in September 1931. Short engaged three Japanese fighters over Shanghai in 1932, destroying two before being shot down himself.

With the P-12/F4B series, Boeing's faith in the biplane ended. The next series of civil aircraft, bombers and fighters were all low-wing monoplanes – the fighter being the well remembered 'Peashooter' or P-26, which saw action in the Philippines during the Second World War, and was reported to have shot down the first Japanese aircraft.

Boeing Stratocruiser *USA:* Every so often an aircraft appears which does more for aviation than its limited production numbers would indicate. This was certainly the case with the Stratocruiser, for only 55 were produced.

Its development began in 1944 with the first flight of a military aircraft, later named the Stratofreighter. This was a large-capacity transport of striking design, although it embodied the wings, engines, tail unit, undercarriage and other components of the Boeing B-29 Superfortress bomber. Over several years, huge numbers were built, many becoming refuelling tankers and serving right up to the present time with the United States Air Force and others.

The Stratocruiser was simply a civil airliner version of the Stratofreighter. It had the same B-29 parts married to the bulbous fuselage, and had accommodation for between 55 and 100 passengers or 28 sleeping berths and five seats. All versions featured a lower-deck lounge and bar – an innovation which, combined with a long range and high speed, made the Stratocruiser a very popular airliner.

As with many great American aircraft, the Stratocruiser was first introduced into service by Pan American World Airways, in 1949, on North Atlantic routes. Pan American owned eventually about half of all Stratocruisers built, although five other airlines operated the type. BOAC took delivery of its first aircraft in the same year as Pan Am, and began transatlantic services in December. They remained as flagships on the Atlantic run until forced out of service by the first generation of long-range jet airliners.

Breguet 14 and 19 *France:* The highly efficient Breguet 14 day/night bomber and reconnaissance biplane was the finest French aircraft of its type in the First World War. It became operational in September 1917, as a French equivalent of the British D.H.4, and remained operational until 1930. It was also flown by Belgian and American squadrons during the war.

Meanwhile, the prototype of the Breguet 19 appeared, (also a single-engined bomber with normal accommodation for a pilot and rear gunner). Intended as a successor to the 14, it made its maiden flight in May 1922, and production aircraft became available from 1925 as landplanes and later seaplanes. Compared with the rather angular 14, the 19 had a large rounded fuselage, and was a sesquiplane – with lower wings of considerably smaller·span and chord than the upper wings. Engines ranging from 375 to 800 hp could be installed, allowing a turn of speed which made the 14's 180 km/h (112 mph) look rather slow.

The Breguet 19 entered service with many air forces and was licence-built by Belgium, Greece, Japan, Spain and Yugoslavia. Some remained operational as bombers and reconnaissance aircraft until 1940, by which time they were totally obsolete. The Spanish 19s fought during the civil war in that country.

During its long and very successful career, the 19 made a number of historic flights, including the first east-west crossing of the North Atlantic and the first non-stop airplane crossing of the South Atlantic. On each occasion the aircraft was flown by Captain Dieudonné Costes.

Bristol 170 Freighter *Great Britain:* One of the major successes of the Bristol Aeroplane Company after the Second World War, the Bristol Freighter was the standard cross-Channel car- and passenger-carrying aircraft of Silver City Airways from 1953 until the 1960s.

Like other manufacturers in 1943–4, Bristol thought ahead to what it was going to build when peace was restored. As in the case of the First World War, it seemed likely that, following a few years of peaceful austerity, commercial aviation would progress well beyond the pre-war levels of activity. Inventions like the jet engine, and other technological achievements, suggested that the faint-hearted would be left behind. With this in mind, Bristol had already begun to plan a large 100-passenger long-range airliner called the Brabazon. But, while work on the Brabazon continued, a less adventurous aircraft seemed essential, for rapid entry into post-war service.

To this end, the Bristol 170 Freighter was designed as a general-purpose aircraft. However, with the campaign against the Japanese in Burma still under way, the two prototype Freighters were ordered as military transports, with the stipulation that the design should be modified to accommodate an army three-ton truck. The forward fuselage was redesigned to have large hinged doors at the nose, and although the war was over by the time the first prototype flew, in December 1945, this nose-loading scheme was to ensure the Freighter's success.

Surveys showed that both cargo- and passenger-carrying aircraft were needed; so the Bristol 170 was made into two versions – the Freighter for cargo carrying, with nose doors, and the Wayfarer with no nose doors but seats for 36 passengers. Best known of all the production variants was the Mk 32 Freighter, a lengthened model ordered by Silver City which could accommodate two to three cars and 23 passengers.

Some of the 214 Bristol 170 Freighters and Wayfarers that were built were still flying in the 1970s. The Brabazon ended on the scrap heap.

Bristol Beaufighter *Great Britain:* When No 29 Squadron of the Royal Air Force became fully operational with the Beaufighter Mk IF in October 1940, it marked the beginning of operations by a night fighter that was completely capable of performing its task. For although the Bristol Blenheim IF, also equipped with the new A.I. airborne interception radar, was operational, the Beaufighter had two qualities which the other lacked – speed and fire-power. Once a Beaufighter had detected a German night bomber, a single short burst from its four cannon was often sufficient to shoot down the enemy.

Built as a company-funded long-range fighter (using major components from the earlier Beaufort torpedo-bomber), the prototype Beaufighter first flew on 17 July 1939 – by which date 300 Mk IFs had already been ordered. This seemingly desperate measure by the Air

Top left Boeing B-29
Superfortress

Centre left Boeing B-52
Stratofortress, camouflaged
for operations over Vietnam

Below left Boeing F4B-4
fighter of the US Navy,
similar to the Army's P-12
series

Opposite above Boeing
Model 247

Opposite below Boeing
KC-97 of the USAF

Ministry was, by 1938–9, not uncommon, as it helped speed up the production of much-needed combat planes.

As production continued, additional versions appeared, differing in engines installed and in other ways. Beaufighters were used in many theatres of war and for varied duties, performing particularly well in the Western Desert thanks to their long range. Coastal Command of the RAF received several torpedo-carrying versions which were responsible for sinking a great deal of enemy shipping. The last and most numerous was the superb Mk X, which could carry a large torpedo or bombs and rocket projectiles, and claimed among its victories several German submarines.

To the Japanese, the Beaufighter became known as 'the whispering death' – which gives some idea of the speed at which one could suddenly appear, strike and turn for home.

Beaufighters were also flown by the air forces of Australia, New Zealand and, in small numbers, the US. In Britain they remained flying as target tugs throughout the 1950s.

Bristol Blenheim *Great Britain:* The first British aircraft to fly over German territory after the outbreak of the Second World War was a Bristol Blenheim Mk IV of No 139 Squadron – which took photographs of German naval ships at Wilhelmshaven on 3 August 1939. This reconnaissance enabled other Blenheim Mk IVs, this time of No 110 Squadron, to attack the vessels on the following day, so recording the first British attack on a German target during the war. These missions indicate the important position the Blenheim light bomber held in the Royal Air Force of the time. Yet its development was something out of the ordinary.

In 1934 Lord Rothermere, owner of the *Daily Mail* newspaper, had ordered from the Bristol Aeroplane Company a six-passenger aircraft for executive transport, asking that it should be the fastest airplane of its kind in Europe. To this brief specification Bristol built the Type 142, a twin-engined monoplane which was first flown on 12 April 1935 and proved to be capable of flying about 65 km/h (40 mph) faster than the single-seat fighters then in military service. Naming the aircraft *Britain First*, Rothermere presented it to the nation. Its speed could not be ignored and so a military version was ordered. By the time the prototype flew in mid-1936, no fewer than 150 production models had already been ordered.

As Blenheim Mk I light bombers, the first of these entered service in early 1937. The Blenheim I was operated mainly in the Western Desert once the war had begun, although some 200 were converted into night fighters, equipped with the new A.I radar to locate and intercept enemy bombers, and with a gun pack under the fuselage. The later Mk IV featured a longer nose and increased armament (the Mk I only having one forward-firing and one rear-mounted machine-gun, plus bombs) and was

Bristol 170 Mk 32 Freighter operated by Silver City Airways

also sent to less active areas such as the Middle and Far East theatres, once aircraft like the Mosquito became available. The final Blenheim variant was the Mk V, which served in North Africa from 1942. Of the Mk Is exported or licence-built abroad, those of Finland probably saw most action during the desperate struggle against the Russians from November 1939.

Bristol Boxkite *Great Britain:* The Boxkite is perhaps the most famous of early British 'stick and string' aircraft – yet it owed more than a little to the French Voisin design, as refined by the English-born Henry Farman.

First built in 1910, the Boxkite showed its true capability only after it was fitted retrospectively with one of the first Gnome rotary engines exported from France. This type of engine, which drove a pusher propeller on the Boxkite, became the outstanding power plant of its time, fitted to many thousands of aircraft up to and during the First World War. In an effort to discover the Gnome-powered Boxkite's full potential, it was taken to Larkhill where, in front of a staggered crowd, it flew to the dizzy height of 45 m (150 ft).

Production of Boxkites was soon under way, and examples were demonstrated in Australia and India. The important step of introducing the type to flying schools also began, with the

Opposite Breguet 19A2 B2 of 1922, powered by a Renault engine

Bristol Beaufighter Mk VI of
the USAAF

Bristol Blenheim I of the
RAF

Right Bristol F.2B Fighter

Below Britten-Norman
Islander

CANT Z.1007*bis* **Alcione** *Italy:* 14 May 1944 was a disastrous day for the Italian Co-Belligerent Air Force serving with the Allies. While returning from a regular supply-dropping mission to Yugoslav partisans, nine Z.1007*bis* Alcione (Kingfisher) bombers strayed from their escort of five Macchi MC.205 and three Reggiane Re 2001 fighters and were easy prey for about 20 Messerschmitt Bf 109Gs which 'jumped' them as they crossed the Yugoslav coast. Five bombers went down into the Adriatic and two others were severely damaged.

After engine problems with the prototype and early production aircraft, the Z.1007*bis* had been evolved with three 1000 hp Piaggio P.IX radials of proved reliability, and all seemed set for mass production by the CRDA CANT concern. However, by the time Italy entered the war on the German side, on 10 June 1940, only four Z.1007*bis* had been taken on charge, with the 47⁰ Stormo (Group). In September of that year a small experimental unit, the 172ᵃ Squadriglia Ricognizione Strategica Terrestre, flew briefly with the Corpo Aereo Italiano from Chièvres in Belgium. Just one mission was mounted against England, in the form of a diversionary raid on Great Yarmouth, in November 1940, resulting in a field day for Royal Air Force Hurricanes. In contrast the

Z.1007*bis* distinguished itself in action over the Mediterranean, the Aegean, North Africa and with the CSIR (Corpo Spedizione Italiano) in Russia.

Operating in widely differing climates, the Z.1007*bis* suffered from warping of the wooden fuselage and wings; consequently, Alcione-equipped units had a low serviceability record. More than 500 were built by September 1943, in two versions with different tail units – one with twin oval fins and rudders, and the other with a large, curved single fin and rudder.

Caproni 1914–18 bombers *Italy:* Unlike most combatant countries that were involved in the First World War, Italy did not declare war on Austria-Hungary until May 1915 and on Germany until August 1916. While still at peace, Italy built up a force of multi-engined heavy bombers which was then unequalled in the British, French or German air forces.

Development of the heavy bomber in Italy had begun in 1913, when Caproni produced the Ca 30, a triple-engined biplane of fairly large dimensions. Neither this aircraft nor the next model entered production. Nevertheless, Caproni continued development and the Ca 32 did reach operational status with the Italian Army Air Service, in August 1915. In all, 161 Ca 32s were built and with them the first strategic and night bombing units were formed.

These biplane bombers, and subsequent biplane and triplane developments, were used operationally almost from the moment that Italy declared war. However, they had one main problem. Their large size, heavy bomb loads and poor defensive armament left them open to

CANT Z. 1007*bis* of the
Italian Air Force

Opposite Caproni Ca 42
triplane bomber

fighter attack. To remedy this, Caproni began building a new series of smaller triple-engined biplane bombers, possessing higher speeds (although shorter ranges and lighter warloads) and with better-positioned defensive machine-guns, known officially as the Caproni Ca 5 series. The main version was the Ca 46, of which 255 were delivered as day and night bombers from early 1918. Ca 46s were also built in France and the US, and more served with the Royal Naval Air Service, as had earlier Caproni bombers.

After the war, some Ca 46s were converted into first-generation airliners, with accommodation for ten passengers, and were used on domestic routes in Italy.

Caproni Ca 101 *Italy:* With the Ca 101, Caproni once again showed his attachment to the triple-engined arrangement, but this is where any similarity to his earlier wartime biplanes ended. More significant was that he had followed a trend of design that was prevalent in the early 1930s – reflected also in the Fokker F.VII/3m series, Ford Trimotor and Junkers Ju 52/3m.

The Ca 101 was a neat and well designed work-horse. In general layout it had a thick high-mounted monoplane wing and square-section fuselage. Its wide-track undercarriage and three powerful engines gave it the ability to lift very reasonable freight loads from fairly rough terrain, making it ideal as a utility transport. However, although operated as a civil transport aircraft, it was as a military bomber and cargo-carrier that it really made its name.

Opposite Caproni Ca 101 of
the Italian Air Force

Following earlier trials, the Ca 101 entered service with the Stormi da Bombardamento (Italian bomber force) shortly before Italy's invasion of Abyssinia (now Ethiopia), in October 1935. During the campaign it was used as a bulk cargo carrier and as a bomber, carrying its weapon load internally in containers or externally beneath the fuselage. Numbers of Ca 101s were normally despatched to attack enemy ground forces, to enable the Italian army to advance without too much opposition.

The poorly-armed Abyssinian soldiers and horsemen quickly crumbled before the power of the bomb and machine-gun and by May 1936 Addis Ababa had been captured and the war won. With the end of the war the Ca 101 gave way to newer and faster bombers, for high speed had never been one of its virtues.

Cessna Model 172 *USA:* The Cessna company was founded in 1911 by Clyde V. Cessna, an early American aviator. It has since built up a world-wide reputation as a manufacturer of light civil aircraft. In 1977, the company offered no fewer than 58 types in this class, the most notable of which is the Skyhawk, or Model 172 as it used to be known.

Overleaf left Early
production Cessna 172

The Model 172 first appeared in the mid-1950s as the middle type in Cessna's range – a four-

seater of good all-round performance and sturdy construction. As with most of Cessna's aircraft, it had braced high wings and a nosewheel type of undercarriage, and soon featured an optional fold-away 'family seat' for one or two children.

With more than 26 869 Model 172/Skyhawks delivered by 1977, it is Cessna's top seller. Of this number, more than 1380 were built under licence in France by Reims Aviation. The Skyhawk versions, which superseded the standard Model 172 completely on the production line in 1976, had been marketed previously as de luxe models of that aircraft.

As well as being flown by owner-pilots throughout the world, Model 172s and Skyhawks are popular in flying schools and aero clubs and can be used to tow gliders into the air. They are also in military service, those of the United States Air Force being known as T-41 Mescaleros. These are used to give student pilots about 30 hours of basic training before they graduate on to primary jet trainers.

Cierva Autogiros *Spain:* By the early 1920s the development of the helicopter had virtually ground to a halt, following the early, moderately successful experiments of Paul Cornu and the Breguet brothers in France in 1907. It was not until the mid-thirties that the first really successful models appeared, heralding the birth of the helicopter as we know it today.

Back in 1920, a Spaniard named Juan de la Cierva had begun experimenting with a new form of rotorcraft which he named the Autogiro. This was a compromise between an airplane and a helicopter, and Cierva's first experimental prototype was produced by fitting a free-turning rotor to a Deperdussin monoplane. The idea was that the airplane's conventional engine and propeller would enable it to move forward in the normal way for take-off. Air flowing past the rotor would turn it like the sails of a windmill, creating sufficient lift on wing-like blades to raise the aircraft into the air and keep it there. This was correct in theory, but Cierva's prototype, the C.1, and two later models, proved more ready to turn over on to their sides while on the ground than fly. The explanation was that the rotor blades advancing towards the airflow, as the Autogiro moved forward, created more lift than those 'retreating' rearward on the other side. The difference in lift made the aircraft unstable. To obviate this, Cierva invented the 'flapping hinge', which allowed the advancing blades to lift themselves up on hinges while moving forward, and so absorb some of their own excess lifting power, and the retreating blades to fall, and so produce the same amount of lift as the advancing blades. Now the rotor was balanced, and on 9 January 1923 Cierva made the first successful flight in an Autogiro in his C.4.

When the C.5 proved equally successful, Cierva received financial help from the Spanish government and evolved the C.6A from an Avro

Caproni Ca 101

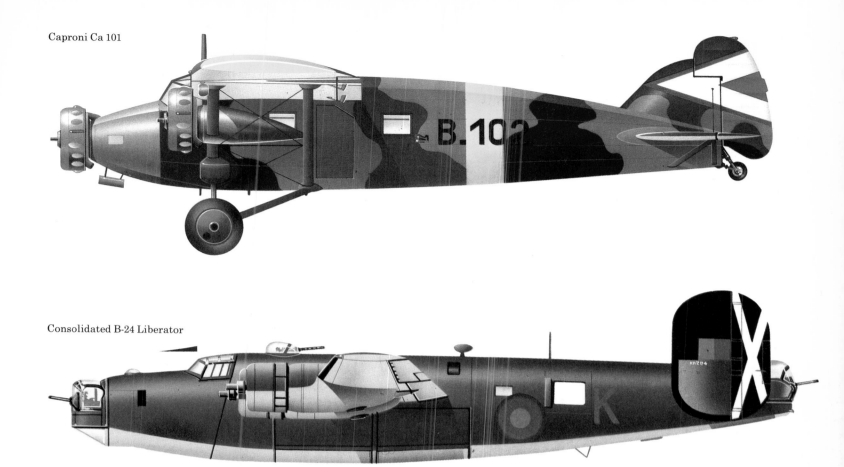

Consolidated B-24 Liberator

Cierva C.19 Mk IVP
Autogiro

Cody British Army
Aeroplane No. 1

504K trainer. This was flown cross-country for 12 km (7½ miles) in 1924, and in the following year Cierva demonstrated this aircraft at Farnborough, England. Success was now assured, and licence production of Cierva Autogiros was undertaken in both England and the US. The C.8L Mk II became the first rotorcraft to cross the English Channel, between Croydon and Le Bourget, on 18 September 1928. Even the Royal Air Force operated numbers of these aircraft as Avro-built C.30 Rotas in the late thirties and early forties.

The Autogiro was short-lived with the military, being superseded by the helicopter with a powered rotor. But small autogyros are, today, very popular among enthusiasts all over the world (*see* Wallis autogyros).

Cody's British Army Aeroplane No. 1 *Great Britain:* Samuel Franklin Cody was born in the United States in 1861 but, after spending many years in England, was made a British citizen at his own request. Like the famous 'Buffalo Bill' Cody of Wild West renown, Samuel Cody was of striking appearance, with long hair, goatee beard and waxed moustache, and he made a great name for himself as a pioneer of British aviation.

Cody began experimenting with heavier-than-air aircraft at the turn of the century, in the form of man-carrying kites. In 1901, he crossed the English Channel in a small boat which was pulled along by one of his box-kites;

Consolidated B-24 Liberator 'Bolivar Jr' flying near Guam in the Mariana Islands in mid-1945

Consolidated PBY Catalina

Overleaf Curtiss JN-4D Jenny, one of the most famous early trainers

by 1904 the War Office had adopted a version of this man-carrying kite for the British Army as an observation platform.

Throughout his career, which ended tragically in an air crash in 1913, Cody worked alongside the Army at Farnborough, now the home of the Royal Aircraft Establishment and the famous bi-annual air shows. By 1908 he had sufficient aeronautical knowledge to build a full-scale powered airplane – the British Army Aeroplane No. 1. In it, on 16 October 1908, he flew a distance of 424 m (1390 ft) at Farnborough, to achieve the first officially recognized powered airplane flight in Great Britain. He crashed the airplane on landing but was unhurt – the first of many such accidents.

Development of Army Aeroplane No. 1 continued, and on 14 May 1909 Cody recorded the first flight in Britain of over one mile – between Laffan's Plain and Danger Hill. By July 1909, Cody had enough confidence in his flying machine to take his wife for a flight, so enabling her to become the first woman airplane passenger in England.

Although real progress in the design of airplanes was taking place all around him, Cody continued to develop later machines on roughly the same 'stick and string' lines, using bigger engines to achieve higher speed. An aluminium replica of the tree to which he used to tether his aircraft, to test their power, stands today at the end of Farnborough's main runway – as a monument to a great man.

Consolidated B-24 Liberator *USA:* Produced in even greater numbers than the other famous Second World War US bomber, the Flying Fortress, the Liberator gained a distinguished war record with its operations in the European, Pacific, African and Middle Eastern theatres. One of its main virtues was a long operating range, which led to it being used also for other duties including maritime patrol, anti-submarine work, reconnaissance, tanker, cargo and personnel transport – Winston Churchill using one as his own transport aircraft.

The aircraft was originally designed to a United States Army Air Corps requirement, and the prototype first flew on 29 December 1939. Meanwhile, orders for production aircraft had also been received from Great Britain and France, who had tried desperately to build up and modernize their air forces for the war which had been inevitable. However, the Liberator was not available to France by the time of its capitulation, and French-ordered aircraft were diverted to Britain.

Among the first Liberators to go into British service were six used as transatlantic airliners with BOAC, while others went to Coastal Command as patrol aircraft. As production in the States continued to expand, taking in other manufacturers to help build the type, versions appeared with varying armament and other differences. Liberators also found their way into the United States Navy, the Royal Canadian Air Force and the armed forces of other countries. In Europe, Bomber Command of the Royal Air Force concentrated mainly on night bombing, while the United States Army Air Force operated mainly as a day bombing force. On 4 December 1942 US Liberators of the 9th Air Force attacked Naples, recording their first raid on Italy, followed on 19 July 1943 by the first raid on Rome by 270 Liberators and Flying Fortresses of the USAAF. Casualties among the US day bombing forces were high, until the perfection of formation flying and the support of long-range escort fighters. This was well illustrated on 17 August 1943 when 59 bombers were shot down while attacking German ball-bearing factories, followed by 60

Convair B-58 Hustler

losses in a similar raid in October. In March 1944 a large force of US Liberators and Flying Fortresses attacked Berlin in daylight, the first of several such raids.

Incredibly, Liberators are recorded as having dropped over 630 000 tons of bombs, while several thousand enemy aircraft fell to their guns. Some were converted to carry the first US air-to-surface, radar-guided missile, the Bat, and in April 1945 a Bat sank a Japanese naval destroyer. After the war the Liberator continued to serve with the United States forces, notably as an air rescue and weather reconnaissance aircraft with the Coast Guard in the 1950s.

Consolidated PBY Catalina *USA:* Active from 1941 until after the end of the Second World War, the Catalina performed a large number of different tasks in the European, Pacific and Atlantic theatres of war. Its appearance in the sky often heralded the destruction of an enemy ship or submarine, by virtue of its heavy load of bombs or torpedoes. Its ability to remain airborne for more than 24 hours on maritime reconnaissance missions also made life difficult for any enemy naval force trying to sail undetected; the enemy knew that once spotted by a Catalina, their presence would soon be known to all Allied warships in the vicinity. A Royal Air Force Catalina of No 209 Squadron was responsible for locating the huge German battleship *Bismarck*, on the run in May 1941, leading to its destruction; another located the Japanese aircraft carrier force in the Indian Ocean in April 1942, which later attacked Ceylon and sank two British cruisers. In contrast, for an Allied convoy at sea trying to elude German submarines it was a protector and for a ditched airman, a life-saver.

The prototype had first flown on 28 March 1935 and a small number of civil examples made some notable exploration flights before the war. Yet it was as a military flying-boat and amphibian that the 'Cat' is best remembered. In all, the US Navy received 2140 Catalinas, while some 660 went to the RAF. Others served with Canada, Australia, the Netherlands, and the Soviet Union, which also built the type as the GST.

Convair B-58 Hustler *USA:* Jet-powered fighters that appeared during the last years of the Second World War left little doubt that the turbojet engine would be the power unit for all major military aircraft of the future.

After the war, air forces all over the world began to re-equip with jets. Fighter units were the first, but as soon as this was under way, the design of jet-bombers was initiated as the next priority. By the early 1950s, the United States Convair company had designed the Delta Dagger fighter for the United States Air Force. A similar delta wing form was selected for a strategic bomber which Convair began designing for the USAF in 1952.

The first of 13 prototypes made its maiden flight in November 1956, and the type was subsequently chosen for production. Becoming operational with the 43rd Bomb Wing of Strategic Air Command in the spring of 1960, the Hustler was the USAF's first supersonic bomber, possessing a maximum speed of over Mach 2.

In all, 86 production B-58 Hustlers were produced, and were unique in that their weapon load comprised a nuclear bomb inside a large metal pod mounted under the fuselage. On early aircraft the container also carried fuel for the outward journey to the target, and was jettisonable; on later Hustlers two smaller containers carried fuel and bomb/fuel/electronic equipment.

Although the Hustler had a short operational

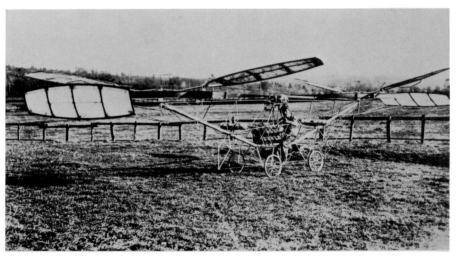

Curtiss pusher being flown by Eugene Ely from the cruiser USS *Pennsylvania* after his first successful landing on deck

Opposite
Above Convair F-106 Delta Darts of the USAF

Centre Convair B-58 Hustler, the world's first supersonic strategic bomber

Below Cornu helicopter of 1907

life, in its time it was rivalled only by the Soviet Tu-22 and the French Mirage IV-A.

Convair F-106 Delta Dart *USA:* Although designed more than 20 years ago, the Convair Delta Dart still plays an active part in the defence of the United States. About 12 squadrons remain operational with Aerospace Defence Command as the heart of the United States Air Force's manned interceptor force.

Designed as a developed version of the earlier F-102 Delta Dagger, the Delta Dart retains most of the Dagger's features, including the delta wings from which they get their names. The most significant change is in the engine, the J75 of the Delta Dart raising the maximum speed from Mach 1.25 to Mach 2.3.

First flight of a Delta Dart was on 26 December 1956 and delivery of production aircraft to squadrons began in July 1959. Altogether some 340 Delta Darts were produced in single and two-seat versions. Subsequent modifications to keep those remaining fully operational have included the fitting of new drop tanks, with flight-refuelling capability, and the installation of a cannon to supplement the air-to-air missiles which are carried in an internal weapons bay.

Although it should not be too long before they are retired from USAF strength, it seems likely that the Darts operational with Air National Guard units will continue for some years,

mainly by virtue of their fairly advanced electronic guidance and fire control systems.

Cornu helicopter *France:* The helicopter built and first flown by Paul Cornu on 13 November 1907 is famed for having made the first true flight of a man-carrying helicopter. This record is sometimes disputed, as the Breguet brothers, also of French nationality, recorded the actual first take-off by a man-carrying helicopter on 29 September 1907. The difficulty arises from having to decide what constitutes a true flight.

The Breguet helicopter was a huge structure of uncovered struts which took on a basic cruciform shape. At the tip of each of the four booms was a four-biplane-blade rotor, all four being powered by a single 50 hp Antoinette engine via belt-drive. The pilot sat under the engine, at the centre of the structure. It managed to take off, but had to be steadied in flight by four helpers armed with long poles.

The Cornu helicopter was much more compact. The 24 hp Antoinette engine drove two two-blade rotors which were mounted at the tips of long front and rear outrigger-booms, and the whole machine rested on a four-wheel undercarriage. Unlike the Breguet machine, it did not require any manual stabilizing in flight, although, to prevent the helicopter from climbing to a dangerous height it was tethered to the ground.

Although tethered aircraft are not normally

credited with free flight, the Cornu helicopter is generally recognized as the first to make a true flight. This lasted about 20 seconds, during which Paul Cornu attained the staggering altitude of about 0.31 m (1 ft). He lacked the resources to continue his experiments after that promising start.

Curtiss F9C Sparrowhawk *USA:* The concept of the parasite fighter – carried by a larger aircraft and launched when needed to defend the mother-craft or to observe or attack targets normally outside the latter's range – has been tried many times. The nearest the concept has come to fruition was during the early 1930s, when the United States Navy ordered two prototypes and, subsequently, six production examples of the Curtiss Sparrowhawk.

The story began in 1929, when two airships were designed for the US Navy as USS *Akron* and USS *Macon*. They were to be the first of a large number of similar rigid airships that would fly ahead of US Navy fleets as scouting aircraft. In the event, only these two airships were built – but from the start they had been designed to act as mother-craft for a purpose-built fighter – the Sparrowhawk.

Both the *Akron* and the Sparrowhawk prototypes first flew in 1931. Following delivery of six production Sparrowhawks in 1932, the first airplane-to-airship hook-on was achieved in June of that year. This involved lowering a trapeze arrangement from the airship, so that the fighter could fly underneath and latch-on, using a 'sky hook' mounted on the upper wing. The fighter could then be lifted inside the airship, which had an internal hangar to house the fighters between flights.

Akron crashed in the Atlantic in April 1933, but without loss of any of the Sparrowhawks. Within two weeks, the second airship, USS *Macon*, had flown and the Sparrowhawks were detached to this craft. Operations with *Macon* were proving a great success when it too was lost, over the Pacific, in February 1935. This was the last straw, and subsequent development of the parasite concept by America was to involve fighter and bomber aircraft. The airship had had its day.

Curtiss JN Jenny *USA:* The Curtiss Jenny ranks with the Avro 504 as one of the world's best-known early trainers, and is the only American-designed landplane to be generally associated with the First World War.

It is not common knowledge that the Jenny was a mixture of both British and US design, Glenn Curtiss having contracted Mr B.D. Thomas (of the Sopwith company) to design an aircraft to his requirements. This was designated Type J. However, Curtiss had also designed a similar aircraft known as the Type N, and the best points of the two designs were merged to produce the JN, known as the Jenny.

The first two production models were built in relatively small numbers, although the Royal Naval Air Service acquired 100 to speed up its pilot training programme for the European war. The next version was the JN-4, and this became the most numerous and best known variant, of which over 6400 were built. Both British air services received large numbers of JN-4s, and these supplemented British trainers in producing the many new pilots needed for the Western Front and other combat areas.

Meanwhile, in the USA and Canada, Jennies were training pilots by the hundred; 95% of all airmen trained in North America during this period were taught on Jennies. The Jenny also became involved directly in a warlike situation, but not in Europe. In March 1916, a Mexican revolutionary named Pancho Villa attacked the town of Columbus, in New Mexico, and killed 17 people. To capture Villa, the US created a punitive expedition of 15 000 soldiers and the 1st Aero Squadron with eight early Jennies, and set off into Mexico. The expedition was doomed to failure, as the large column could not catch up with the fast moving and easily hidden revolutionary forces. Even when the aircraft were on reconnaissance, the pilots found that the high mountains, treacherous air currents, dust and even snow prevented them from carrying out their missions. Within two months all eight Jennies had either crashed, been vandalized or were unfit for service and scrapped.

After the First World War, hundreds of ex-military and unpacked Jennies were sold off to civil flying clubs and barnstormers; others were used on route-proving flights, like the first one across the Canadian Rockies made in August 1919 by Ernest C. Hoy.

Curtiss P-40 Warhawk *USA:* The Curtiss P-40 served during most of the Second World War with one air force or another, and under several different names including Tomahawk and Kittyhawk in Britain and Warhawk in the United States.

The prototype P-40 took to the air in the autumn of 1938, and production was initiated in the following year. Performance of the first version of this single-seat fighter had not really come up to expectations, but as several air forces were desperate for new aircraft, the type was welcomed into service. The US had delayed modernizing its Army Air Service until the last minute, so P-40s made up a large part of their equipment during the first years of war. Britain and France also ordered P-40s to contend with the German Luftwaffe, but in the case of France, deliveries came too late and their P-40s were diverted to the Royal Air Force – to be known as Tomahawks. Similarly, the Soviet Union's outdated air force had fared badly at the hands of the Germans, and P-40s were also sent there.

Not particularly good technically or in performance, though very durable, P-40s continued to be produced until the end of 1944,

Opposite Curtiss Kittyhawk I, a version of the Warhawk flown by the RAF during the Second World War serving also with air force units of Turkey, South Africa, Canada, Australia and New Zealand. Later versions were known as Kittyhawks to the RAF and its Allies. Not usually realized is that the name Warhawk applied only to the United States Army Air Force P-40s starting with the P-40F version, a much improved plane with a licence-built version of the British Rolls-Royce Merlin engine installed.

Many US volunteer pilots flew on behalf of Britain, the Soviet Union and China before the United States entered the war. A group of them, equipped with P-40s, went to help the Chinese in their struggle against the Japanese in 1942, where they became known as the 'Flying Tigers' because of their uniquely painted aircraft. This group later became part of the USAAF proper, and P-40s were thereafter used widely in the Pacific.

Curtiss pusher biplane *USA:* Glenn Curtiss was prominent as a leading designer, constructor and pilot throughout the 'pioneering' period of early aviation in the United States – but his aircraft achieved no greater fame than

Curtiss P-40F Warhawk of the USAAF

when they carried out the first take-off and landing on a ship (foreshadowing the aircraft carrier).

The first of these historic events took place on 14 November 1910, when a Curtiss biplane, piloted by Eugene B. Ely, successfully took off from a 30 m (83 ft) wooden platform that had been built over the bows of the light cruiser USS *Birmingham*. In the event, Ely lost so much height after taking off that he touched the water, but managed to keep control and made a safe touch-down on nearby land.

The second historic event took place on 18 January 1911, when a Curtiss biplane, again piloted by Ely, successfully landed on the rear section of the cruiser USS *Pennsylvania*, which had a wooden platform built on its stern, 40 m (119 ft 4 in) in length. The cruiser was anchored at the time in San Francisco Bay. It had been planned originally to attempt the landing while under way, but this was considered impossible as the huge vessel needed more room in which to manoeuvre. The Curtiss biplane came to rest after travelling along only

one-third of the platform, to the cheers of the ship's crew, who had climbed onto every available viewing point – including the flagpoles. Having had lunch with the officers on the *Pennsylvania*, Ely flew off the ship and returned to land.

Although the US continued development of the aircraft carrier, the lead it built up with these flights was soon lost to Great Britain. The first pilot to take off from a moving ship was Commander Charles Rumney Samson, Royal Navy, who in May 1912 took off in a Short S.27 biplane from the battleship HMS *Hibernia*, while it was steaming at $10\frac{1}{2}$ knots off Portland. British carrier development moved rapidly, and the Royal Navy commissioned the first vessel to carry airplanes, HMS *Hermes*, in 1912, followed by the first ship built to carry airplanes, HMS *Ark Royal*, the first officially recognized aircraft carrier, HMS *Furious* in 1917, and the first flush-deck carrier, HMS *Argus* in 1918.

Curtiss F9C-2 Sparrowhawk fighter, fitted with airship hook-on attachment on upper wing

D

Dassault Mirage III *France:* One of the most widely operated interceptor and fighter-bomber types in the world, the Dassault Mirage III is an all-weather aircraft capable of exceeding Mach 2 at high altitude and Mach 1 at very low altitude. It set the pattern for many modern French combat aircraft, with its delta wings, no horizontal tail surfaces, and a single, fairly large, turbojet engine.

The prototype flew for the first time on 17 November 1956, powered by an engine far smaller than those fitted to production aircraft, but its potential as a lightweight fighter was obvious. If any further proof of this was needed, pre-production Mirage III-As were fitted with auxiliary rocket motors which boosted their speed to Mach 2.2 and let them climb to a staggering 25 000 m (82 000 ft). Such perform-

ance, combined with the ability to take off in a very short distance (even on grass), made the Mirage III ideal to replace the outdated Dassault Mystères.

The Mirage III, in various forms, became the main combat type on which France depends for its defence. Initial production Mirage III-Cs became operational in 1961, followed by two-seat training, fighter-bomber and intruder, and reconnaissance versions. Similarly, the air forces of Israel, South Africa, Australia, Switzerland and others in South America, Asia, the Middle East and Europe fly Mirage IIIs. Those of Israel have seen the most combat, faring particularly well during the Arab-Israeli Six Day War of mid-1967 when, with other combat types, they gained a massive victory over Eastern bloc aircraft, including MiG-21s.

Also in French service, and with other air forces around the world, is the Mirage 5, a ground attack development of the Mirage III capable of carrying up to 4000 kg (8820 lb) of weapons (including two Sidewinder air-to-air missiles in an interceptor role). Belgium is among the largest operators of this aircraft. The

Departure of the first BOAC Comet 1 on a passenger service, with BOAC staff and the press looking on

Dassault Mirage F1, a higher-performance development of the III-E, is a multi-mission fighter with attack capabilities. Major changes in design include the use of swept wings.

Dassault Mirage IV-A *France:* The Mirage IV-A, with its atomic bomb load, became the French nuclear deterrent in the mid-1960s. It had been developed to carry France's original atomic bomb, a free-fall weapon carried semi-recessed in the underfuselage, and was based on the Mirage III configuration (although considerably enlarged and with a maximum take-off weight well over double that of the fighter).

Deployment by France of its own atomic weapons appeared necessary mainly because it had withdrawn its military forces from NATO. It had done this because President Charles de Gaulle refused to have United States nuclear attack aircraft based in France under conditions which did not give the French government control over their operation.

As supersonic strategic bombers, the 62 Mirage IV-As delivered to the French Air Force were designed to be kept in bombproof shelters, from which they could take off directly in an emergency. As the French Navy received its submarine-launched nuclear missiles – and silo-based ballistic missiles also became operational – the Mirage IV-A's importance was reduced. The aircraft now have two roles, as low-level nuclear strategic bombers or conventionally-armed tactical attack aircraft.

De Havilland Comet *Great Britain:* The career of the Comet family was punctuated by triumph and tragedy. For what began as the world's finest and most revolutionary airliners soon ended as several shattered wrecks at the bottom of the sea. Yet, despite the setbacks, the Comet rose again, phoenix-like, to fly with major airlines throughout the world.

The concept of the Comet dated from the mid-war years, when a committee was formed to draw up details of a whole range of civil airliners that could be put into production after the war. Most exciting of the series of types specified was a jet airliner which would take advantage of Britain's leadership in jet-engine development. Design and construction of this aircraft, named the Comet, was entrusted to de Havilland and the first flight of the prototype took place on 27 July 1949. After some modification to the design, BOAC took delivery of its first aircraft and opened the world's first scheduled passenger service with turbojet-powered airliners on 2 May 1952, between London and Johannesburg. In all, BOAC bought nine Comet 1s. Seating 36 passengers, they could cruise at the then remarkable speed of 788 km/h (490 mph). More importantly, they could fly above most bad weather.

The pressurized cabin, apart from being necessary at high altitude, added greatly to all-round comfort. Yet, it was the pressurization system that also caused the Comet's quick downfall. Comet 1 flying was going well, and many other airline companies wanted the plane until, on 2 May 1953, a BOAC Comet crashed soon after take-off from Calcutta, India, and all 43 people on board were killed. On 12 January 1954, a second Comet 1 plunged into the sea off Italy, killing 35 people. Parts of the wreckage were recovered, and it was established that metal fatigue had been caused by the constant increase and decrease of pressure inside the cabin. Meanwhile, on 8 April a third Comet had broken up and crashed, killing 21 people, and all Comet airliners were grounded instantly.

Despite these tragedies, lessons had been learned of value to the aircraft industry. These resulted in some redesign of minor details of the Comet and the use of heavier-gauge metal on the fuselage. Everyone was satisfied that the same kind of accidents would not recur, and BOAC ordered a fleet of what proved to be highly successful Comet 4s, the first of which flew in 1958. Other airlines ordered Comet 4s, 4Bs and 4Cs – examples of which are still flying with Dan-Air.

De Havilland D.H.2 *Great Britain:* The de Havilland D.H.2 was as important to the Royal Flying Corps in 1916 as the Hawker Hurricane was to the Royal Air Force during the Battle of Britain in 1940.

By 1915, aircraft had proved their worth as observation and bombing machines but, to the surprise of the Allies, in the autumn the Germans began shooting down their plodding, poorly-armed and over-stable aircraft in droves. Throughout the winter of 1915/16 air services like the RFC were hammered by the new Fokker Eindecker fighter which had the ability to fire ahead, between the blades of its revolving propeller, by using a synchronized machine-gun.

Still suffering huge losses, the RFC began to receive its first real single-seat fighters in the form of D.H.2s in early 1916. Although these were still pusher fighters (with rear-mounted engine and propeller) – because a synchronized machine-gun arrangement had not yet been perfected by the Allies – the D.H.2 was a very effective machine, with good speed, manoeuvrability and endurance. Armed with one forward-firing machine-gun, which could be pivoted up and down, the D.H.2 could meet the Eindecker face-to-face, and win.

So the Allies gained a measure of air control, but not for long. A replacement for the D.H.2 was too long coming, and it was not finally withdrawn from service until mid-1917, by which time the Germans had regained air superiority with fighters like the Albatros D.I and D.II. (Those D.H.2 squadrons based at home, in Palestine, Macedonia and in other areas did not have to face new German machines quite so quickly.)

Again the Allies faced overwhelming odds, and the courage of the pilots was often rewarded only by being shot down in flames, in an age when parachutes were not issued to pilots of either side. So there was a feeling of tremendous relief when, in the latter part of 1916, the Sopwith Pup and SPAD VII arrived on the scene.

It was while flying a D.H.2 that Major L. W. B. Rees RFC won a Victoria Cross in 1916. Flying alone, he forced down two German bombers and broke an entire formation of ten, after flying towards them in the mistaken belief that they were British aircraft!

De Havilland D.H.4 *Great Britain:* The de Havilland D.H.4 is rated by most aviation historians as the finest single-engined bomber flown in the First World War. This is not surprising, as it was fast enough to outrun all opposing German fighters. Even when intercepted, it could defend itself with forward-firing and rear-mounted machine-guns. It was also a high-flyer for its day, with a service ceiling far greater than the aircraft built to replace it, the D.H.9. It had just one shortcoming, in that the cockpits of the pilot and rear gunner were set too far apart, which made communication difficult. This had been done deliberately, so that the pilot would have the best possible downward view during a bombing run, while the gunner had a clear field of fire in most directions. However, as conversation between crew members was often essential during a dogfight, this arrangement was not satisfactory.

Production D.H.4s were first used on bombing missions by the Royal Flying Corps and Royal Naval Air Service in the spring of 1917. This gave grim pleasure to the British public, as they were being terrorized by bombing raids on southern England by German Zeppelins, and later by Gotha bombers. D.H.4s were also employed as photographic and reconnaissance aircraft, and for anti-submarine and anti-Zeppelin missions. For this last role, the D.H.4 was fitted with upward-firing guns, so that it could fly underneath the airship and hit its belly with fire – a method conceived to offset the fact that Zeppelins could fly at greater altitudes than most aeroplanes.

By far the biggest users of the D.H.4 were the Americans, who had 628 on active service in France at the end of hostilities and went on to build 4846 by 1919. These were licence-built with Liberty 12 engines, and were the first genuine combat aircraft to be mass produced in the US (and the only US-built landplanes to see action during the war).

After the war D.H.4s continued to fly in the United States for many years. Two D.H.4Bs carried out the first successful air-to-air refuelling experiments in mid-1923, while others helped to establish the US transcontinental airmail service.

De Havilland D.H.9A *Great Britain:* After the success of the D.H.4, it was decided to build an improved aircraft, the D.H.9, which would not only give better service (if that was possible) but

De Havilland D.H.2 fighter of the First World War

would overcome the few shortcomings of the earlier type. One major improvement was the bringing together of the two cockpits, to allow communication between the pilot and observer during flight.

To power this aircraft, the new Siddeley Puma engine was chosen. This had a lower power output than the Eagle VIII of the D.H.4A, but was seen as a suitable power plant available in good numbers. Unfortunately, the Puma had not been tested adequately, and encountered endless trouble in service. Thus the unsatisfactory bomber began a period of widespread service on the Western Front and in the Middle East.

As the basic fault lay not with the D.H.9 itself but with its engine, Westland Aircraft was given the task of developing it into the D.H.9A, with a new set of larger wings, a wire-braced fuselage and, most important, a US Liberty engine with a frontal radiator.

However, as no Liberty was available in the UK at the time for the prototype D.H.9A, an Eagle VIII of the type fitted to the D.H.4 was installed. Success was at last achieved, the D.H.9A proving considerably faster than the D.H.9, with a longer range and ability to carry a heavier bomb load. Meanwhile, D.H.9s were still fighting at the Front. Early production D.H.9As, still powered by Eagle engines, became operational in late August and it was only a short time before Liberty-powered D.H.9As were flying. By the Armistice, 885 D.H.9As had been built, although only a small proportion of these had seen active service.

After the war, D.H.9As continued as the standard Royal Air Force general-purpose bombers, serving in Russia against the Bolsheviks in 1919 and later as policing/air control aircraft with the RAF in Iraq, on the north-west Frontier of India, and in Aden. They finally gave up their place with the RAF when the Westland Wapiti, designed for the purpose, became available in the late 1920s. D.H.9As were also licence-built in Russia as R-1s, some still flying in the 1930s.

Overleaf A fine example of a de Havilland Tiger Moth that is still flying today

American de Havilland
D.H.4, operated for many
post-war years as a general
purpose biplane

De Havilland Mosquito *Great Britain:* When
the first Mosquitos became operational with the
Royal Air Force in 1941, the type was already
seen as a multi-purpose aircraft, as the initial
batch of 50 included night fighters, photo-
reconnaissance aircraft and bombers. Yet
nobody could have envisaged that Mosquitos
would also be used as intruders, day fighters,
fighter-bombers, anti-shipping, pathfinder, training and target-towing aircraft.

The prototype had first been flown by
Geoffrey de Havilland Jr on 25 November 1940
and several factories eventually built the type
in Britain, while others were licence-built in
Canada and Australia.

The first Mosquito sortie was made on 20
September 1941, when a single aircraft made a
reconnaissance flight over France. At home, the
Mosquito night fighter, carrying A.I Mk IV
airborne radar, began to take over from the
Bristol Blenheim. By late 1942 the Mosquito
was becoming operational in ever increasing

De Havilland D.H.9A of
No 30 Squadron RAF
photographed during the
1920s. Note the spare wheel
carried on the nose.

numbers, and its unique qualities of very high
speed and long range were clearly ideal for a
particular mission then being planned.

It had been decided that an attack should be
made on the German Gestapo headquarters in
Oslo, Norway, which contained records of
members of underground resistance organ-
isations. Such a mission would, if successful,
help protect those who were supplying Britain
with secret information. Therefore, on 25
September 1942, Mosquitos carried out a long-
range attack on the HQ, accurately bombing
the building and then returning home at high
speed.

Later, in mid-1943, the Mosquito FB Mk VI
was becoming operational. As well as the usual
RAF duties, it was used by Coastal Command as
an anti-shipping aircraft, armed with eight 60 lb
rocket projectiles. More unusual weapons
carried by some Mosquitos included a 57 mm
cannon for ground attack (this devastating gun
was capable of destroying any armoured vehi-

French Dewoitine D 520 fighter

cle), and the 4000 lb 'block-buster' bomb. Even with this bomb on board, the Mosquito could outfly most German night fighters, and on numerous occasions it attacked far-off Berlin and German V1 flying-bomb sites.

Mosquitos were active on D-Day, and right up to the end of the war. Production did not end in Britain until late 1950.

De Havilland Moth *Great Britain:* It is impossible to list everything that the little Moth achieved after it first appeared in 1925, but it had as much influence on the course of aviation as any of the great civil or military aircraft of history.

The Moth was a product of the wave of enthusiasm for low-cost sport flying that existed in Britain in the early 1920s. Captain Geoffrey de Havilland realized that most of the types designed for private flying were too low powered to be practical. The only aircraft that came near to meeting the needs of the potential market was his Humming Bird. But this tiny monoplane was a single-seater, designed originally to take part in a competition organized by the *Daily Mail* newspaper for ultra-light aircraft. So he initiated the design of a rugged and dependable biplane that would be easy to fly and suitable for use as a trainer at flying clubs. When the D.H.60 Moth appeared, it was basically a scaled-down D.H.51, which had been designed as a touring biplane of fairly large proportions. An unusual feature was its engine, which had started life as a large 120 hp power plant, but had been cut in half, given a new crankcase, and named the Cirrus.

The Moth was an instant success, and the Air Ministry set up five new flying clubs equipped with the type. If extra publicity was needed, it came on 29 May 1925, when Alan Cobham (who made several famous long distance flights between the wars) piloted the modified prototype from Croydon to Zurich and back in a single day.

Opposite above De Havilland D.H.115 Vampire T.11 two-seat trainers of the RAF photographed in 1954

Opposite below De Havilland Beaver seaplane

Then, after many Moths and Cirrus engines had been produced, and others licence-built abroad, production switched to a version with a completely new engine, the Gipsy. With this installed, the D.H.60 became the Gipsy Moth and went on to even greater triumphs.

Gipsy Moths were used for sport and flying instruction all over the world, in both civil and military guises. The most famous was named *Jason*, in which Amy Johnson flew from Croydon to Darwin between 5 and 24 May 1930, recording the first England to Australia solo flight by a woman.

Production of Moths continued for many more years, leading to the most prolific, the Tiger Moth, which is still flown today.

De Havilland Vampire *Great Britain:* The first jet aircraft in the world to land and take off on the deck of an aircraft carrier, HMS *Ocean*, on 3 December 1945, the Vampire was also Britain's second jet fighter, after the Meteor, to enter service.

The prototype made its maiden flight on 20 September 1943, powered by a de Havilland Goblin turbojet engine which was installed aft of the pilot's cockpit in the short fuselage. Twin tailbooms were fitted to the aircraft (allowing the engine to exhaust between them) and each carried a tail fin between which the tailplane was attached. The wings were, like those of the Meteor, straight. Such a design enabled the pilot's cockpit to be positioned well forward, giving him an excellent view.

As an 870 km/h (540 mph) single-seat fighter with excellent manoeuvrability, the Vampire F Mk 1 entered Royal Air Force service in 1946, with No 247 Squadron. The Mk 1 was followed by several later versions, including the first fighter-bomber variant the FB Mk 5, in 1949. This was able to carry up to 900 kg (2000 lb) of bombs or rockets on underwing pylons, and an export version was built as the Mk 52. The final single-seat Vampire was the FB Mk 9, powered by an uprated Goblin engine and incorporating several refinements. There was, however, an experimental long-span aircraft which established for Britain a new world altitude record of 18 119 m (59 446 ft) on 23 March 1948.

Of the two-seat versions, the night fighter NF Mk 10 served with the RAF, although it had been produced originally for export only. All other two-seaters were trainers.

Meanwhile a Sea Vampire had been produced by converting an early F Mk 1, and production was later undertaken as F 20s for the Fleet Air Arm. It was a Sea Vampire which made that first-ever jet landing on a carrier.

De Havilland Canada DHC-2 Beaver *Canada:* The Beaver pioneered de Havilland Canada's now extensive range of short take-off and landing (STOL) aircraft, and first flew soon after the end of the Second World War, on 16 August 1947. It had been developed mainly to satisfy the need for a utility aircraft that could

cope with the harsh terrain and climate of Canada, but found huge sales potential overseas, eventually being exported to more than 60 countries around the world. Of the 1657 Beavers produced, the majority went for military service, notably with the US Army and Air Force.

Usually equipped to carry six passengers or about 500 kg (1100 lb) of freight, the Beaver can be flown with a wheel, float or ski undercarriage, and has operated in the Arctic with the American forces. In 1963 a new version known as the Turbo-Beaver appeared, powered by a turboprop instead of a piston engine. This helped to improve the overall performance, and the Turbo-Beaver can carry up to ten persons (including pilot) or the equivalent freight.

De Havilland Canada Twin Otter and Otter *Canada:* The name of de Havilland, although synonymous with first-class military, commercial and light aircraft (from before the First World War to well after the Second), has now disappeared from the aircraft manufacturing scene in Britain. However, in 1928 Geoffrey de Havilland set up a subsidiary of the company in Canada, which still trades under its original name.

In 1951 the prototype of the Otter, a new single-engined utility transport aircraft, designed by the Canadian company, flew for the first time. In all, 460 were produced and among its purchasers were the US Army and the Canadian Armed Forces, which use Otters with wheel, float and ski undercarriages.

In 1965 de Havilland Canada produced as a private venture a STOL-performance twin-engined development of the Otter, named the Twin Otter. The first production aircraft was delivered in 1966, and ten years later, in July 1976, the five-hundredth Twin Otter was handed over ceremonially to Metro Airlines.

With normal accommodation for between 13 and 20 passengers – although special interiors are available for executive, air ambulance, rescue or survey use – the Twin Otter is flown by military and civil operators. To supplement interior space in the freight-carrying role, a ventral pod can be fitted to the underfuselage. However, the Twin Otter's most exciting task is perhaps fire-bombing. For this role, a rectangular tank is carried underneath the fuselage. Over the forest fire that is to be put out, the water or liquid chemical inside the tank is released in spectacular fashion.

Rugged and dependable, despite its pleasing lines, the Twin Otter flies in some regions of the world where no other aircraft can go, landing on all kinds of surface, by means of the various different undercarriages that are available. Some are flown in the Canadian Rocky Mountains, while those operated by Air Alpes of France fly tourists to ski resorts.

Above De Havilland Mosquito B 35

Opposite De Havilland Twin Otter of norOntair

Dewoitine D 520 of the French Air Force

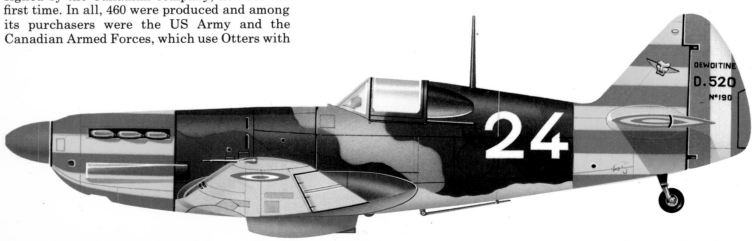

Dornier Do 217K-2, basically a development of the Do 17 with a greatly increased bomb load and powered by two BMW 801D radial engines of 1700 hp each

Dewoitine D 520 *France:* First flown in October 1938, the D 520 could have proved a major headache to the invading Germans in 1940 had sufficient numbers been produced to give the French Armée de l'Air a sporting chance. As it happened, the large number of alterations made to the fighter before production got underway – insisted on by air force technical officials – meant that only 430 were built before the capitulation of France. The French Navy also received about 40.

The D 520 was fast and deadly, and was a better aircraft than its contemporary, the Morane-Saulnier 406. In the event, the more numerous MS 406 played a more important part in France's defence, although D 520s managed to destroy over 145 German aircraft.

After France's surrender, the pro-German Vichy French government chose the D 520 for its air force units, and another 180 of the fighters were produced. After the Germans invaded the southern part of France, many of the D 520s were pressed into German and Italian service as fighter trainers. Some were passed on later to Bulgaria and Romania.

In 1944, when France was liberated by the Allies, the few surviving D 520s were then flown by a newly-formed French fighter unit, which must have enjoyed the irony of flying against the Luftwaffe in French fighters that had been produced by permission of the Germans.

Dornier Do 17 *Germany:* When the Second World War started in September 1939, the German Luftwaffe had three main types of bomber in service: the Heinkel He 111, the Junkers Ju 88 and the Dornier Do 17. However, neither of the first two had created quite as much speculation or even panic before the war

as the Dornier Do 17. This was understandable, for at the 1937 International Military Aircraft Competition held in Zurich, a Dornier Do 17 had outclassed in performance a French fighter thought to be the finest in Europe, the Dewoitine D 510. This must have given rise to considerable concern among French air force officers, although it was later revealed that the German bomber had been specially prepared with boosted engines.

The Do 17, or 'Flying Pencil' as it was nicknamed, had originally been designed as a high-speed mail carrier for operation by the German airline company Deutsche Luft Hansa. Unfortunately, the few civil examples constructed did not prove successful; so the aircraft was modified and taken up by the military as a medium bomber. By 1938, a number were flying operationally in Spain, on behalf of the Nationalist forces, as the Germans saw Spain as a useful proving ground for their servicemen and aircraft.

When the Second World War began in the following year, the Luftwaffe had both bomber and reconnaissance Do 17s in service, and progressively improved versions were to remain on strength right through the war. The first German aircraft to be shot down by Royal Air Force fighters was a Do 17, on 30 October, by the pilot of a Hawker Hurricane. Again, the worst aircraft losses in a day were those inflicted on the Luftwaffe, on 10 May 1940, when British, French, Belgian and Dutch aircraft and ground forces, accounted for over 300 German aircraft, 26 of them Do 17s. However, the attrition rate of Do 17s simply indicates the extent of their service. Do 17s were operated also during the war as night fighters and intruders, with four nose-mounted machine-guns and a cannon.

The extraordinary Dornier Do X twelve-engined flying-boat

A development of the Do 17 was the Do 217, which had the distinction of sinking the surrendered Italian battleship *Roma* with an air-launched radio-controlled bomb, in September 1943. This was the first major operational success achieved by such a weapon.

Dornier Do 24 *Germany:* Based on the earlier Dornier Do 18 twin-engined flying-boat – which had been designed for mail carrying across the Atlantic – the first prototype Do 24 made its initial flight on 3 July 1937. It was intended for the Royal Netherlands East Indies Naval Air Service, although two of the three prototypes passed into Luftwaffe service as transports. Eleven of the Dutch Do 24Ks had been delivered by 1939, and were joined in the East Indies by 26 more, licence-built in Holland. When Germany attacked Holland and forced it to capitulate in May 1940, those Do 24s still on the assembly line were completed and pressed into Luftwaffe service. They were followed by Dutch-built Do 24Ts, produced for German use. Others were also built in occupied France.

By this time, the Do 24Ks in the East Indies had been virtually wiped out by the Japanese, although a handful escaped destruction and managed to fly to Australia, where they were

Overleaf
Top left Dornier Do 17Z of the Luftwaffe

Top right Dornier Do 24 used formerly by the Spanish Air Force for search and rescue duties

Below Douglas Dakota 4 operated by Intra of Jersey

flown until the end of the war. Do 24s 'liberated' from the Germans in 1944 were used by the French Navy into the fifties. Others sold to and licence-built in Spain were highly regarded and operated from 1944 to well into the sixties.

Dornier Do X *Germany:* On 25 May 1929, the first flight took place of an aircraft that was not only the largest in the world but had a passenger capacity several times greater than any other airplane of that time. Known as the Dornier Do X, it was a product of Germany's shackled but thriving aircraft industry, which was restricted by the Treaty of Versailles to producing only civil planes.

Powered originally by 12 German-built Bristol Jupiter engines, mounted in tandem pairs atop the huge monoplane wing, the Do X was a flying-boat with a massive hull fitted with sponsons (short stabilizing surfaces) on each side at water level. The passenger cabin was situated on a lower deck, beneath the crew compartments.

On 21 October 1929 the Do X took off with no fewer than 159 passengers on board – nine of whom were stowaways – as well as a full crew of ten. This flight, together with an epic trans-atlantic journey in stages from Germany to

81

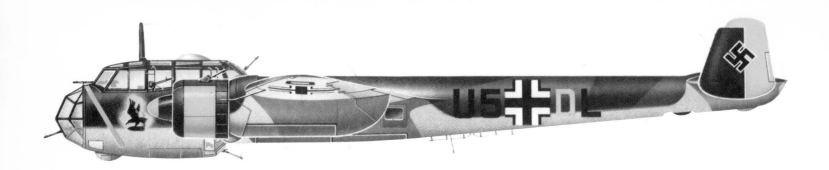

New York, which took nearly ten months from November 1930, captured the imagination of people all over the world. Earlier long-distance, record-breaking flights had usually been made in specially prepared aircraft, by rather special people. The Do X, on the other hand, looked the kind of aircraft in which ordinary passengers could fly in the wake of the pioneers.

Unfortunately, all had not gone as well as appeared on the surface. Problems with the original engines had forced a re-fit with US Curtiss Conquerors, and the transatlantic flight had been dogged with misfortune. A wing had been damaged by fire in Lisbon and the hull had sustained damage in the Canary Islands. Both were repairable, but the Do X never achieved any commercial success.

Douglas DC-1, 2 and 3 *USA:* The early 1930s saw a complete transformation of commercial air transport with the introduction of the Boeing Model 247. At last the majestic but lumbering biplane was giving way to the sleek low-wing, all-metal monoplane airliner. However, such was the interest in the 247 that Boeing could guarantee delivery only to United Airlines, who had ordered the first sixty.

Transcontinental and Western Air (TWA) therefore issued a requirement to other manufacturers for a similar airliner – a challenge which Douglas accepted. It built the DC-1, in many ways a more refined aircraft, although it flew for the first time on 1 July 1933, only four months after the Model 247 entered service. When it was handed over to TWA, it flew in record time between Los Angeles and New York. Impressed, the airline placed an immediate contract for 28 more Douglas airliners, but in an even more refined form.

History owes a lot to TWA, for the production airliner delivered by Douglas was the DC-2, which began operations in July 1934. At that time it was the best passenger aircraft in the world, and other operators soon began queuing up to place orders. First of the non-US airline customers was KLM, which began flying the type in the autumn of the same year, and the DC-2 seemed set for a long production run.

However, even greater acclaim was to come Douglas's way when it attempted to fulfil yet another requirement, this time from American Airlines. This company operated sleeper aircraft on its trans-America flights and, wanting to keep abreast of the latest developments, asked Douglas for a suitable airliner. Their answer was the DC-3, a direct but slightly larger development of the DC-2. The prototype first flew on 17 December 1935, and the design was soon being produced in two versions for American Airlines – the 14-passenger DST sleeper and a 21-seat 'daytime' airliner. Services with DC-3s started in June of the following year.

What was to become perhaps the most important airliner in history, quickly established its reputation with this and other operators, including the military. During the Second World War, the DC-3 (named Dakota by Britain) was mass produced as a utility transport in C-47, C-53, and other versions, known also as Skytrains and Skytroopers, and was licence-built in large numbers in Russia as the Lisunou Li-2. Used in all imaginable roles, from freight and personnel transport to glider tug and ambulance, the type was active in all theatres of war, notably during the D-Day landings in Normandy and subsequent assaults by Allied airborne forces.

After the war the military flying continued, while production of the civil version restarted. DC-3s became the mainstay of worldwide passenger and freight services for many years, although as larger-capacity piston-engined airliners and then jet airliners became available, DC-3s were gradually turned over to smaller operators.

Douglas Dauntless *USA:* The Dauntless first entered service in mid-1939 – yet by the time the war with Japan began in December 1941, it was already obsolete.

Designed as light bomber and reconnaissance aircraft, Dauntless monoplanes served during the war with the US Marine Corps, the Army and the Navy, production not finally coming to an end until 1944, by which time nearly 6000 had

The famous Douglas DC-1 of TWA

Douglas Dauntless of the US Marine Corps

Douglas World Cruiser *Chicago*. Note the 'World Flight' emblem on the fuselage side

been built. Their first real test came on 7 May 1942, when the US aircraft carriers USS *Lexington* and USS *Yorktown* faced three Japanese carriers in the Battle of the Coral Sea. During the battle, which lasted two days and was the first naval battle in which victory was decided by aircraft alone, Dauntless dive-bombers fought well alongside other US aircraft. Each side lost one carrier (the Japanese carrier *Shoho* being sunk by Dauntless and Devastator bombers), but the US had stopped the Japanese ships from supporting an invasion of Port Moresby, New Guinea, and the proposed air assault on Australia.

Next came the great Battle of Midway in June, again between United States and Japanese ships. This time US naval aircraft, spearheaded by Dauntless dive-bombers, destroyed four Japanese carriers, a cruiser and 250 aircraft, for the loss of one US carrier, a destroyer and 150 aircraft. This battle turned the tide of war against the Japanese in the Pacific.

Dauntless aircraft accounted for many Japanese aircraft shot down in air-to-air combat, and finished their wartime career as anti-submarine bombers and as attack aircraft, carrying depth charges and rocket projectiles respectively.

Douglas World Cruiser *USA:* The 1920s are remembered as a time of route proving and long-distance flying. The prestige of air forces could be enhanced by such flights, which were sometimes made by individual aircraft and sometimes by large formations. Among the countries that participated widely in this exciting pioneer flying were Great Britain, Italy, France, the Soviet Union and the United States – and it was the US which gained the distinction of making the first successful flight around the world.

The story of the world flight really began in the early 1920s, when the Douglas Aircraft Company was given a contract to produce an aircraft suitable for such an attempt. It produced the World Cruiser, a heavy two-seat biplane, based on its DT-2 naval torpedo-bomber and the famous Liberty engine. A novel feature of the design was that removal of the undercarriage was made simple, so that wheeled or float landing gears could be interchanged rapidly as the next stage of the future journey would dictate.

Arriving at Seattle in March 1924, the four World Cruisers were prepared for the start of the round-the-world attempt, which began on 6 April. The first stage of the flight took the planes to Prince Rupert, on the coast of British Columbia in Canada. They covered the hop of 973 km (605 miles) in $8\frac{1}{4}$ hours. Following the planned route, the aircraft next flew in stages to Alaska, where one of the World Cruisers (named *Seattle*) crashed at Dutch Harbor, without injuring the crew. The others continued, via the Aleutian Islands, Japan, China, Indo-China, Burma, India, Persia, Iraq, Turkey, Romania, Hungary, Germany, France, Great Britain, Iceland and Greenland, back to Canada and across the United States to Seattle. Unfortunately, only two of the World Cruisers, the *Chicago* and *New Orleans* completed the journey, *Boston* having ditched in the North Atlantic. Luckily, the crew were saved. The two aircraft which arrived at Seattle on 28 September 1924 had covered 44 342 km (27 553 miles) in 371 hours and 11 minutes of actual flying time.

E

English Electric Canberra *Great Britain*: The Canberra is one of the oldest types of jet bomber to remain in first-line service anywhere in the world. The 100 or so Canberras still in service with the Royal Air Force now operate in reconnaissance, ECM (electronic counter-measures), training, utility and target-towing roles. However, many of the countries that were supplied with new or refurbished ex-RAF aircraft continue to use them as tactical light bombers, in addition to other roles. Among the dozen or so foreign users, India, Pakistan, Australia and New Zealand have all flown the Canberra in combat, during the Indo-Pakistan War, in Vietnam and in Malaya. The United States Air Force and the South Vietnam Air Force also flew Canberras operationally during the Vietnam War, these having been produced under licence in the States by the Martin Company as the B-57. Altogether, 403 B-57s were delivered in various forms.

Design of what was to become Britain's first turbojet-powered bomber began in 1945, and the prototype made its initial flight on 13 May 1949. Modified to carry an extra crew member, production Canberra B.2s had accommodation for a navigator/plotter, over-target navi-gator/bomb-aimer, and the pilot. The B.2 en-tered RAF service in May 1951, initially with 101 Squadron, replacing Avro Lincolns. With a maximum speed nearly double that of the old piston-engined Lincoln, the RAF then had both modern jet fighters and bombers in service.

British production of the Canberra totalled 903 aircraft, in 14 versions, another twelve versions being added by subsequent modifi-cation of existing aircraft. A further 48 aircraft were licence-built in Australia, which also operated seven trainers.

English Electric Lightning *Great Britain*: The Lightning was Britain's main interceptor fighter for well over a decade after it entered Royal Air Force service in 1960 – yet it never achieved its full potential as an export fighter. As a prototype it had been, perhaps, the most potent fighter in the world, but by the time production was under way other types had been evolved which could match it in performance.

Its development dates back to 1947 when a Ministry of Supply requirement was issued for a new fighter to replace earlier RAF types like the Hunter. By way of development, the P.1A research aircraft was built, embodying the general lines of the later Lightning production aircraft. There followed a great deal of super-sonic research, which culminated in the first flight of a pre-production aircraft on 4 April 1957.

The single-seat Lightning first entered RAF service in 1960, with No 74 Squadron, as the first British fighter capable of supersonic speeds in level flight. Subsequently, it equipped other squadrons based in Britain, Germany and Cyprus. It was very successful, for not only could later variants fly at over Mach 1 without afterburning, but they could also accelerate from Mach 1 to Mach 2 in a little over three minutes and fly at over Mach 2 while carrying British-built Firestreak and Red Top air-to-air missiles. Long-range ferrying flights could be undertaken using two unusual over-the-wing auxiliary fuel tanks.

The Lightning still retains a role today in the defence of the British Isles. But, as Jaguar aircraft have become available for attack duties, so US-built Phantom fighters have been transferred from this work to take over as the main interceptors of the RAF.

Although export versions of the Lightning were not successful, a number of new aircraft and a few ex-RAF types were purchased by Saudi Arabia and Kuwait as multi-role fighters for their air forces. However, it is doubtful whether these will remain operational for much longer.

Above English Electric Lightning F.6 of the RAF

Opposite English Electric Canberra B.2 operated by the Venezuelan Air Force

Fairey IIIDs of No 481 Flight based in Malta during the 1920s

F

Fairchild A-10A *USA:* Unique in the United States Air Force inventory is the A-10A, a newly-conceived type of aircraft for the old role of close support. Operations by the USAF in Vietnam emphasized the stupidity of trying to use multi-million dollar fighter-bombers to attack small concentrations of armoured vehicles in dense jungle, or guerilla units supplied by loads carried on bicycles. Expensive aircraft proved an embarrassment to the USAF, coming into their own only when matched against other jet aircraft in dogfight situations, or for conventional bombing duties. Because of this, the USAF reverted to use of outdated piston-engined aircraft like the Skyraider, able to carry heavy weapon loads at speeds which gave their crews time to spot an elusive enemy. In USAF and South Vietnamese service the old-timers proved effective until the enemy began using shoulder-fired, homing anti-aircraft missiles.

Bearing in mind all the lessons learned in Vietnam, the USAF then announced, in 1967, a requirement for a purpose-built close support aircraft, for which the Fairchild design was chosen. The first prototype Fairchild A-10 made its initial flight on 10 May 1972, and production examples have since entered service as A-10As.

Ugly but completely functional, the A-10A is powered by two fuselage-mounted turbofan engines and is capable of carrying a huge warload up to 7257 kg (16 000 lb) in weight, including retarded, cluster, laser-guided, electro-optically-guided, incendiary and general-purpose bombs, missiles and gun pods. However, its most important armament is a fuselage-nose-mounted 30 mm rotating seven-barrel cannon which is a real 'tank buster'. Able to fire up to 4000 depleted uranium shells per minute, it has shown itself capable of destroying any known battle tank.

The A-10A has a maximum speed of only 729 km/h (453 mph), which critics of the aircraft say leaves it wide open for anti-aircraft missiles. However, it has to be detected first, and this can

Fairey Battle flown by the Royal Australian Air Force

The much-loved Fairey
Flycatcher naval fighter

be prevented by low-level flying and the use of ECM (electronic countermeasures) jammer systems.

Fairey IIID *Great Britain:* A great deal of confusion has existed for many years concerning precisely when the Fairey IIID reconnaissance and general-purpose biplane entered service with the Royal Air Force, the Fleet Air Arm, and those countries that received export versions.

Basically, the IIID was a direct descendant of the Fairey IIIA, B and C, produced during the First World War. The prototype flew in August 1920, and before any British unit received production examples, considerable numbers were exported. The recipients included Australia, the Netherlands, Sweden and Portugal – and a IIID of the Portuguese Navy (named *Santa Cruz*) has been famous since 1922 as the first aircraft to cross the South Atlantic. In fact, it crashed at an island refuelling stop on the way and was replaced by another IIID, which also crashed. So the flight was completed by a third Fairey seaplane.

By this time at least one IIID was being test flown from the British aircraft carrier HMS *Argus*, using the technique of fitting jettison-able wheels underneath the aircraft's floats, so allowing it to fly from the carrier deck. When IIIDs first entered Fleet Air Arm service in 1924, they were operated with wheeled undercarriages from the carrier, using at first the arrester hook technique for landing, and with float undercarriages from other naval vessels. Once firmly in British service, the IIID quickly built up a reputation for reliability and strength, and was ideal for policing duties abroad. RAF IIIDs of a special unit flew a series of long-distance flights from March 1926, the first covering more than 22 370 km (13 900 miles) between Egypt and Cape Town, South Africa, then back via Greece and France to England.

When the last of the IIIDs were withdrawn from British service in 1930, they had seen little real drama, although a few had been sent to Shanghai in 1927 to help the authorities during the Chinese rebellion.

Fairey Battle *Great Britain:* With war looming up, aircraft development in the latter half of the 1930s moved at a faster rate than in any previous inter-war period. Caught right in the middle of all this was the Battle, for although it had been put into production as an urgent, modern replacement for the Hawker Hart and

89

Hind biplane light bombers in 1936, it was all but obsolete by the outbreak of war in 1939.

The Battle was designed to a Ministry specification issued in 1933, and was powered by the new and highly-acclaimed Rolls-Royce Merlin engine. Like most modern aircraft, it was a low-wing monoplane, and carried a crew of three in tandem under a long enclosure. Numbers 52 and 63 Squadrons of the Royal Air Force were the first to become operational on Battles in 1937, with 13 other squadrons forming by the following year.

With such a commitment to the type, there was no way the Battle could be quickly replaced. With only one forward-firing gun and one rear-mounted gun, it was almost helpless against the faster German fighters at the beginning of the war. Yet, ten squadrons of Battles were sent to France in September 1939 as the first element of the Advanced Air Striking Force. It was the rear gunner of a Battle who shot down the first German aircraft on the 20th of that month – and the RAF's first two Victoria Crosses of the war were won by Battle crews on 10 May 1940 during an attack on the Maastricht bridges. However, Battles suffered appalling losses.

Following their withdrawal from service in 1941, many Battles were sent to Canada under the Commonwealth Air Training Scheme, and became trainers (and target tugs), to provide pilots for the growing British air forces.

Fairey Flycatcher *Great Britain:* Few aircraft typified the British spirit of the twenties better than the Flycatcher. This fighter had a 'cocky' appearance which seemed right for a nation that had emerged unbroken from a terrible war and now governed the greatest empire the world had ever known.

During the First World War Britain had pioneered the aircraft carrier with HMS *Furious*, and later HMS *Argus*, which was the first carrier to have a flush deck. Nobody doubted the carrier's worth. Wartime operations from *Furious*, and from turret platforms on other naval vessels, had proved beyond doubt that aircraft were essential at sea. Nevertheless, the Fleet Air Arm had to wait until 1923 to receive the first of its new Flycatcher fighters. Unusually, the wings did

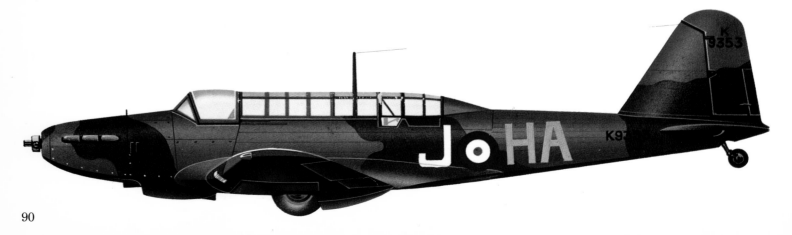

not fold for storage, the airframe being designed
to be taken apart in manageable sections.

When the Flycatcher finally arrived, it
proved fast and highly manoeuvrable. Pilots
found it easy to fly, and it had none of the vices
of the rotary-engined fighters of the war years.
Altogether, 192 were built, serving on all
British aircraft carriers, from turret platforms
on major ships, and from naval shore stations,
operating on both wheel and float undercarriages. They had the distinction of being the
first Fleet Air Arm fighters with hydraulic
wheel brakes, which enabled them to dispense
with the need for an arrester hook to stop them
after landing on deck. Although they were well
outdated by the time they retired from service in
1934, many pilots missed their delightfully aggressive handling qualities.

Fairey Fox *Great Britain:* The Fox entered
Royal Air Force service in 1926, with No 12
Squadron based at Andover. It gave that unit a
definite edge over all other light bomber
squadrons in the Air Force, for here was an
aircraft that could outpace contemporary bombers and fighters alike. Yet history shows that
the Fox did more than just give the RAF a new,
high-speed combat aircraft. It achieved its
impressive performance by having unpreceden-
tedly clean lines, made possible by the closely-
cowled Curtiss inline engine which gave the
forward fuselage a near-pointed form. This was
a complete breakaway from the traditional
radial engines, and the drag they generated,
and led the way to the Hawker Hart and Fury
series of bombers and fighters of the 1930s.

The Fox had started life as a private venture,

built at a time when money for new aircraft was
short. The prototype flew for the first time on 3
January 1925, and in October of that year was
demonstrated in front of Air Chief Marshal Sir
Hugh Trenchard. On seeing its performance, he
immediately ordered sufficient aircraft to main-
tain a single squadron – these 28 Foxes were the
only aircraft of their type built for the RAF.
Some were later re-engined with Rolls-Royce
Kestrels and redesignated Mk IAs.

If the RAF did not want any more, there were
those who did. From 1933 the Belgian
Aéronautique Militaire operated two advanced
versions of the Fox that were built in fairly
large numbers under licence in that country.
They were the all-metal Fox IIM and Fox VI, the
latter with an enclosed cockpit and an 860 hp
Hispano-Suiza engine.

Fairey Rotodyne *Great Britain:* Another
example of British quality design and invention
that was axed because of a lack of finance, the
Rotodyne could so easily have been the world's
first vertical take-off airliner to enter service.

The short history of the Rotodyne really
starts in December 1947, when the Fairey
Gyrodyne flew for the first time. This small
four/five-seat experimental helicopter was
powered by a single piston-engine, which drove
both the main rotor (when powered) and a
tractor propeller mounted on a stub wing.
Unfortunately, having earlier set up a new
international speed record for helicopters of 200
km/h (124.3 mph), the prototype crashed in
April 1949 and the crew were killed.
Subsequently, the second Gyrodyne became
the Jet Gyrodyne, with tip-jet rotor drive.

Many lessons had been learned from the Gyrodynes; so, in the mid-1950s, Fairey began the design of a much more adventurous aircraft that would combine principles from the helicopter, autogyro and airplane. Named the Rotodyne-Y, this aircraft first flew on 6 November 1957 and was described as an experimental VTOL transport convertiplane, although it was in fact the prototype of the proposed Rotodyne-Z production aircraft for airline operation.

The Rotodyne had more in common with the Jet Gyrodyne than with the earlier Gyrodyne, for its huge main rotor was powered by four pressure-jets mounted at the blade tips, where air and fuel were burned together to produce thrust for rotation. For forward flight in autorotative mode, with the tip-jets switched off and the rotor freely turning, two turbo-prop engines and propellers were installed under the wings. The complete arrangement thus allowed the Rotodyne to take off vertically or as a STOL aircraft and, with the rotor autorotating, to fly at reasonably high speeds as an autogyro-cum-airplane by means of its wings and tractor engines.

The Rotodyne-Y had accommodation for 40 passengers, whereas the Rotodyne-Z would accommodate up to 70; even so it was highly successful. The first transition from vertical to horizontal flight was made on 10 April 1958, and several potential customers became interested. However, the project was cancelled in 1962 for lack of finance to complete development.

Fairey Swordfish *Great Britain:* Known affectionately as the 'Stringbag', because of its profusion of bracing struts and wires in an age when most aircraft were cantilever monoplanes, the Swordfish was a torpedo-bomber of the very highest quality. It was first flown in prototype form on 17 April 1934, and initial production aircraft were delivered to the Fleet Air Arm in 1936.

With a maximum speed of only 222 km/h (138 mph), the Swordfish was anything but fast – yet its reliability and strength of construction partly made up for this. It usually carried a crew of three, in open cockpits, and was armed with a single torpedo, carried under its fuselage. Alternatively, it could carry a mine or bombs, and two machine-guns were provided for defensive use. All in all, it looked like something more suited to the First World War than to the late thirties. This must have been in the Air Ministry's mind when in 1938 the first flight took place of the aircraft designed as its successor, the Fairey Albacore. Although put into production, the Albacore was in fact withdrawn from service before the Swordfish, which lasted out the war.

In September 1939 there were 13 Swordfish squadrons and these soon entered the war. In November 1940 Swordfish were responsible for the crippling of Italian warships at Taranto. Later, they were instrumental in bringing

about the destruction of the German battleship *Bismarck*. This great ship was the pride of the German Navy, a vessel with larger guns than any British contemporary – a point amply demonstrated when it sank one of Britain's finest warships, HMS *Prince of Wales*. Although shadowed after this action by other British ships, at a safe distance, the *Bismarck* was lost until spotted by a Catalina on 24 May 1941. Now it was the Swordfish's turn. Attacks were made which damaged the *Bismarck* sufficiently to slow it down until British warships could close in to attack and sink Germany's 'unsinkable' ship. The entire operation lasted four days.

The Swordfish that made the attack on the *Bismarck* flew from an aircraft carrier, HMS *Ark Royal*, and it was for such operations that the Swordfish is best known. However, the biplane did not always have things all its own way. Many times its squadrons suffered very heavy losses, mainly from German fighters – and an attack on the cruisers *Scharnhorst* and *Gneisenau*, during their dash to safety through the English Channel in February 1942, led to the annihilation of six Swordfish.

Farman Goliath *France:* The Farman Goliath was designed originally as a heavy bomber for service with the French Air Force – but with the end of hostilities in November 1918 the manufacturers decided to convert it into a passenger airliner.

The first Goliath airliner was a no-frills, minimum-effort conversion of the bomber and was not well received by potential customers. Few improvements had been made in the interests of comfort, and the passenger seats were flanked by the internal bracing members that were used to strengthen the bomber fuselage. Learning from their mistakes, the manufacturers set about redesigning the interior of the passenger cabin, with lavish furnishings that became the vogue in post-war

Farman Goliaths parked at Le Bourget, France, in the early 1920s

Felixstowe F.2A

Europe. The price of the airliner increased, inevitably, to the equivalent of $7480 (£4,250)!

With its blunt-nosed fuselage and massive trousered undercarriage legs, the Goliath was not a pleasant-looking airliner, but it was efficient. About 60 were produced, including five built in Czechoslovakia. Goliath operations began in early 1919, and it became one of the most important aircraft associated with European air travel, serving for a whole decade.

The first Paris-to-London flight by a Goliath was made on 8 February 1919, when military personnel were transported on a special flight to Kenley. A regular Paris-to-Brussels service began in March 1919, and a regular Paris-to-London service in March 1920, operated by Cie des Grands Express Aériens. Early routes were proving a success. Then, on 7 April 1922, disaster struck when a Goliath of Grands Express Aériens collided with a de Havilland D.H.18 of Daimler Airway over the French town of Thieuloy-Saint-Antoine, killing seven

people. Both pilots had been navigating by following the same road, at the same height, but in opposite directions.

Despite this setback, Goliaths continued to be a familiar sight throughout Europe, and could often be seen at London's main air terminal, Croydon Airport.

Felixstowe F.2A *Great Britain:* The name Felixstowe referred to the Royal Naval Air Service station where the F.2A was developed from an American Curtiss design. But, it was naval officer John C. Porte who contributed most to the outstanding performance and service record of this aircraft.

Porte had been introduced to Curtiss flying-boats through a British company that had acquired an agency for them. In 1914 he travelled to the US to join Glenn Curtiss, who was then working on a completely new type of flying-boat for a projected transatlantic crossing. The aircraft was named *America*, and

Above A French-built example of the Fieseler Storch in wartime Luftwaffe markings, British registered for flying at air shows

Opposite above The immortal Fairey Swordfish carrying a torpedo under the fuselage

Opposite below Fiat C.R. 42 Falco biplane fighter

Porte was to be the pilot. Instead, only a month after the *America* had been completed, Porte returned to England and joined the RNAS, as the war in Europe had begun.

Because of his experience, Porte soon found himself at Felixstowe, charged with developing a flying-boat for the RNAS. Using the *America* as a starting point for his much improved F.1, he designed a new hull and used Hispano-Suiza engines. Only a few F.1s were produced, but subsequent work on a new hull and tail unit for the larger Curtiss H.12, plus Rolls-Royce engines, resulted in the Felixstowe F.2 design. This went into production as the F.2A in 1917, and nearly 100 were produced before the end of the war, possessing much improved hydrodynamic qualities compared with the H.12.

Operating on anti-submarine and patrol missions, each F.2A could carry two 104 kg (230 lb) bombs under the lower wings, and was defended by machine-gun positions in the nose and three mid-fuselage stations.

F.2As were responsible for the destruction of several German U-boats and Zeppelin airships, and such was their success that Porte devised a scheme by which F.2As could be towed behind naval vessels on special lighters (small wide beam boats), to increase their area of operation.

Fiat C.R. 42 Falco *Italy:* After the First World War, the Fiat company began the production of a series of biplane fighters which became the mainstay of Italian fighter squadrons. By 1932 the series had culminated in the C.R. 32, which subsequently flew in the civil war that raged in Spain from July 1936. This gave the C.R. 32 a chance to prove itself in combat, and it was soon regarded as the main fighter in Franco's forces,

Below Fieseler Fi 156 Storch in Luftwaffe markings

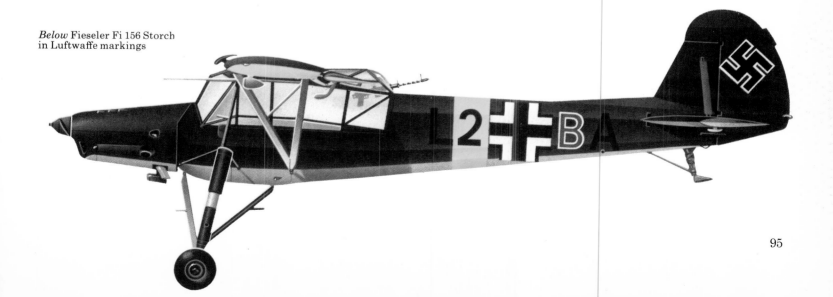

Focke-Wulf Fw 200 Condor
anti-shipping aircraft

even replacing early German fighters.

By the late 1930s, most of the more prominent air forces were gradually re-equipping with low-wing monoplane fighters. Fiat still believed there was a place for the biplane, and designed the C.R. 42, of which the prototype made its first flight in 1939. The C.R. 42 was ordered into quantity production, and by 1942 no fewer than 1784 had been built, some to fulfil orders placed by other European countries.

In Italian service C.R. 42s were used as fighters, escort fighters in the Mediterranean theatre, night fighters for home defence, and fighter-bombers in the desert campaigns, carrying two 100 kg (220 lb) bombs. As development continued, maximum speed was raised from 430 km/h (267 mph) to 518 km/h (322 mph). However, even though the C.R. 42 could match the speed of most modern monoplane fighters, performance in other respects fell short of what was required in the Second World War, and this was the last biplane fighter to enter Italian service.

Fieseler Fi 103 (V1) *Germany:* When the British intelligence services first heard that Germany was working on pilotless aircraft, they thought they might have been subjected to an elaborate hoax. It therefore became vital to discover as quickly as possible whether or not they had stumbled on one of Hitler's so-called 'terror weapons'.

The story of the V1, or 'doodlebug' as it became known in Britain, began in 1939, when the Argus Motorenwerke proposed that a missile should be built using a new type of engine which it was developing. This engine, called a pulse-jet, took in air at the front, through flap valves, behind which petrol was injected at very short intervals and ignited. The resulting combustion closed the flap valves momentarily, producing thrust. As the gases exhausted from the rear, another charge of air entered the front, keeping the process going,

Opposite above Piloted version of the V1 flying bomb

Opposite below Focke-Wulf Fw 190

with consequent raucous noise from the repeated ignitions.

The project was put in the hands of Fieseler Werke in 1942 and a secret test site was built at Peenemünde. The first Fi 103 was test flown in December of that year, having been air-launched from an aeroplane and, after initial problems had been rectified, a start was made on constructing launching sites. Meanwhile the Fi 103 had become V1 at Hitler's suggestion, the V symbolizing *Vergeltungswaffe*, or reprisal weapon.

The main concentration of launching sites was in the Pas de Calais area, where long ramps were erected along which to launch the V1s. Despite intensive action by the RAF to locate these sites and destroy them, more that 8600 V1s were launched against England between 13 June and 4 September 1944, nearly half of which were stopped short by Tempests, Spitfires, Meteors and other fighters, barrage balloons and anti-aircraft units. Many more V1s were launched against other European targets.

By January 1945 the last V1s had been launched against Britain, as the 'Fatherland' itself was now in danger.

A manned version of the V1 was developed in Germany, which was to be air-launched and piloted to its target. Prior to diving, the pilot was to bale out, although in fact this version was little more than a suicide aircraft.

Fieseler Fi 156 Storch *Germany:* Overshadowed by Germany's high-performance fighters and hard-hitting bombers, the Storch was nevertheless one of the most successful aircraft built in Germany before the Second World War.

Its design originated in 1935 – the year that Hitler officially confirmed the existence of the new Luftwaffe – with the intention of producing a light aircraft suitable for army co-operation duties. For this role, the aircraft would need to accommodate at least two persons in a cabin with extensive glazing for ground observation, would need to be able to take off and land in very short distances and would have to possess low landing and stalling speeds. To aid short take-off and landing, the wings were fitted with extensive slots and flaps. The crew sat in tandem, surrounded from waist height by windows, the side panels of which overhung the lower fuselage to allow a clear downward view. Perhaps the most noticeable feature of the aircraft was its long undercarriage legs.

The prototype Storch made its first flight in 1936, and the type immediately went into production, the first examples going into Luftwaffe service in the following year. Altogether 2549 Storchs were built, after 1941 in factories in occupied France and Czechoslovakia.

The type was operational in nearly every battle area from North Africa to the Eastern front of Russia, being also used for reconnaissance, utility, ambulance and staff trans-

port duties.

Perhaps the best known exploit involving a Storch was the hazardous rescue of the Italian dictator Benito Mussolini from a hotel situated high up in the Gran Sasso mountain range, where he was being held, on 12 September 1943.

Focke-Wulf Fw 190 *Germany:* Ranking with the Supermarine Spitfire, Vought Corsair and North American Mustang as one of the best fighters of World War Two, the Focke-Wulf 190 was the work of a team of German designers headed by the famous Kurt Tank. It was evolved basically as a successor to the Messerschmitt Bf 109 fighter, although the official view was that it would never be capable of matching the operational prowess of the 109. How wrong this

Above Fokker D.VII, based in the United States of America

Above right Replica of a First World War Fokker Dr. I Triplane fighter

Left Replica of the famous Fokker E.III Eindecker fighter

proved!

The Fw 190 prototype first flew on 1 June 1939 and production deliveries began in late 1940. Within a year, Fw 190s were making low-level sweeps over southern England in daylight, against which the Spitfire Vs then in service achieved little success. The situation did not improve until the Royal Air Force received more powerful Spitfire IXs, in partnership with four-cannon Typhoons.

Meanwhile, the Fw 190 was also proving a good fighter-bomber, carrying a reasonable bomb load or, in some cases, rocket projectiles. The new war started by Hitler on the Eastern Front resulted in most of the new production Fw 190s being thrown into the fighting against the Russians. Others were needed equally urgently by Rommel in North Africa, to combat the Western Desert Air Force and Allied ground forces who, by the latter part of 1942, were pressing hard at Alamein.

During 1943, the Fw 190 was encountered frequently in Europe while performing night fighter missions. About the same time, the first Fw 190s came off the production line fitted with inline, rather than radial, engines. General appearance stayed the same, because of the use of an annular radiator at the nose.

As RAF and USAAF bombing raids got heavier and heavier in Europe, new tactics were employed by some German fighter units flying Fw 190s. Against US heavy bombers on daylight raids, several Fw 190s would form a queue and approach from the rear of the bomber formation. At very close range, the fighters would then 'open up', so giving the rear gunners in the bombers very little chance of firing methodically at all the attackers.

By the end of the war, more than 20 000 Fw 190s had been built, about one third as fighter-bombers.

Focke-Wulf Fw 200 Condor *Germany:*

Because the Treaty of Versailles, signed in 1919, prevented the Germans from having an air force, when the Nazis reformed the Luftwaffe in the early 1930s they did it illegally and in secrecy. To this end many of the transport aircraft that appeared in Germany at that time were really disguised bombers.

Ironically, one of the finest German long-range maritime-reconnaissance bombers of the war, the Condor, was built originally as a 26-passenger civil transport aircraft, with no intention of its use for any combat role. First flown in 1937, a prototype made several long-distance demonstration flights before the war, taking in destinations like New York and Cairo. Early production aircraft were delivered to airlines, including seven to the German airline Deutsche Luft Hansa.

As a result of Japanese interest in the aircraft as a bomber for the Army Air Force before the war, the Fw 200C version was adapted for the role of maritime-reconnaissance bomber; even then the first production aircraft went first to serve with the Germans in Norway as transports. Once used in the more aggressive role, the Condor quickly built up a reputation as a highly effective anti-shipping aircraft, working in co-operation with German U-boat packs in the North Atlantic and other seas. This combination heralded the sinking of huge amounts of vital Allied shipping, curtailed only when the Allies introduced long-range aircraft, like the Bristol Beaufighter, to clear the skies, and expendable Hurricane fighters carried on CAM merchant ships.

By 1943, newer, purpose-built German aircraft were replacing Condors for maritime reconnaissance missions and they were relegated to transport duties. The surprisingly small production run of 263 aircraft did not end until 1944.

Fokker D.VII *Germany:* The penultimate

fighter produced by Fokker during the First World War, the D.VII, was the finest aircraft to serve with the German forces, matched in combat only by the British Sopwith Snipe and French SPAD XIII. Its design began in 1917 when Reinhold Platz, Fokker's chief designer, produced the V.11. This prototype took part in a fly-off competition with other German fighter prototypes in the following January, and was rushed immediately into quantity production as the Fokker D.VII.

D.VIIs became operational from April 1918, and not a moment too soon for the Germans. Fighters like the Albatros D. V and Fokker Dr. I Triplane were being hounded by British and French fighters, whose development had continued at a high rate since the early disastrous days of the 'Fokker scourge' (see Fokker Eindecker). Such was the D.VII's superiority in performance and manoeuvrability over the Albatros fighter, that the Albatros company was ordered, in February 1918, to abandon its own design and concentrate on manufacturing Fokker D.VIIs.

By the autumn of 1918 more than 40 Jastas (German squadrons) flew D.VIIs, and they quickly began to shoot down all but the latest Allied aircraft encountered in combat. The D.VII's maximum speed was considerably slower than that of the French SPAD XIII, but faster than that of the British Sopwith Camel – but its service ceiling was higher than that of either type.

When the First World War ended, in November 1918, the Allies worked out the Versailles Treaty of Peace. This forbade the Germans from having an air force or producing military aircraft, and noted that all D.VIIs were to be surrendered (the only aircraft specifically mentioned). In defiance of the Treaty, Anthony

Fokker, who owned the Fokker company, smuggled into Holland a large number of D.VIIs and spare parts, and these were sold to Switzerland and Belgium. At the same time a new production line was set up in Holland to produce D.VIIs for the Royal Netherlands Air Force.

The greatest loss of Fokker D.VIIs to a single Allied pilot in one day can almost certainly be attributed to the French 'ace' Capitaine René Paul Fonck. Flying a SPAD XIII, on 26 September 1918, he shot down four D.VIIs, as well as an Albatros D.V and a two-seat biplane.

Fokker Dr. I Triplane *Germany:* Probably the most famous of all First World War German aircraft, the Fokker Dr. I counted among its pilots the 'ace of aces', Manfred von Richthofen. It was, in fact, in such an aircraft that Richthofen finally fell to the machine-guns of Captain A. Roy Brown's Sopwith Camel in April 1918, after gaining 80 victories.

The Dr. I (Dr for *Dreidecker* or triplane) was the result of the German authorities' demand that a triplane fighter should be built to equal or better the success that the British Sopwith Triplane was achieving on the Western Front against the latest Albatros fighters. The order was not easy to comply with – so drastic and virtually untried design features appeared on the first Fokker Triplane that was rolled out in the spring of 1917. This prototype fighter, known originally as the F.I., had cantilever wings needing no interplane struts or bracing wires. Flight testing, however, revealed that the wings vibrated dangerously, so the design was modified to include conventional light struts.

With great expectations, the German air service received its first production Dr. Is in

An historical photo illustrating the interest aroused by the revolutionary Fokker E.III Eindecker fighter

August 1917, but all was not well. Under combat conditions the wing structure still gave cause for concern and within two months the Dr. Is were withdrawn from service. Finally, the problem was cured, and the type re-entered squadron service in December. By then, the modifications had left it with a poor turn of speed compared with other new enemy aircraft, although it had high manoeuvrability and rate of climb.

Remaining in first-line fighter service until the summer of 1918, the German fighters were often seen flying with other types in large formations over the Western Front, sometimes painted in rich colours, which gave rise to the term 'flying circus' that was often applied to Richthofen's formation. With the outclassing of the Dr. I came the deaths of most of the remaining high-scoring German 'aces'.

Fokker Eindecker *Germany:* The 'Fokker scourge' of the autumn and winter of 1915–16, which virtually drove the Allied air forces from the skies of the Western Front, was the result of a single type of aircraft entering German service – the Fokker E (*Eindecker*, or monoplane).

At the beginning of the war, aircraft were generally used only for reconnaissance, artillery spotting and light bombing missions. The largely unexpected success in these roles soon led to other aircraft being armed with machine-guns to shoot down enemy reconnaissance machines before their reports could be given to land forces and artillery batteries. How to fit a machine-gun on an aircraft to ensure the greatest possible effect was the problem. The Allies got round it by designing fighters with pusher engines, so that the gun could be fired forward. However, this arrangement led to poor aircraft performance. Other ideas included fitting a gun to the fuselage at an angle, so that it could fire outside the propeller arc of a tractor-engined aircraft. Eventually, a French pilot, Lt. Roland Garros, had the idea of fitting metal deflector plates to the propeller of his Morane-Saulnier Type L monoplane, so that he was able to fire between the blades of the revolving propeller to get a straight shot at the enemy. Any bullet which would have hit and damaged his propeller was now deflected off the metal plates.

With this arrangement he met a German Albatros two-seat observation biplane and quickly shot it down, following this victory with two more during the next 14 days. Unfortunately, whilst on patrol over enemy lines on 19 April 1915, he was hit by anti-aircraft fire and was forced to land behind the German front line. Although the Morane-Saulnier was badly burnt, there was no possibility of hiding the deflector plates and gun.

Anthony Fokker was asked to produce a copy of this idea for use on German aircraft. Instead, he initiated the design of a proper interrupter gear, which timed the machine-gun to fire between the revolving propeller blades, so making deflector plates unnecessary. Successful testing of this gear on a Fokker M.5K monoplane heralded the production by Fokker of a developed monoplane for first-line service as a fighter.

In all, four versions of the Fokker Eindecker were built, designated E.I to E.IV, production totalling about 400 machines. The first version, with an 80 hp Oberursel engine, proved too slow. The next two versions each had a 100 hp engine, the E.III becoming the major production variant. The last version, the E.IV, was fitted with a 160 hp Oberursel engine and was armed with two Spandau machine-guns. However, as the all-up weight had been

Fokker F.VIIB/3m trimotor *Southern Cross*, which made the first trans-Pacific flight between the US and Australia in mid-1928

increased so much by the larger engine and extra gun, the E.IV could not match the performance of earlier versions and very few were built.

Eindeckers began appearing on the Western Front in the autumn of 1915, and their presence was felt immediately. Allied pilots, not knowing of the forward-firing capability of the Eindecker, were caught unawares as it approached from the rear, and were often shot down before taking any action. Even when they understood the attack capability of the Eindecker, they could do little about it. Huge losses were sustained by the Royal Flying Corps and other Allied air services during the autumn and winter of 1915–16 and the Eindecker gave the Germans near-total air supremacy over the battle zones.

It became a matter of the highest priority to end the reign of the small German monoplane. As the winter progressed the French began to receive the Nieuport 11, which was armed with a single machine-gun mounted on the upper wing, so that it fired outside the propeller arc. Soon afterwards the British began to re-equip with higher-performance pusher types, in the form of D.H.2s and F.E.2bs, later also receiving Sopwith 1½-Strutters fitted with a British-made interrupter gear.

Gradually, control of the skies slipped away from the Germans, but only after appallingly high losses had been suffered by the Allies. The air services were, by 1916, no longer just the eyes of the army, but seemed as if they could one day have the power to win or lose battles for either side.

Fokker F.VII *Netherlands:* First flown on 4 September 1925, the Fokker 'trimotor' was one of the most successful transport aircraft of the inter-war period, enjoying a reputation that was enhanced by its choice for several historic flights of the later twenties.

After appearing initially as a single-engined aircraft, a Fokker F.VII was fitted with three Wright Whirlwind engines to take part in a Ford Reliability Tour in America, and was redesignated F.VIIA/3m. The first trimotor is famous not only for being the forerunner of many production examples, but because it was used by Lt Commander Richard E. Byrd (United States Navy) and Floyd Bennett for the first flight over the North Pole, on 9 May 1926.

Production of F.VII/3ms was started, and the type was soon being operated in several countries as a ten-passenger or freight transport. It was also adapted into a bomber and torpedo-bomber, and small numbers of these served in the Dutch East Indies, and with the Spanish and Polish air forces. A few other F.VII/3ms saw limited service in Holland as general transport and training aircraft.

Probably the most famous flight of the civil trimotor's career took place between 31 May and 9 June 1928, when an F.VIIB/3m named *Southern Cross* was used by Captain Charles Kingsford Smith and C.T.P. Ulm for the first flight across the Pacific Ocean, between California, USA, and Brisbane, Australia.

By the early 1930s, trimotors were flying in over 12 countries, including a few licence-built in Britain; but were gradually replaced by new low-wing monoplane airliners.

Fokker F.27 Friendship *Netherlands:* The name of Fokker came to the forefront of aviation in the First World War when aircraft bearing that name become the mainstay of the Imperial German Air Force fighter units. After that war, Anthony Fokker smuggled examples of his finest fighter, the D.VII, into Holland – where he originally came from – and set up a new factory under his name. Although his company produced some very notable civil and military aircraft before the Second World War, Fokker fighters saw only limited action during 1939–40. However, after that war the company again became prominent as the producer of a small range of excellent civil transport aircraft with military potential, one of which is the F.27 Friendship.

This short/medium-range aircraft is one of the most popular of the smaller airliners flying today. The first prototype made its maiden flight back in November 1955 and delivery of production aircraft started in late 1958. In addition to the production line in the Netherlands (orders totalling 451 by mid-1977), Fairchild Industries built a further 205 Friendships in America, before production ended.

Several versions of the F.27 are available, the standard models for civil operators accommodating between 44 and 52 passengers, seated four-abreast. There is also the F.27 Combiplane, which can be flown as an all-cargo transport or with a mixed load of cargo and passengers, and a special aerial survey version, packing two super-wide-angle cameras and known as the F.27 Cartographic. While the military versions are basically similar, they can carry between 45 and 50 paratroops, 24–30 stretchers and several attendants as an air ambulance, or military freight. A special maritime patrol version has also been built which is ideal for coastal and oil rig patrols and surveillance, search and rescue, fishery patrol, etc.

Usually flown by the smaller airlines of the world, the normal civil F.27 has proved most successful and cost-effective to operate. A typical user is the British airline Air Anglia, which changed from old Douglas Dakotas to Friendships from 1972.

Ford Trimotor *USA:* The Ford Trimotor is an example of a type of transport aircraft that became the vogue from the mid-1920s until the mid-1930s – a three-engined, high-wing monoplane with a fixed wide-track undercarriage. Despite its similarity to the Fokker F.VII/3m, the Trimotor deserves mention as the aircraft that carried four men on the first flight over the South Pole, on 28/29 November 1929.

Opposite Fokker F.27 Friendship of East-West Airlines

Opposite This Ford Trimotor was still flying in Island Airways insignia in the 1960s

In 1926, Lt. Commander Richard E. Byrd and Floyd Bennett had been the first men to fly over the North Pole, in a Fokker F.VII/3m named *Josephine Ford*. The success of that flight led Byrd to start planning a similar flight over the South Pole. But the expedition had to be mounted on a massive scale, as the nearest vestiges of civilization would be so far from the necessary base camp in the Antarctic. Thus, in 1928, two ships sailed for the region, carrying four aircraft and 60 men.

It was a Ford 4-AT Trimotor, named *Floyd Bennett* after Byrd's original pilot who had died of pneumonia, which was the aircraft for the historic flight. After setting up an advanced refuelling camp, Byrd and three other men took off and flew over the South Pole, the round trip taking some 19 hours. And, but for prompt action by the pilot – Bernt Balchen, who ordered that the emergency equipment and stores should be thrown overboard to lighten the aircraft and so enable it to clear a mountain range – the attempt might well have ended in disaster.

Of the 200 or so Ford Trimotors built up to 1933, most had stopped flying by the beginning of the war in 1939.

General Dynamics F-16 *USA:* The new F-16 represents a complete break away from the traditional US fighter concept of a heavy and elaborately-equipped aircraft, and for the first time indicates that the United States has accepted for deployment fast and highly manoeuvrable lightweight aircraft. Although the F-16 must be seen as a fighter on a level beneath that of aircraft like the Tomcat and Eagle, it is nevertheless a highly sophisticated aircraft that is able to carry a real 'sting' in the form of two or more air-to-air missiles, a multi-barrel cannon and underwing hardpoints for bombs, etc.

First flown on 20 January 1974, the YF-16 was the winner of a competition held in the States for a lightweight, low-cost, air-superiority fighter, and the US Air Force will eventually receive about 1338 examples. The type was also chosen by the air forces of Belgium, Denmark, the Netherlands and Norway as a replacement for the ageing F-104 Starfighters.

Another lightweight fighter, the McDonnell Douglas F-18, was chosen by the US Navy. This is a development of the earlier Northrop YF-17, which lost the United States Air Force competition to the YF-16. Both the F-16 and F-18 should become operational in the early 1980s.

General Dynamics F-111 and FB-111 *USA:* One of the most controversial military aircraft to go into production, the F-111 multi-purpose swing-wing fighter has, nevertheless, proved its unique capabilities under actual combat conditions.

The US Department of Defense held a design competition between Boeing and General Dynamics to develop a new type of Mach 2 fighter. General Dynamics were awarded the contract in 1962 – to produce 18 development F-111As for the United States Air Force, and five F-111Bs for the United States Navy. The first F-111A made its maiden flight on 21 December 1964, followed by the first flight with the variable-geometry wings operating on 6 January 1965. In October 1967 the first F-111As were handed over to an operational unit of the USAF, and production of this version subsequently reached 141 aircraft (not including development F-111s).

The 'A' was followed by 94 F-111Es for the USAF, with modified air intakes, which raised the maximum speed to Mach 2.5. This was the first version to be deployed in Europe, flying from Upper Heyford in Great Britain. Despite its designation, the F-111D was the next version; 96 were produced, with improved electronics. Production for the USAF was completed with 106 F-111F fighter-bombers.

Although Britain had ordered 50 F-111s as strike-reconnaisance fighters, the order was later cancelled; but 24 F-111C strike-fighters were delivered to the Royal Australian Air Force.

Congress terminated the naval F-111B programme, but features of this model were incorporated into 76 FB-111As, delivered to Strategic Air Command of the USAF as supersonic strategic bombers. The FB-111A, which became operational in 1969, is capable of carrying up to six nuclear bombs, or six SRAM short-range nuclear attack missiles, or up to 14 288 kg (31 500 lb) of conventional bombs.

Another version is the EF-111A, basically an F-111A converted to provide attack forces with ECM (electronic countermeasures) jamming over a wide area.

The F-111's proving ground was Vietnam, which gave the aircraft a chance to show whether the USAF's confidence was justified. Two of the first six F-111As sent to war were lost in the first week of operations. The fault was, however, more the planners' than the aircraft's – the USAF quickly learned that fast and expensive advanced fighters were not at all ideal for jungle warfare. But later F-111As flying at very low level over the mountains, using terrain-following radar, bombed North Vietnam heavily.

Gloster E.28/39 *Great Britain:* It may seem odd that the Gloster E.28/39 is covered by an entry in this book and not the Heinkel He 178, for the German aircraft is usually recorded by historians as the first jet-powered aircraft to fly, on 27 August 1939. However – although the Gloster followed the Heinkel into the air, becoming the first British jet-powered airplane to fly – Frank Whittle, the creator of the engine that powered the British aircraft, had designed the very first aircraft jet engine to run anywhere in the world, which it did for the first time as 12 April 1937.

The story of the E.28/39 really goes back to 1928, when Whittle, as a cadet at the Royal Air Force College, Cranwell, wrote a thesis entitled *Probable Future Developments in Aircraft Design*. In this, he set out his ideas and basic equations for a jet engine; only to have the whole thing regarded as science fiction by the sceptics. This is not surprising, as he suggested that a jet aircraft could cruise at 800 km/h (500 mph) at heights far beyond those attained by the finest fighters of the day, which flew at around 240 km/h (150 mph). Undeterred, he took out a patent on his design, which was awarded in 1932.

Things might not have progressed much further had it not been for another ex-Cranwell cadet named R. D. Williams, who got the money to exploit Whittle's ideas through a new company called Power Jets Limited. Whittle began the design and construction of his first engine, the U Type, and in April 1937 it was tested successfully. Now, the Air Ministry had to take notice and in 1938 ordered a new engine that could power an aircraft to be produced by the Gloster Aircraft Company.

Work progressed rather slowly and, in the meantime, the German Heinkel 178 had flown. The Gloster E.28/39, which first flew on 15 May 1941, was a much more refined aircraft. By then the Second World War was raging in Europe; so within three years Gloster developed and rushed into service a jet-powered fighter, known as the Meteor.

Gloster Gladiator *Great Britain:* On 11 June 1940 the Regia Aeronautica (Italian Air Force) began its air attacks on the island of Malta, which was an important target as it could threaten the sea routes between Italy and the German and Italian forces in North Africa. This was only the second day of the war for Italy, and its air force stood at over 2500 operational aircraft, of which a large proportion was directed against Malta. To defend the island there were just four Fleet Air Arm Sea Gladiator biplane fighters, soon reduced to three, which the Maltese named *Faith, Hope* and *Charity*. They had been assembled rapidly from their packing cases, which had been standing at the dockside, and kept the Italian Air Force at bay, unaided, until relief forces came to their aid on 28 June. This was undoubtedly the finest episode in the career of the Sea Gladiator.

The Gladiator was the last biplane fighter used by the Royal Air Force and resembled in many ways the older Gloster Gauntlet. However, it represented a half-way stage between the Gauntlet and the later Hawker Hurricane, in that it had an enclosed cockpit for the pilot, packed four guns instead of the two on the earlier type, and had an engine powerful enough to make it the fastest biplane fighter ever operated by the British services. The prototype first flew in 1934 and production examples began to equip RAF squadrons in 1937, followed by the first Fleet Air Arm Sea Gladiators in 1939.

Although their service life was brief, being largely superseded in the RAF by 1939, and in the FAA by 1940, a Gladiator claimed one of the first German aircraft (a Heinkel He 111) shot down over the British Isles. A little later, following Germany's invasion of Norway in April 1940, HMS *Glorious* sailed there with a Gladiator squadron on board, and these aircraft were sent to Lake Lesjaskog in central Norway where they landed on the frozen surface. Subsequent operations had to be flown against overwhelming odds and, although they shot down 14 enemy aircraft without loss in the air, almost the entire squadron was wrecked by enemy bombing. The pilots returned to Britain, but were soon back in northern Norway, where they added 36 enemy aircraft to their tally while employed in giving air cover to the British forces. After the evacuation was ordered, they re-landed on the aircraft carrier, which headed for home waters, only to be sunk en route.

RAF Gladiators served in Greece and the Middle East, and the type was exported to Belgium, Norway, Finland, and elsewhere.

Gloster Meteor *Great Britain:* Although Germany was first to fly a jet-propelled aircraft, the Heinkel He 178, on 27 August 1939, Britain soon caught up, and the Royal Air Force had its first operational jets as soon as the Luftwaffe. Britain's Gloster Meteor was a twin-engined fighter, armed with four cannon, and it embodied experience gained with the earlier Gloster E.28/39 experimental aircraft. A Meteor prototype first flew on 5 March 1943, followed by a small production run of 20 Mk Is, one of which was shipped to the United States in exchange for an example of the first US jet fighter, the Bell Airacomet. Sixteen of the remaining aircraft entered RAF service, from July 1944, with No 616 Squadron.

Meteor operations began on 27 July, when aircraft from the squadron flew from Manston to intercept German V1 flying bombs launched against southern England, a task normally carried out by Tempests and Spitfires. Problems with the guns meant that this first sortie was unsuccessful, although on 4 August a V1 was destroyed by one of the squadron's pilots, who drew alongside the flying bomb and sent it off course, by tipping its wing with his own wingtip. Later on the same day, another Meteor pilot destroyed a V1 with his guns.

By 1945 the Mk III Meteor was in RAF service, with Rolls-Royce Derwent instead of Welland engines, which increased its speed well above that of any piston-engined fighter. This version was more widely operated. Meteors were used in Europe as the Allies advanced into Germany, although they never met German Messerschmitt Me 262 jet-fighters in air combat.

After the war, production for the RAF and the air forces of other countries continued, including night-fighter, ground-attack and photo-reconnaissance variants. British Meteors set up a series of official and unofficial speed records, culminating in September 1946 in a world absolute speed record of 990 km/h (615 mph) by a Meteor F.4. Meteors of the Royal Australian Air Force were the only British-built jet-fighters to serve in the Korean War of 1950–53. It was several more years before the Meteor was retired from RAF strength.

Gotha G series *Germany:* When the Frenchman Louis Blériot crossed the English Channel in 1909, there could be heard, amidst the jubilation, the voices of those who spoke of Britain as no longer an island protected by a stretch of sea and the might of the Royal Navy. Far-sighted strategists viewed Blériot's success as an embryo bridge that could bring new dangers to hitherto impregnable shores. Their fears seemed likely to be realized with the beginning of the First World War when, almost

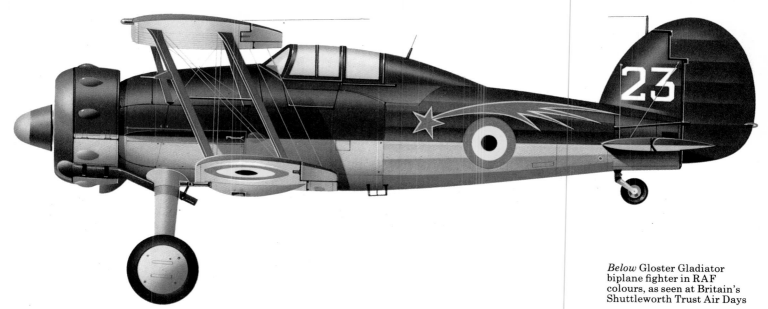

Above Gloster Gladiator of the Belgian Air Force

Opposite above General Dynamics F-111E fighter-bomber

Opposite below General Dynamics F-16 lightweight fighter armed with advanced Sidewinder air-to-air missiles on the wingtips

Below Gloster Meteor F.8 jet fighter

Below Gloster Gladiator biplane fighter in RAF colours, as seen at Britain's Shuttleworth Trust Air Days

Above Gloster E.28/39, the first British jet-powered aircraft to fly, shown above in modified form

Left Heinkel He 178, the world's first turbojet-powered aircraft to fly

Opposite German Gotha G.V heavy bomber of the First World War

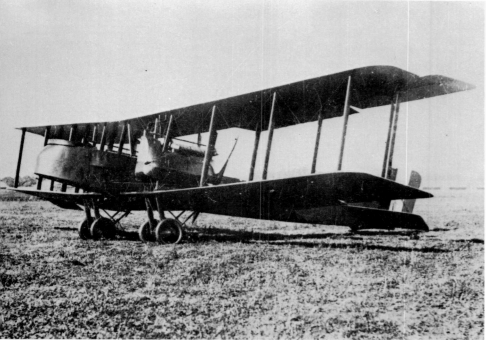

immediately, light bombing attacks on continental targets were made by small German aircraft such as the 'bird-like' Etrich Taube.

Soon, at night, new silent raiders began bombing attacks over Britain, in January 1915. They were the menacing Zeppelin airships, each capable of carrying enough bombs to cause widespread damage to homes, factories, railway stations and other military targets. By 1917 the Zeppelins were being mastered by the defences, only to be joined by the most terrible of all aircraft in the form of Gotha heavy bombers.

Although smaller than the gigantic German Zeppelin R-type bombers, which were also flown against English targets, Gothas were responsible for dropping the greatest tonnage of bombs on England. Twin-engined machines, carrying up to 500 kg (1100 lb) of bombs, Gothas became operational with the German Air Force in 1916. After a few minor raids on England, the first mass Gotha attack was made in daylight on 25 May 1917, when 21 aircraft flew over Folkestone and Shorncliffe and bombed the towns. They killed 91 people and injured many others. On 13 June 1917, 14 Gothas made the first mass bombing raid on London, resulting in 162 deaths and 432 injuries.

Hastily, British aircraft were brought back from France to act as home defence fighters, compelling the Gothas to switch from day to night raids by the spring of 1918. Even under cover of darkness they were pursued relentlessly by British fighters like the S.E.5a and Sopwith Camel. The first Gotha to be shot down at night fell to the guns of a Camel of No 44 Squadron, Royal Flying Corps, in early 1918.

Fighter successes, and accidents caused by the Gotha's need for specially prepared airfields to land on at night, led to the cessation of raids on England in May 1918. The attacks had had one unintentional effect on the course of the war. Terrified by them, the British public had demanded that the same treatment should be meted out by the RFC on German targets. This encouraged the setting up of the Independent Force of the newly-formed Royal Air Force for bombing.

Grumman A-6 Intruder *USA:* The Intruder is a distinctive-looking carrier-borne attack bomber and is currently operational with the US Navy and Marine Corps. It was developed to carry a wide range of nuclear or conventional weapons, and to be able to attack targets at long range in all weathers or in total darkness. These attributes make the Intruder a most formidable aircraft.

The first version of the Intruder, the A-6A, was delivered to the US Navy from February 1963, and in all some 482 were eventually produced. Many were used in action during the Vietnam War with success, but continuing development will eventually bring all remaining A-6As up to the latest A-6E standard. Some have already been converted into other versions, such as EA-6As equipped to jam and

confuse enemy electronic countermeasures and for electronic intelligence; A-6Bs which carry Standard ARM anti-radiation missiles; A-6Cs with increased night attack capability; and KA-6D flight-refuelling tankers.

The A-6E Intruder has improved avionics, and became operational in 1972. By 1976 about 58 had been built as new aircraft, and a much larger number had been produced by converting earlier A-6As.

Grumman E-2 Hawkeye *USA:* Not in the strict sense a combat aircraft, yet very necessary for the protection of naval forces, the Hawkeye is the US Navy's standard early warning aircraft. The first production version was the E-2A Hawkeye, which made its maiden flight in April 1961, and became operational on USS *Kitty Hawk* in 1965. Since then the improved E-2B and E-2C versions have appeared, the latter becoming operational in 1973, and featuring an advanced radar. Hawkeyes currently serve on all large United States aircraft carriers.

Among the highly sophisticated electronic equipment that the Hawkeye carries (to enable it to detect approaching missiles and high-speed enemy aircraft in all weathers and in an electronic jamming and ground clutter environment) it has a large saucer-like rotodome on top

of the fuselage which houses an antenna system. This rotates slowly to give an all-round picture. The information that the antenna provides is processed on board the aircraft and then relayed to a Naval Tactical Data System, which is responsible for alerting interceptor-fighters or launching missiles, if necessary, to counter the threat.

Production of the E-2C Hawkeye for the US Navy will continue into the 1980s.

Grumman F4F Wildcat *USA:* From 1931 until 1936 Grumman produced a series of classic biplane fighters for the United States Navy, all of which had uniquely-retracting undercarriages. When the Navy requested designs for a new carrier-borne fighter in 1935, Grumman won the contract with yet another biplane. But as work on the XF4F-1 progressed it became clear that existing F3F biplane fighters could match its performance if re-engined.

Grumman started again and, instead of the new biplane, produced the prototype XF4F-2 monoplane fighter, which first flew on 2 September 1937. This aircraft did not appear to be as good as the Brewster F2A Buffalo (the first monoplane fighter of the US Navy, and later to prove a disappointment) and no orders for it were placed. Nevertheless, Grumman was awarded a contract for another prototype, the

Grumman Martlet II carrier-borne fighter of the Royal Navy

Previous pages Grumman E-2C Hawkeye early warning aircraft, escorted by two Grumman F-14A Tomcats

Grumman FF-1, the first US Navy fighter with a retractable undercarriage

XF4F-3, using a later Twin Wasp engine with a two-stage supercharger. In this form it first flew on 12 February 1939, and the first production contract was awarded just before the outbreak of war in Europe.

At this time France was looking around desperately for any modern aircraft; so it ordered a fairly large number of G-36A export versions of the F4F-3. Powered by a Wright engine, the G-36A was not delivered in time to help France, and the contract was taken over by Britain. This is how the Fleet Air Arm began to receive the first of a large number of Grumman fighters, which it named Martlets, in the latter half of 1940.

From the late autumn of 1941, Martlets were delivered with foldable wings, to aid stowage on board ship. However, while the Martlets' performance was better than that of the British carrier-borne fighters they were replacing, the narrow-track undercarriage gave their pilots many anxious moments while landing on the decks of carriers. This did not prevent Martlets from being widely used by the FAA for convoy protection duties in the Atlantic and Mediterranean.

Meanwhile, the United States had entered the war in December 1941, and the US Navy's F4Fs, known as Wildcats, immediately went into action, shooting down their first Japanese bomber just two days after outbreak of war with Japan. From that point the Wildcat was never out of the fray, forming the fighting spearhead of the US carriers involved in the great sea battles of the Coral Sea and Midway. Wildcat production continued until the autumn of 1945, the FAA adopting the US name for its Mk V and VI models.

Grumman F-14A Tomcat *USA:* The late 1960s and 1970s have proven extremely difficult times for military planners in the West. While countries like the Soviet Union have been producing many hundreds of new military aircraft each year – in the West inflation, some public opinion and political pressures have caused the replacement of outdated aircraft to take second place.

Occasionally a government's hand is forced into action, as was the case with the Tomcat. In the 1960s, news reached the West of a new Soviet fighter, the MiG-25, which was capable of flying at over three times the speed of sound. A specially-prepared version of this aircraft set up impressive height and speed records.

Quickly the US Navy arranged a design competition for a new high-performance multi-role fighter, and in 1969 Grumman was selected to produce prototypes of what became the F-14 Tomcat. The first flew on 21 December 1970, but

113

was lost in an accident. Development continued, and aircraft carrier trials were started in 1972. Deployment of operational aircraft to the US Navy began later that year, and between 1974 and 1975 Tomcats became operational on board the carriers USS *Enterprise* and USS *John F. Kennedy*.

By 1977 well over 234 Tomcats had been delivered to the Navy, and these have proved excellent multi-role fighters, their fine high-and low-speed flying characteristics and superb manoeuvrability resulting from use of variable-geometry or swing wings. During one test firing of the aircraft's Phoenix missile, the weapon was launched while the small pilotless jet target was still 200 km (126 miles) away, flying at supersonic speed and using jammers to confuse the missile's homing equipment. This did not prevent Phoenix passing so close that it would have destroyed the target had it been fitted with a live warhead.

Tomcats have also been supplied to the Imperial·Iranian Air Force, which ordered 80 aircraft.

Grumman FF-1 *USA:* The Grumman FF-1 has two major claims to fame – as the United States Navy's first fighter aircraft with a retractable undercarriage, and as the only American fighter to be flown in the Spanish Civil War.

It was the first aircraft designed by the Grumman Aircraft Engineering Corporation, which had been founded in December 1929 and began by producing floats to convert naval seaplanes into amphibians. The quality of workmanship, and the enterprising manner of

the company, quickly led to a US Navy order for an example of a fighter aircraft that Grumman had designed. Known as the XFF-1, this was a two-seat biplane, intended for operation from aircraft carriers and powered by a large radial engine. For highest possible performance, the main undercarriage wheels were made to retract into wells in the forward fuselage, and an enclosed cockpit was fitted.

This aircraft first flew in late 1931 and, after being re-engined, achieved over 320 km/h (200 mph). This was considerably faster than any single or two-seat fighter then in service, so the Navy ordered an initial batch of 27 more. Others followed, with different engines, including dual-control operational trainers.

The FF-1 first became operational in June 1933, and served initially on board the USS *Lexington*. The FF-1 had also stirred up interest in Canada, and was licence-built there as the Goblin I for the Royal Canadian Air Force. Forty Canadian FF-1s were exported to Turkey – which passed on its aircraft to the Republican forces when the civil war started in Spain in 1936. One FF-1 went to Japan where it was tested for ideas which could be incorporated into the nation's own aircraft – and one went to Nicaragua.

Grumman TBF Avenger *USA:* The Grumman Avenger was designed as a replacement for the Douglas Devastator, a torpedo-bomber of 1937 vintage which caused considerable damage to Japanese ships during the early sea battles of the Pacific War.

The prototype Avenger first flew in 1941 and

Overleaf Grumman Avenger torpedo-bomber of the US Navy

Grumman A-6E Intruder from USS *Enterprise*

Grumman Wildcat of the US
Navy

America's nuclear-powered
aircraft carrier USS
Enterprise, with Grumman
F-14A Tomcat fighters and
Sikorsky Sea King
helicopters on the stern, and
other Grumman aircraft
forward, including E-2
Hawkeye early warning
aircraft

joined the United States Navy just in time to take part in the Battle of Midway in June 1942. Compared with the aircraft it was replacing, the Avenger was much faster, was able to carry twice the warload and was better defended, having a power-operated rear turret as part of its five machine-gun armament. In addition to Avengers of the US Navy, a very large number went into British service from 1943, being known originally as Tarpons. However, the aircraft had been designed to carry an American 22 inch torpedo internally, and British torpedoes would not fit properly – so Fleet Air Arm Avengers operated mainly as bombers with loads of up to 900 kg (2000 lb), as attack aircraft armed with rocket projectiles or as minelayers. They were employed against German sea and land targets and against Japan. A small number were also flown by the Royal New Zealand Air Force.

During the war years, US Navy Avengers were, understandably, the most active and claimed many victories, including the sinking of the Japanese aircraft carrier *Hiyo* near the Mariana Islands on 19 June 1944. With the war won, America continued flying Avengers until 1954, many with special modifications such as a huge under-belly radar for anti-submarine and other duties. The FAA flew the type even longer, on similar duties, as did Canada, the Netherlands and France. Ironically, the Japanese Maritime Self Defence Force was also provided with anti-submarine Avengers.

Handley Page H.P.42 *Great Britain:*
Beginning in 1916, Handley Page became
famous for the construction of giant aircraft –
its bombers of the First World War starting a
line which, by 1930, led to the H.P.42 commercial airliner built for Imperial Airways.

This aircraft was often described by Handley
Page as the first real airliner, although this
claim is hard to substantiate in view of the
earlier introduction of aircraft like the
Armstrong Whitworth Argosy. The H.P.42 was,
nevertheless, an extremely fine and significant
airplane. Eight were built, in two versions – the
'E' or Eastern (Hannibal class) and the 'W' or
Western (Heracles class) – the first example
flying initially on 14 November 1930. The 'E'
model, with seating for 24 passengers, was
designed for operations in semi-tropical climates along the air-mail routes from Egypt
eastwards to India and southward to Kenya.
The 'W', with 38 seats, was flown to the
continent from Croydon Airport.

Apart from its incredible STOL performance
and reliability, the H.P.42 was above all famous
for its passenger comfort, although the design
created tremendous drag, which reduced speed.
The two main passenger cabins were positioned
fore and aft of the wings, the centre portion of
the fuselage accommodating the baggage hold
and the kitchen. The cabins themselves looked
like the interior of a royal railway coach. The
two pilots sat high in the nose of the aircraft,
and originally found it so difficult to get
orientated that a metal structure was temporarily mounted on the nose of the first H.P.42
to indicate the horizon. It was soon removed
and the H.P.42s built up an unrivalled reputation for safety and reliability. They never
killed a passenger until the last of them
disappeared during a wartime flight in the
Middle East in 1940.

Handley Page Halifax *Great Britain:* Of the
three main types of four-engined heavy bombers
which served with Royal Air Force Bomber
Command during the Second World War, the
Halifax was the second to begin operations
against German targets. It never quite earned
the reputation of the later Lancaster, but

logged more than 75530 wartime missions
between 10 March 1941 and 25 April 1945.

Designed to an Air Ministry requirement of
1936, the first prototype made its maiden flight
in October 1939, a month after the war in
Europe had started. Deliveries were made
initially to No 35 Squadron, at Leeming in
Yorkshire, in November 1940; production
thereafter running at a high rate until 6176 had
been built. The Mk VII was the last bomber
version. Subsequent variants were the Mks VIII
and IX unarmed transports.

The Halifax bomber made its first raid on
Berlin on the night of 17/18 April 1941, in
company with Avro Manchesters and Short
Stirlings. In a change of tactics at the end of
June, a number carried out an attack on Kiel in
daylight; but the vast majority of operations
took place at night. By November 1941, the
Halifax was well established in service and took
part in one of the heaviest raids against
Germany up to that time – a 400-bomber attack
on Berlin, Cologne and Mannheim, which was
achieved at fairly high cost. When the 1000-
bomber raids on Germany were mounted,
Halifaxes were among the main participants.
The last really heavy raid in which the type
took part was probably that against Dortmund,
when Halifaxes and Lancasters released 4800
tons of bombs over the target in mid-March
1945.

A number of Halifaxes also operated in the
Middle East and with Coastal Command, and
were used for dropping paratroopers and for
reconnaissance missions. The Halifax was also
the main type used to tow Horsa and Hamilcar
troop-carrying and freight-carrying gliders to
France on 6 June 1944 – D-Day.

Handley Page Hampden *Great Britain:*
Distinctive for its 'flying panhandle' fuselage,
the Hampden was the result of trying to design a
bomber that would carry a heavy warload, and
have a long range, while being fast and
manoeuvrable. Compared with its Royal Air
Force contemporaries, it certainly offered speed
and manoeuvrability, but only at the expense of
bomb load and crew comfort, the fuselage being
less than 1m (3ft) wide at its broadest point.
Another serious shortcoming was that its
machine-guns in nose, dorsal and ventral
positions, plus a single forward-firing fixed gun,
were inadequate to defend it properly.

The prototype Hampden first flew in June
1936, and large numbers of production aircraft
were ordered soon afterwards. Delivery to the

Handley Page Halifax III

RAF began in 1938, and there were eight full Hampden squadrons by the beginning of the war, intended primarily for day bombing. These units also carried out the first British mining operations off the Danish coast as early as April 1940. Losses were generally so heavy, however, that the Hampdens were transferred to night bombing duties – and with improved armament performed reasonably well. Hampdens, flying alongside Wellingtons and Whitleys, carried out many attacks on Germany, and on Italy from the latter part of 1940, including participation in the first 1000-bomber raid on Cologne; but in September 1942 they were retired from such missions.

From that time the Hampden reverted to minelaying, but now with Coastal Command. It also performed well as a torpedo-bomber, until withdrawn completely in 1944.

A version of the Hampden with Napier Dagger engines was the Hereford, but this served mainly as a training aircraft.

Handley Page O/400 *Great Britain:* Developed from the Handley Page O/100 heavy bomber, of which 46 were built, the O/400 was similar in most respects but had more powerful engines and better-positioned fuel tanks. These two bombers were the largest landplanes used by the British during the First World War.

The O/100 established a reasonable war record in France from 1916, as a day and, later, night bomber. Early losses during day operations had been caused by the inability of the lumbering bombers to fly at greater speeds and altitudes than opposing German fighters. Development of the improved O/400 was initiated to reduce vulnerability to attack; but the official view was that day bombing by smaller and faster aircraft could better achieve the required results. When further work on the O/400 was cancelled, it seemed to be the end of the big bomber until, of all people, the Germans helped to change the official attitude.

In the summer of 1917, air raids by German Gothas caused considerable damage to British targets, including London, and the cry of the British public was for revenge. This they got, for O/400s were ordered in sizeable numbers and soon began to reach France. No fewer than seven squadrons of the specially-formed Independent Force eventually used the type for strategic bombing raids on German targets. Particularly memorable were events on the night of 14/15 September 1918, when a formation of 40 O/400s bombed the Saar region, in Germany. By that time their weapons included a huge 1650 lb 'block-buster' bomb.

An O/400 was the first aircraft to be flown from Britain to Egypt, in August 1918. After the war several O/400s were delivered to the Chinese Aviation Service.

Handley Page Victor *Great Britain:* Adaptability for other duties has always been a major asset of military aircraft when they have become obsolete in their original roles. This is certainly true of what were once Britain's finest and most formidable combat aircraft, the Victor and the Avro Vulcan.

The Victor was one of three types of modern jet-powered medium bombers, built in the early 1950s, that gave Britain its original nuclear deterrent capability. The prototype first flew on Christmas Eve 1952, and featured an unusual crescent wing, originally flight tested in scaled-down form on the Handley Page H.P.88 research aircraft. By 1958 Bomber Command of the RAF was receiving its first production examples, as Victor B.Mk 1/1As, followed in 1961 by much improved Victor B.Mk 2s. From 1964, the Mk 2s carried Blue Steel, Britain's first nuclear stand-off bomb.

When Mk 1 aircraft were gradually retired, they were converted into flight-refuelling tankers. Likewise, when responsibility for Britain's nuclear attack capability was transferred to the Navy's Polaris submarines, the Victor Mk 2's role was changed from low-level attack to flight refuelling. The Mk 2 then began replacing the Mk 1, carrying more advanced equipment capable of servicing three aircraft at once. In this role it continues to serve today.

Hawker Fury *Great Britain:* The Hawker Fury single-seat fighter was developed along the same lines as the Hawker Hart bomber, gaining its high speed by virtue of its 525 hp Rolls-Royce Kestrel in-line engine which, closely cowled, gave the aircraft a beautifully streamlined fuselage. This was coupled with the very careful design of the aircraft as a whole, to reduce drag to a minimum.

When it entered Royal Air Force service in 1931 as the Fury I, going first to No 43 Squadron, it became the first fighter to be capable of more than 322 km/h (200 mph) in level flight – considerably faster than the then current Gloster Gamecocks and Bristol Bulldog Mk IIs.

Handley Page Hampden I

119

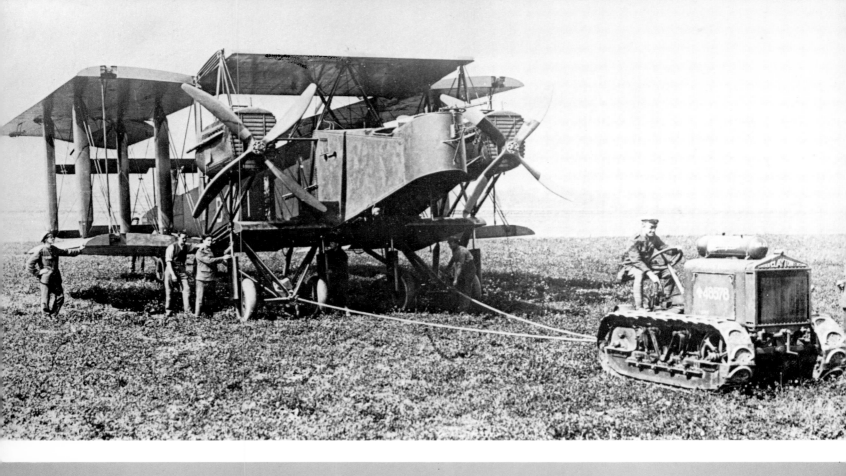

Opposite above Handley Page
O/400 heavy bomber of the
Independent Force being
towed with its wings folded

Opposite below One of
Imperial Airways' majestic
H.P.42 biplane airliners at
Croydon Airport in the 1930s

Right Handley Page
Hampden bomber, known as
the 'flying panhandle'

Below Handley Page Halifax
III heavy bomber

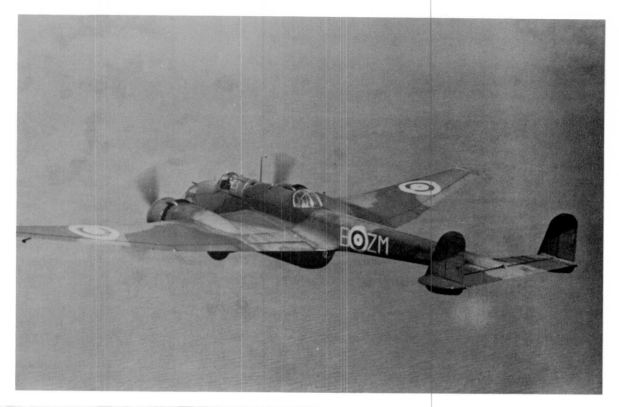

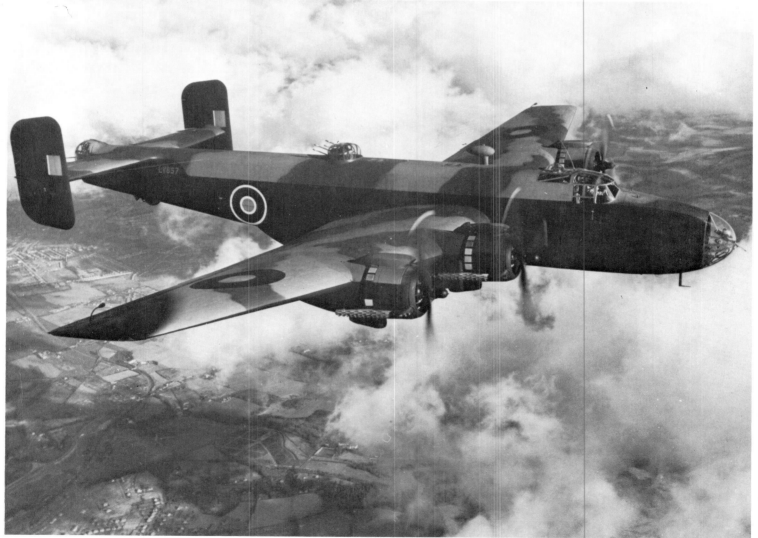

The RAF was proud of the Fury and sent a service flight to the centennial celebrations held at Toronto.

Fury Is remained in RAF first-line service until 1939, by which time they were thoroughly outclassed by the latest Hawker fighter, the 521 km/h (324 mph) Hurricane. However, production Furies had been exported to other countries, the largest sales being to Persia (Iran), which operated 20 aircraft powered by large radial engines.

After several years of operational flying, and because the expansion programme of the RAF was underway, a new version of the aircraft appeared as the Fury II. This was basically an interim fighter to serve until sufficient numbers of Hurricanes had been produced to take over as the main interceptor fighters of the RAF. Yet, because of its larger 640 hp Kestrel engine, it was able to fly at 359 km/h (223 mph), and increased the already good rate of climb by about a third. Fury IIs first went to No 25 Squadron in 1937 and subsequently equipped a total of six squadrons. Their operational life with the RAF was very brief, extending only through 1937 and 1938.

Fury IIs were also exported, the greatest number going to Yugoslavia which purchased ten.

Hawker Hart *Great Britain*: How much the Hart day bomber owed to the earlier Fairey Fox cannot be judged – what is certain is that the Hart's streamlined fuselage shape, and consequent high speed, resulted from the use of a closely-cowled in-line engine – a feature pioneered by the Fox in Britain. Otherwise, the Hart was far superior in both design and performance, proving such a sturdy, adaptable type that it inspired all subsequent Hawker designs until the Hurricane monoplane, which retained a Hart-like fuselage.

The prototype Hart bomber flew for the first time in mid-1928 at Brooklands, and was faster than most fighters then in service. Coupled with the fact that it could carry 225 kg (500 lb) of bombs (then regarded as a good load), it was clearly a desirable aircraft. Following a small development batch of Harts, production bombers were delivered to No 33 Squadron, Royal Air Force, in January 1930. In all, production totalled 983 aircraft, and included versions for service in India (where Harts continued flying right up to 1939, on the troublesome north-west frontier), a specially equipped version for tropical flying, a communications version and a dual-control trainer. Harts were also exported to five countries, of which Sweden also licence-built 42 examples.

The same basic design formula was used by Hawker in several other of its 'between wars' aircraft, including the Fury, Demon fighter, Nimrod carrier-borne naval fighter, Osprey naval-reconnaissance fighter, Hardy and Audax general-purpose aircraft, Hartbees ground attack aircraft and Hind light bomber.

Hawker Hunter *Great Britain*: The Hunter is still regarded today as one of the best ground-attack aircraft in military service, yet it was as an interceptor that it first entered Royal Air Force service in mid-1954. The prototype, known as the P.1067, had first flown on 20 July 1951, and subsequent production covered several different versions for operation with the RAF, Royal Navy, and the air forces of other countries. In particular, Switzerland received a number of new aircraft during the production phase, and as late as 1970 ordered a total of 60 more refurbished Hunters for its air force.

In its initial operations, the Hunter, with its very high subsonic speed, represented a major improvement over the Gloster Meteors, previously the RAF's standard jet-fighters. In fact, a Hunter had regained the world speed record for Britain in 1953, from the US Sabre. Hunters became standard equipment of many squadrons, and were among the aircraft based in Malta and Cyprus for operation during the Suez crisis of October/November 1956. RAF Hunters were also used in action during the Aden troubles.

Since then, Hunters of other air forces have seen plenty of action, during the wars between India and Pakistan, and in the Middle East with Jordan. Hunters are still flying as fighter-bombers around the world, but those with the RAF remain mainly as trainers.

Hawker Hurricane *Great Britain*: Often underrated in favour of the Spitfire, the Hurricane was the main victor of the Battle of Britain, as the Royal Air Force had at that time 32 Hurricane squadrons, compared with 19 Spitfire squadrons. This meant that 620 Hurricane and Spitfire fighters (with another 84 assorted fighters like the Gloster Gladiator) had to face the German air threat of 3500 bombers and fighters.

The Hurricane was the work of Sydney Camm, who began its design in 1934. The prototype first took to the air on 6 November 1935, at Brooklands, and the initial production Hurricane I entered RAF service in December 1937, with No 111 Squadron. Powered by the famous Rolls-Royce Merlin engine, it became the first RAF monoplane fighter with an enclosed cockpit and retractable undercarriage, its first fighter capable of a level speed in excess of 483 km/h (300 mph), and its first eight-gun fighter.

During the Battle of Britain, which began in earnest on 8 August 1940, Hurricanes concentrated mainly on the destruction of the German bombers, as these were the aircraft that would cause the most damage if allowed to get through. The only Victoria Cross ever awarded to a Fighter Command pilot was won by Ft Lt James Nicolson, a Hurricane pilot of No 249 Squadron who, on 16 August 1940, while attacking a German aircraft in front of him, was pounced on from above and behind by other German aircraft. Nicolson's aircraft caught

Opposite Handley Page Victor tanker of the RAF, about to refuel a Hawker Siddeley Harrier

Opposite Hawker Fury I of No 1 Squadron, RAF

Opposite below Hawker Fury of the Yugoslav Air Force

Handley Page O/400

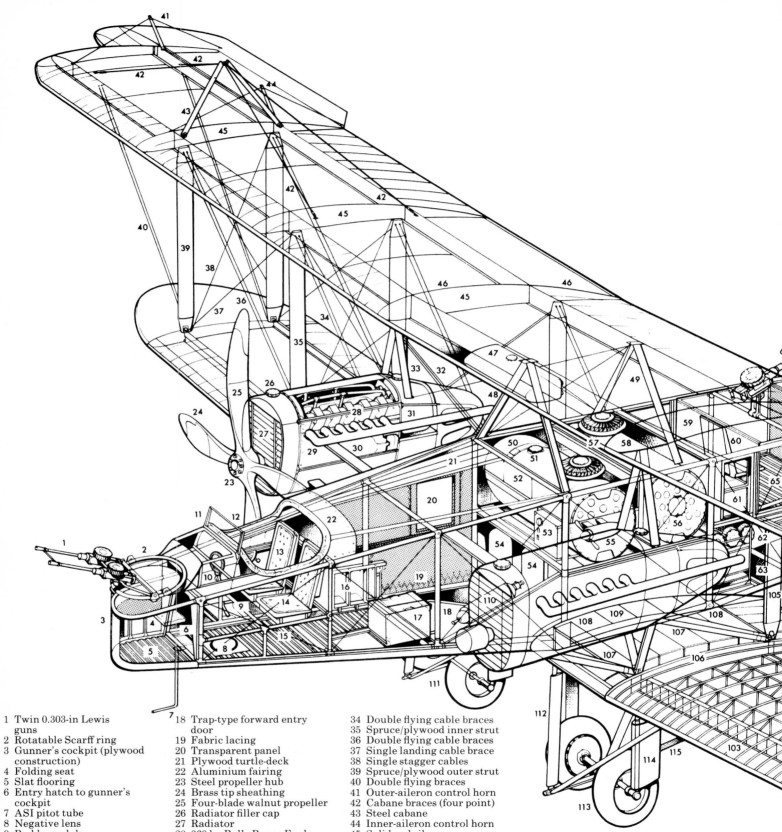

1 Twin 0.303-in Lewis guns
2 Rotatable Scarff ring
3 Gunner's cockpit (plywood construction)
4 Folding seat
5 Slat flooring
6 Entry hatch to gunner's cockpit
7 ASI pitot tube
8 Negative lens
9 Rudder pedals
10 Control wheel
11 Clear Pyralin windshield
12 Padded cockpit coaming
13 Pilot's seat
14 Observer's seat
15 Slat flooring
16 Light-bomb rack (manual)
17 Batteries

18 Trap-type forward entry door
19 Fabric lacing
20 Transparent panel
21 Plywood turtle-deck
22 Aluminium fairing
23 Steel propeller hub
24 Brass tip sheathing
25 Four-blade walnut propeller
26 Radiator filler cap
27 Radiator
28 360 hp Rolls-Royce Eagle VIII engine
29 Exhaust manifold
30 Nacelle bracing strut/control spar
31 Oil tank, 15 Imp gal (68 l) in each nacelle
32 Rigging lines
33 Streamlined steel struts

34 Double flying cable braces
35 Spruce/plywood inner strut
36 Double flying cable braces
37 Single landing cable brace
38 Single stagger cables
39 Spruce/plywood outer strut
40 Double flying braces
41 Outer-aileron control horn
42 Cabane braces (four point)
43 Steel cabane
44 Inner-aileron control horn
45 Solid end ribs
46 Wing dihedral break-line
47 Gravity-feed fuel tanks in leading edge, two of 12-Imp gal (54.5 l) capacity
48 Centre-section streamlined forward cabane strut
49 Centre-section streamlined aft cabane strut

124

50 Forward cylindrical fuel
   tank (held by web straps),
   capacity 130 Imp gal (591 l)
51 Filler cap
52 Cross member
53 Engine control pulley
   cluster
54 Centre-section main bomb-
   bay
55 Six volt wind-driven
   generator (port and
   starboard)
56 Perforated baffle plate
57 Air-driven fuel pumps
58 Aft fuel tank, capacity 130
   Imp gal (591 l)
59 Solid rib at dihedral break-
   line
60 Upper gunner's seat
61 Transparent panels
62 Ammunition racks
63 Ventral gunner's hatch
64 Clear Pyralin panels
65 Gunner's slatted flooring
66 Plywood bulkheads
67 Single dorsal 0.303-in Lewis
   gun
68 Fabric lacing
69 Control cable pulleys
70 Fuselage frame
71 Multi-strand cable bracing
72 Elevator control cable
73 Interplane streamlined
   spruce strut

74 Starboard rudder
75 Fabric-covered upper
   tailplane
76 Elevator control horn
77 Fixed surface centre-section
78 Fabric-covered elevator
79 Port rudder spruce frame
80 Port lower elevator frame
81 Fabric-covered lower
   tailplane
82 Rudder hinge spar
83 Plywood tail covering
84 Rear navigation light
85 Interplane strut
86 Vertical stabilizer
87 Steel attachment point
88 Faired struts
89 Tailskid

90 Removable fabric panel
91 Lifting points (stations 10
   and 12)
92 Port steel cabane
93 Rear upper mainplane spar
94 Forward upper mainplane
   spar
95 Plywood covering
96 Steel fitting
97 Solid drag strut
98 Wing structure
99 Port aileron structure
100 Port outer interplane struts
    (plywood-covered spruce)
101 Lower mainplane end rib
102 Wing structure
103 Leading-edge rib
    construction

104 Port inner interplane struts
    (plywood-covered spruce)
105 Hinge strut
106 Lower mainplane dihedral
    break-line
107 Steel tube engine nacelle
    support struts
108 Wing/fuselage attachment
    points
109 Wing root walkway
110 Fire extinguisher
111 Starboard undercarriage
112 Undercarriage forward
    strut
113 Port twin mainwheels
114 Faired rubber cord shock
    strut
115 Aft strut

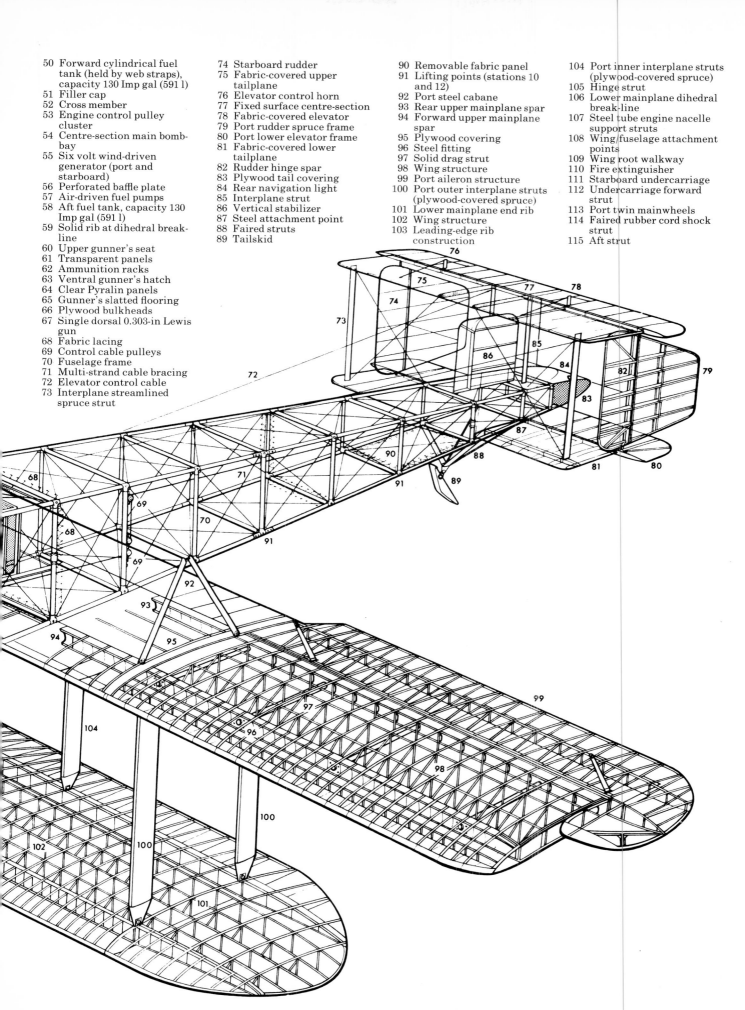

Hawker Hurricane

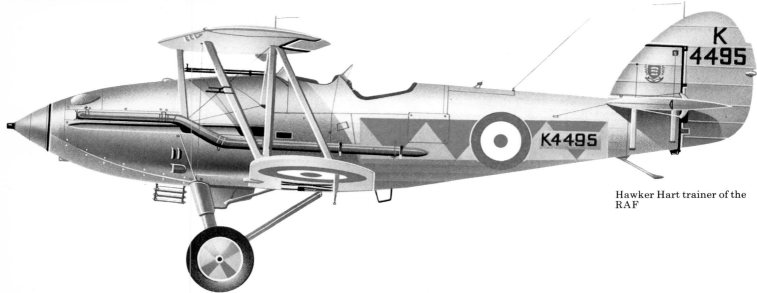

Hawker Hart trainer of the RAF

fire, but he continued his attack until he had shot down his original target, then parachuted to safety. The highest scoring Allied pilot of the battle – a Czech named Sergeant Josef Frantisek, who claimed 17 victories – was also a Hurricane pilot.

When it became clear that the Hurricane was becoming outclassed as a pure fighter, other duties were assigned to it. In October 1941 the 'Hurribomber' fighter-bomber came into being, carrying either two 113 kg (250 lb) or two 226 kg (500 lb) bombs under its wings. The Mk IID of 1942 was fitted with two 40 mm cannon for tank busting and two machine-guns, and was operated mainly in North Africa against Rommel's desert forces and in Burma against the Japanese. Other Hurricanes carried rocket projectiles as alternative ground attack weapons.

Perhaps the most important sub-variant was the Sea Hurricane. This operated from aircraft carriers, being fitted usually with catapult spools and arrester hook. However, most Sea Hurricanes were not newly-built fighters but converted RAF types, and were deployed originally not for aircraft carrier operations but to protect merchant shipping. To combat German maritime-reconnaissance bombers, some ships were converted into CAMs (catapult aircraft merchantmen) which meant that a Hurricane fighter could be launched from the ship when danger approached. The biggest problem was

RAF Hawker Hunter F.4 fighter

Hawker Hurricane Mk I

that the fighter could not re-land on board, and so the pilot had to ditch it in the sea. The main areas of operation for the 'Catafighters' were in the Mediterranean and Baltic, but by 1943 the Sea Hurricane had all but disappeared from service.

Of the 14 533 production Hurricanes built, some had gone for service with other air forces. In particular, nearly 3000 were despatched to the Soviet Union to aid its fight against the Germans on the Eastern Front. The first Hurricane sorties in Russia were made on 11 September 1941 in defence of Murmansk, pilots from France, Britain and America helping the Soviets in their task.

Hawker Typhoon *Great Britain:* The Typhoon was the Royal Air Force's first fighter with a speed of over 644 km/h (400 mph), yet its initial performance was so poor that it might well have been withdrawn from service.

It had originally been designed as a replacement for the Hawker Hurricane fighter which, by 1941, was becoming outclassed. The prototype made its maiden flight on 24 February 1940 and production aircraft began to equip RAF squadrons by July 1941. In 1940 the Air Ministry had urgently requested a new fighter that could catch and deal with the German Focke-Wulf Fw 190 fighters that were by then making low-altitude attacks on Britain. The

Hawker Hurricane IIC of the Portuguese Air Force

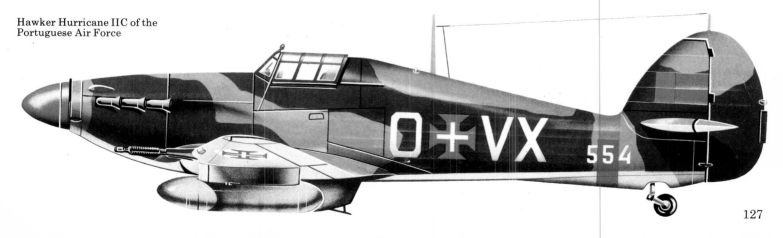

127

Typhoon had the necessary speed and, armed initially with 12 machine-guns but later four 20 mm cannon, also had the fire power. Unfortunately, in service it was found that the Napier Sabre engine was unreliable and gave the aircraft a poor rate of climb and inferior high-altitude performance. Nevertheless, the Typhoon was employed against the Fw 190s until the latter part of 1942, and did the job quite successfully.

Next, Typhoons began to make their own raids on Europe and on enemy shipping, and for this attack role they were eminently suited. Carrying up to two 454 kg (1000 lb) bombs or rocket projectiles, the Typhoon was able to attack anything from tanks to ships at low level and soon built up an excellent reputation. Perhaps the best remembered single achievement of the Typhoon came in August 1944 when advancing American forces trapped what remained of 16 German divisions near Falaise in France. The RAF Typhoons were called in, and on one day alone waves of Typhoons destroyed 137 German Panzer tanks. The Typhoon attack continued for some days, eventually laying waste all the German armour, until the remaining force was captured.

Hawker Siddeley Buccaneer *Great Britain:* The Buccaneer was designed in the early 1950s, to satisfy a Royal Navy requirement for a low-level strike aircraft that could fly at just under the speed of sound and operate from aircraft carriers. The Blackburn company (later part of Hawker Siddeley) evolved it as the B.103, the first of which flew in April 1958.

Production of the Buccaneer for the Navy was in two main versions, the S Mk 1 with two Gyron Junior 101 engines and the S Mk 2 with Rolls-Royce Spey engines. Naval squadrons began receiving Buccaneers from July 1962, which were flown from Britain's aircraft carriers and naval shore bases. Armed with nuclear or conventional bombs, and Bullpup or Martel air-to-surface missiles, they were capable of making long-range attacks on surface targets, approaching at a height of only 60 m (200 ft) above the land or sea.

Late in the Buccaneer's career, the Royal Air Force also decided to use them, and the first of several squadrons became operational in July 1970. Two of the RAF Buccaneer squadrons are currently based in Germany. With a maximum weapon load of up to 7257 kg (16 000 lb), carried on a rotating weapons bay door and externally, the Buccaneer packs a greater warload than the basic Lancaster four-engined heavy bomber of the Second World War. The South African Air Force also operates a small number, each fitted with an auxiliary rocket engine to boost performance.

Still with a major role in the defence of Britain, and as part of the NATO force in Europe, the Buccaneer will remain operational for some years. However, when the Royal Navy's last big aircraft carrier, HMS *Ark*

Royal, is decommissioned at the end of this decade, it will spell the end of Buccaneer flying at sea.

Hawker Hart light bomber showing clearly the observer's rear-mounted gun

Hawker Siddeley Harrier *Great Britain:* The Hawker Siddeley Harrier was the world's first operational vertical take-off and landing airplane, and remained unique until the introduction of 'Forger' into Soviet service in 1976. What is not generally known is that this single-seat attack aircraft, which normally flies just below the speed of sound at low altitudes, has engaged in and often won simulated dogfights against the best US fighter.

Developed from the Hawker Siddeley Kestrel experimental V/STOL tactical fighter, which first flew in October 1960, the Harrier took to the air on 31 August 1966. Six prototypes were constructed, followed by the first production Harrier GR Mk 1 for the Royal Air Force. In RAF service this and subsequent versions have been operational as close-support and tactical reconnaissance aircraft since 1969, serving both at home and in Germany.

The biggest user of Harriers is the United States Marine Corps. The first of its aircraft, known as AV-8As, were delivered to the United States in 1971. The AV-8A has provision for launching Sidewinder air-to-air missiles, and initially 102 were ordered. With the USMC, Harriers have been stationed in the USA and Japan, and have been carried on board the USS *Guam*.

The McDonnell Douglas company of America holds the right to licence-build AV-8As, and is developing a version for the US Navy designated AV-8B, with a supercritical wing and increased weapon load. The Spanish Navy, in fact, ordered AV-8As and trainers from America, and these operate under the name Matador.

The Royal Navy is to be equipped eventually with 25 Sea Harriers, from the late 1970s. These will be operated mainly from the new 'through-deck cruisers' of the HMS *Invincible* class, while others will serve on HMS *Hermes* for anti-submarine work.

The Harrier normally carries up to 2270 kg (5000 lb) of weapons, including 30mm guns, bombs, rockets and missiles, plus reconnaissance or similar equipment, although 3630 kg (8000 lb) of stores have been carried experimentally. One of its major assets is that it can be concealed under trees or camouflage nets, so enabling it to advance with ground forces and make surprise attacks on the enemy. It can take off from virtually any ground surface, including areas that are too small or otherwise unsuitable for conventional aircraft.

Whereas most other experimental VTOL aircraft (and 'Forger') have relied on vertically-mounted engines for vertical take-off, the Harrier uses only a single horizontally-mounted engine for both jet lift and forward propulsion. Vertical lift is achieved by rotating to a downward position four exhaust nozzles, mounted two each side of the fuselage – the resulting thrust then lifts the aircraft off the ground. For transition to forward flight, the nozzles are gradually rotated rearward.

Hawker Typhoon IB armed with four cannon

Hawker Siddeley Hawk *Great Britain:* The Hawk is a small jet aircraft designed to operate as a basic and advanced trainer with the Royal Air Force. Accommodation is provided for two persons, on Martin-Baker rocket-assisted ejection seats. The front seat is normally used by the pupil, with the instructor to the rear. As a secondary role, the Hawk can also be used as a single-seater for ground attack missions, the armament then consisting of a fuselage-mounted gun pack and rockets or bombs on six underwing pylons.

Design of the Hawk was initiated when the UK Ministry of Defence announced a requirement for an aircraft to replace eventually the Jet Provost, Gnat and Hunter, all of which have been standard RAF types since the 1950s. The first pre-production model made its maiden flight on 21 August 1974. By the autumn of 1976 nine Hawks had been built, and the type entered RAF service at the end of the same year.

Initial contracts cover the manufacture of 176 Hawks for the RAF, and 50 have been ordered by Finland, the first overseas customer. In British service, the aircraft are used for basic and advanced flying training, including operation as radio, weapon and navigational trainers.

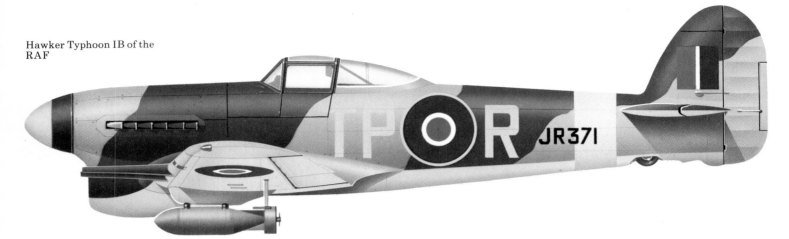

Hawker Typhoon IB of the RAF

Left Hawker Siddeley Harrier, the world's first operational VTOL aircraft, fitted with the new laser-nose which incorporates laser-ranging and marked target-seeking equipment. This Harrier is based in Germany.

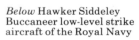

Below Hawker Siddeley Buccaneer low-level strike aircraft of the Royal Navy

Hawker Siddeley Hawk
operational trainer being
towed to the runway

Hawker Siddeley Nimrod *Great Britain:* One of the most advanced maritime patrol aircraft in the world, the Nimrod was produced for Royal Air Force Strike Command as a replacement for the old piston-engined Avro Shackleton. The latter was the standard RAF long-range maritime patrol aircraft from 1958 to 1969.

Based on the de Havilland Comet 4C airframe, the external appearance of the aircraft has been changed considerably from that of the airliner. The Nimrod has an unpressurized pannier under the normal cabin area, and this houses the bomb bay, radome and other operational equipment, while electronic support measures and magnetic anomaly detector equipment are carried in a fairing at the top of the fin and in a rear-mounted tailboom respectively. A great deal of sophisticated equipment is also carried internally for anti-submarine, surveillance and anti-shipping roles – while day

or night photography and ground attack using stand-off missiles, rockets, bombs or cannon are possible. A special version of the Nimrod has also been ordered for airborne early warning and control missions, with large bulges at the nose and tail which house the scanners.

The photographic role was well demonstrated when, in company with a Canberra, a Nimrod took photos of the new Soviet aircraft carrier *Kiev* as it sailed into the Mediterranean in 1976. A less talked about employment for certain RAF Nimrods is reported to be electronic reconnaissance, including the monitoring of foreign radio and radar transmissions.

Not all the Nimrods' duties are so combat orientated; they are often employed for search and rescue and fishery protection duties, and can even be used to transport personnel. During the 'Cod Wars' with Iceland, Nimrods helped warn the British fishing fleets and naval vessels of Icelandic gunboat activity.

Hawker Siddeley Trident *Great Britain:* Work on the Trident was started by the old de Havilland company, under the designation D.H. 121. It was designed to fulfil a requirement of British European Airways for a short-range jet-powered airliner with a maximum cruising speed of about 965 km/h (600 mph).

No prototypes were built, and the first flight, on 9 January 1969, was by a production Trident 1 airliner for BEA, one of 24 ordered. They were followed by 15 Trident 1Es, with 115 instead of 103 seats and more powerful Spey engines. Trident 1Es are currently operated by several airlines, including British Airways and CAAC (of China).

In 1965, BEA ordered 15 Trident 2Es, with better take-off performance by virtue of more powerful Spey engines, increased range, and a higher take-off weight. BEA began scheduled services with their 2Es in April 1968. CAAC and Cyprus Airways also bought some. These

Hawker Siddeley Nimrod
showing clearly its ECM
equipment pod on top of the
tail-fin and the extended tail
housing MAD equipment

Opposite
Above Sopwith Aviation Company's Kingston works building Snipe and Salamander (foreground) biplanes for the RAF, 1918

Below The same works in 1976 producing Hawker Siddeley Harrier VTOL strike aircraft

aircraft were fitted with Autoland – the first airliners in the world with equipment for all-weather, all-visibility, automatic landing capability.

Next came the Trident 3B, a development of the 1E which, as well as accommodating 180 passengers in a lengthened fuselage, had a Rolls-Royce RB 162-86 turbojet engine in the tail as a booster during take-off in hot climates. BEA ordered 26 (now operated by British Airways), and CAAC ordered two improved performance Super Trident 3Bs, each accommodating 152 passengers, which were delivered to China in July 1975.

Heinkel He 111 *Germany:* During its career with the German Luftwaffe, the Heinkel He 111 went through several changes of engine, forward fuselage design and armament. Despite this, the bomber failed to keep up with subsequent aircraft development during the Second World War and was really obsolete before it went out of production in Germany in 1944.

It had been designed in 1934–5 as a dual-purpose aircraft, of which different versions could serve as military medium bombers and as fast civil transports for ten passengers and mail. The first of the four prototypes was in bomber guise, though Nazi propaganda tried to persuade foreigners that the He 111 was a civil aircraft. This first prototype flew in early 1935, and was soon joined by another, which became the real prototype of the first production He 111s. Early production bombers, with BMW VI engines, were tested by the Luftwaffe in 1936, but were not accepted as their performance was too low.

To put the situation right, a new version of the bomber appeared as the He 111B, with Daimler-Benz DB 600 engines, which entered Luftwaffe service in time to be among the earliest German aircraft to fight with the Condor Legion in the Spanish Civil War. Faced with mostly outdated biplane fighters, the He 111 found the going easy in Spain.

By the outbreak of the Second World War, improved versions of the bomber had been delivered to the Luftwaffe, including the He 111P. This represented the first major redesign,

with a heavily-glazed, smoothly curved flush nose which took in the pilot's cabin. A little later came the last and most successful version, the He 111H. Powered by Junkers Jumo 211A engines, many sub-variants of the 'H' appeared from then until 1944.

Although an He 111H was the first German aircraft to be shot down over Britain during the Second World War, in October 1939, the Heinkel's easy victories during the Spanish Civil War had left the Germans believing that the bomber had no need of a strong fighter escort. This belief was short lived, however, when the Luftwaffe came up against Hurricanes and Spitfires during the Battle of Britain. Even last-minute increases in defensive armament did not save them, and the Luftwaffe changed tactics by using them for night bombing and minelaying.

However, in early 1942, a new version became operational as a torpedo-bomber, armed with two torpedoes, a role in which it proved highly successful. Unusual tasks performed by other He 111s included the air-launching of V1 flying-bombs, the first of which fell on East Anglia in September 1944, and Henschel glider bombs. The final variant of the He 111 was an eight-paratroop transport.

After the war He 111s continued to be flown in Spain, where the type had been licence-built since 1945, under the designation CASA C2111. Ironically those that were still flying there in the early 1970s were powered by British Merlin engines – the power plant of Hurricanes and Spitfires!

Heinkel He 177 Greif *Germany:* German bomber production during the Second World War was devoted almost exclusively to medium bombers and dive-bombers, although from time to time other types did appear. One such aircraft was the Greif, a heavy bomber which saw only limited service but earned the name of 'Flaming Coffin'.

Heinkel designed the Greif to a German requirement for a heavy bomber for anti-shipping duties. It was a large aircraft of very much heavier all-up weight than the standard Luftwaffe bombers of the time, and among its advanced features was the use of two coupled

Below left Heinkel He 177A-5 Greif, captured and in British markings

Below right Henschel Hs 123

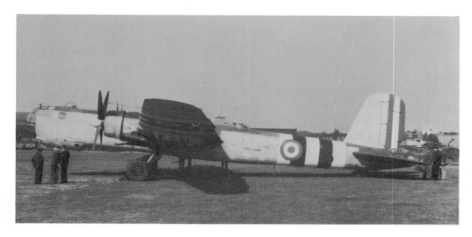

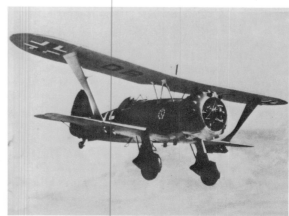

engines. Thus, the aircraft appeared to be twin-engined, as only two propellers were fitted, but each propeller was driven by two engines mounted side-by-side. The first prototype flew initially in November 1939 but quickly experienced overheating problems with its engines. Then two others of the first batch broke up while airborne and one caught fire. However, despite these and later accidents, the Greif entered Luftwaffe service and was used operationally from 1942 until the end of the war. Overheating of the engines and subsequent fires caused more losses than actual combat. Nevertheless, although very unpopular with their crews, over 1000 Greifs of all versions were built.

Henschel Hs 123 *Germany:* The Henschel Hs 123 is one of the few successful German warplanes that have been given less credit than they deserve. Designed solely as a stop-gap dive-bomber until the Junkers Ju 87 'Stuka' was ready for operational service, the Hs 123 was a single-seat biplane, first displayed in public near Berlin in May 1935.

The prototypes proved far better than their rival, the Fieseler Fi 98, but suffered early setbacks when two of the first three aircraft broke up in the air during diving trials. The cause of the structural failure was clear and, following some redesigning of the wings, production Hs 123A-1s equipped the first Luftwaffe dive-bomber unit in October 1935.

The civil war in Spain gave the Hs 123 a chance to prove itself, and in December 1936 a handful arrived there. Although designed as dive-bombers, it was in the ground attack role that these proved a success, soon being joined

by others supplied from Germany. However, by 1937 production versions of the vastly superior Ju 87 began to appear and Luftwaffe units began converting to the newer type.

By the beginning of the Second World War, the Ju 87 was by far the most important dive-bomber of the Luftwaffe, the Hs 123 remaining operational only for ground attack. Despite obvious obsolescence, it continued to perform valuable work during the Polish campaign, then against Belgium and France, finally ending up on the Eastern Front, where it remained until mid-1944. Here, as in the earlier battle zones, the Hs 123's original heavy 551 lb bomb had given way to weapon loads more suitable for its ground attack duties, namely four 110 lb bombs, anti-personnel bombs or twin cannon.

Top Hawker Siddeley Trident 3, operated by BEA from April 1971

Above Well-camouflaged Heinkel He 111 bomber that was licence built in Spain as the CASA C2111

I

IAI Kfir (Lion Cub) *Israel:* Following the refusal of the French government to deliver Mirage 5 fighter aircraft for which Israel had already paid, Israel Aircraft Industries looked into the possibility of manufacturing aircraft of generally similar design. As a start, it undertook production of spare parts for Mirage III fighters in service with the Israeli Air Force. Next stage was manufacture of an aircraft named the Nesher (Eagle) which was similar to the Mirage but fitted with Israeli electronics and equipment. About 40 Neshers are said to have been ready in time to take part in the Yom Kippur War of October 1973.

IAI next had the more difficult task of adapting the basic airframe to take a much more powerful General Electric J79 afterburning turbojet (as fitted in the Israeli Air Force's Phantom fighters). The rear fuselage had to be shortened and increased in diameter. At the same time the front fuselage was enlarged and flattened to take more advanced navigational, weapon delivery and radar equipment. The undercarriage was strengthened, the cockpit redesigned, fuel capacity increased, and provision for Israeli-designed Shafrir air-to-air missiles added. The resulting aircraft was named Kfir (Lion Cub), and was first shown at Ben-Gurion Airport, Lydda, on 14 April 1975. For ground attack missions, the Kfir can carry a wide variety of weapons, including an Israeli Luz-1 air-to-surface missile. Israel now hopes to export Kfirs, as well as satisfying its own requirements.

In 1974 production began of the Kfir-C2, an improved multi-purpose version for the IAF and for export. Main differences include the addition of fixed canard surfaces and other airframe refinements. The C2 is now the main production version of the Kfir.

Ilyushin Il-2 *USSR:* The Soviet Union lost a great deal of time in modernizing its air force in the thirties – but it seemed temporarily safe after signing a surprising non-aggression pact with Germany. This agreement only appeared to be strengthened when Soviet forces helped Germany to divide up Poland in September 1939.

Numbers of new fighters were adding to Soviet strength at this period, but by far the most important aircraft for the future of the Soviet Union itself entered service as the Ilyushin Il-2 Shturmovik. This was a single-seat ground attack monoplane, armed with two forward-firing cannon and two machine-guns, and could also carry bombs or rocket projectiles. The pilot was surrounded by armour-plating in his cockpit.

In June 1941 the inevitable happened, and Germany invaded Russia. On the first day alone over 400 Soviet aircraft were destroyed, some of them Il-2s, for although it was proving highly successful in its ground attack role, it was vulnerable to fighter attack from the rear. To remedy this, a two-seat version of the Il-2 appeared in 1942 with a rear cockpit for a gunner who faced backwards, armed with a machine-gun.

Now the Il-2 could operate with less fear of enemy fighters, and got on with destroying vehicles and trains, ground strafing and bombing. In all about 35000 Il-2s were produced, and they served throughout the war, recording the lowest casualty figures of any Soviet-built aircraft. Stalin described them as being 'as essential to the Soviet Army as air and bread'.

Below left The Kfir, Israel's first production supersonic jet fighter

Below right Ilyushin Il-2 type 3 ground attack aircraft

Ilyushin Il-2 of the Soviet Air Force

135

J

Junkers F13 *Germany:* The Junkers F13 holds a very special place in the history of commercial aviation, as it was one of the first purpose-built airliners. It was of advanced design for its time, with both the cantilever low wings and the fuselage covered in corrugated metal (which was to be a trademark of Junkers transport aircraft). The well-upholstered and enclosed cabin provided seats for four passengers, although the crew of two were still expected to brave the elements in their open cockpit.

The ancestry of the F13 goes back to 1915, when Hugo Junkers produced his first all-metal monoplane as the J1 or Tin Donkey – not to be confused with the Junkers J1 armour-plated attack biplane. From the J1 was evolved, in 1918, another monoplane known as the J10, intended for attack missions. This was converted after the war into a make-shift two-seat civil transport, which was used on regular flights between two German cities, but proved uneconomical. A purpose-built airliner was needed, so Junkers produced the F13, which first flew on 25 June 1919.

Between 1919 and 1932 no fewer than 322 F13s were built, in more than 60 variants, and these provided early airlines with reliable and economical small aircraft. Such was their worth that some were purchased by air forces as general-purpose cargo-carriers, the F13 bought by Persia (Iran) in 1922 being that country's first military aircraft. The F13 was the first aircraft of its type to be fitted with safety belts, and was operated on wheel, float and ski undercarriages. The very first example built was still flying at the outbreak of the Second World War, offering short-distance joy-rides in Berlin.

Junkers G38 *Germany:* Although only two were built, the G38 was a remarkably successful aircraft and a giant among its contemporaries. Built in Germany at a time of great depression and inflation, it served in Luft Hansa colours from 1931 to the outbreak of the Second World War.

Hugo Junkers, the designer, had built up an envied reputation through his aircraft with cantilever wings of thick section, and by the use of corrugated metal (*see* Junkers F13). He was also an advocate of the 'flying wing' concept, an idea which he came near to realizing with the G38.

Design of the G38 began in 1928, as a 34-passenger airliner. Its most notable feature was its huge monoplane wing, which was 1.7 m (5 ft 7 in) thick at the root (the point where the wings meet the fuselage). Powered by four Junkers Jumo engines mounted in the wing leading-edge, the first G38 (D-2000, later named *Deutschland*) made its initial flight at Dessau on 6 November 1929. Although delivered to Luft Hansa in the following year, it did not enter service on air routes from Berlin until 1932. The passenger accommodation was some-

Opposite above Junkers G38 airliner of Luft Hansa

Opposite below Junkers G38 named *von Hindenburg*, showing clearly the passenger windows in the nose and inner wings

Junkers F13 all-metal monoplane airliner, one of the first new aircraft to be produced for commercial flying after the First World War

what unusual, in that there were two seats in the extreme nose and three in each wing root, plus those in the cabin.

A second G38 (D-2500) appeared in 1931 and differed from the first in having two main passenger decks and a smokers' room at the tail. Soon, both aircraft were flying to more and more destinations, including London and Copenhagen. In 1936 the first one crashed at the place where it had made its maiden flight more than six years earlier, leaving the second, now named *Generalfeldmarschall von Hindenburg*, to ply the civil routes until the autumn of 1939, when it was pressed into military service. Under its new operator, the Luftwaffe, it continued to give good service until it was destroyed in an air raid by the Royal Air Force in 1940. The biggest passenger landplane of its time, the G38 possessed many advanced features, including full-span trailing-edge flaps which allowed the landing speed to be kept to a mere 93 km/h (58 mph).

Junkers Ju 52 *Germany:* The Junkers designation Ju 52 applies to two distinctly different aircraft – the Ju 52/1m single-engined civil transport and the three-engined Ju 52/3m, sometimes known as the 'Iron Annie'. The latter is by far the most famous, beginning in 1934 as a civil airliner which served all over Europe, and

elsewhere (notably in South America), for many years in both landplane and floatplane forms.

Meanwhile, in Germany a new air force was being formed illegally, and Ju 52/3ms were pressed into service as temporary bombers as well as transports. When the Spanish Civil War started in 1936, Luftwaffe Ju 52/3ms were immediately employed by the Nationalists to ferry about 10 000 Moorish soldiers to help in the revolt. Soon other Ju 52s arrived in Spain, this time as bombers, until replaced by purpose-

Junkers Ju 87 'Stuka' of the Italian Air Force, with underwing gun pods

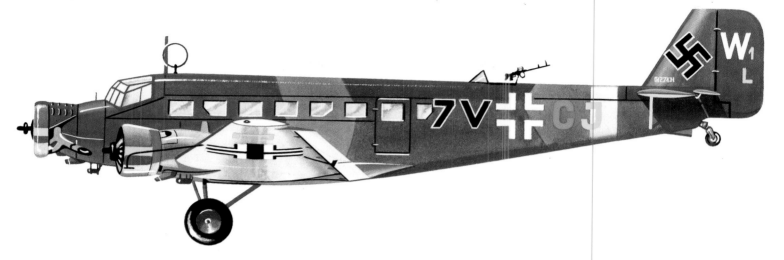

Opposite and above Junkers Ju 52/3m in full Luftwaffe markings

built bombers like the Heinkel He 111 and Junkers Ju 86.

When the Second World War started, Ju 52/3ms equipped the bulk of the Luftwaffe's transport units and were used in virtually every major operation. On 10 May 1940, the day in which the Luftwaffe lost more aircraft in 24 hours than any other air force before or since, 157 of the 304 aircraft destroyed during the invasion of the Netherlands and Belgium were Junkers Ju 52/3ms. Production totalled more than 4800 by 1944 – a few remaining operational to this day in the Swiss Air Force.

Junkers Ju 87 *Germany:* Ask any schoolboy to name three Second World War German aircraft and you can be sure that one would be the Stuka (abbreviation for *sturzkampf-flugzeug*, meaning dive-bomber).

As with many Axis aircraft used against inferior air forces, the Ju 87's early reputation far exceeded its actual merits. Admittedly, it was effective and greatly feared in Poland, France, part of Russia and other countries, where the screaming sounds of diving Stukas usually heralded heavy attack from German air and land forces. Nevertheless, when opposed by the Royal Air Force, its weaknesses and extremely poor defensive armament showed up, and it proved useless as a weapon with which to 'Blitzkrieg' Britain.

Although dive bombers had been designed in most aircraft manufacturing countries in the early 1930s, only Germany (and Japan to a lesser degree) really went ahead with the type as mass-produced, fully-operational aircraft for army support. The Ju 87 was designed and built to take part in a dive-bomber competition held in 1936, and eventually won against stiff and arguably better opposition. Production got underway immediately, and the first of about 5000 Ju 87s entered Luftwaffe service in the spring of 1937.

For testing under actual battle conditions, a detachment of early Ju 87s was sent to Spain to fight with Franco's forces in the civil war. On the basis of this experience, a few design

changes were made to the aircraft, and by the outbreak of the Second World War about 335 were operational with the Luftwaffe. On 1 September 1939 Germany invaded Poland, commencing the *Blitzkrieg* tactics of heavy bombing.

A similar fate befell several other countries, and even the Germans began believing reports of the invincibility of the Ju 87s. It therefore caused no surprise when, in summer 1940, waves of these aircraft were sent to attack British targets. However, this time they met a well-equipped and fully prepared air force, and huge numbers of Stukas were destroyed.

The Stuka, defeated in the Battle of Britain, was withdrawn to other theatres of war and was encountered right up to the final Allied victory in 1945.

With its cranked wings and large fixed undercarriage, the Stuka was not an attractive plane but represented a thoroughly nasty and battle-tested war machine. Nevertheless, in the early days of the war, it proved to be an immensely effective military and psychological weapon.

Junkers Ju 88 *Germany:* Except for the Messerschmitt Bf 109 and Focke-Wulf Fw 190 single-seat fighters, it is true to say that the Junkers Ju 88 was the most important aircraft to serve with the Luftwaffe throughout the Second World War.

Designed originally as a high-speed medium bomber, the first prototype took to the air on 21 December 1936. The prototypes were followed by pre-production Ju 88A-Os, of which some were in service together with production Ju 88A-1s in September 1939. These, and A-2s and -3s, were flown during the Battle of Britain but, like other German bombers, were underarmed and suffered badly at the hands of the Royal Air Force. This experience led to the Ju 88A-4, which embodied many modifications including greater-span wings, more protective armour-plating, a heavier bomb load and four or five guns instead of the three fitted previously. Other A-series aircraft were fitted out for

1 Spinner
2 Pitch-change mechanism housing
3 Blade hub
4 Junkers VS 11 constant-speed airscrew
5 Anti-vibration engine mounting attachments
6 Oil filler point and marker
7 Auxiliary oil tank (5.9 Imp gal/26.8 l capacity)
8 Junkers Jumo 211J-1 12-cylinder inverted-vee liquid cooled engine
9 Magnesium alloy forged engine mount
10 Coolant (Glysantin-water) header tank
11 Ejector exhaust stubs
12 Fuel injection unit housing
13 Induction air cooler
14 Armoured radiator
15 Inertia starter cranking point
16 Ball joint bulkhead fixing (lower)

17 Tubular steel mount support strut
18 Ventral armour (8 mm)
19 Main oil tank (9.9 Imp gal/45 l capacity)
20 Oil filling point
21 Transverse support frame
22 Rudder pedals
23 Control column
24 Heating point
25 Auxiliary air intake
26 Ball joint bulkhead fixing (upper)
27 Bulkhead
28 Oil tank (6.8 Imp gal/31 l capacity)
29 Oil filler point and marker (Intava 100)

30 Fuel filler cap
31 Self-sealing starboard outer fuel tank (33 Imp gal/150 l capacity)
32 Underwing bombs with *Dienartstab* percussion rods
33 Pitot head
34 Spherical oxygen bottles
35 Wing skinning
36 Starboard navigation light
37 Aileron mass balance
38 'Double wing' aileron and flap (starboard outer)
39 Aileron hinge
40 Corrugated wing rib station
41 Reinforced armoured windscreen
42 Reflector sight

43 Padded crash bar
44 Signal flare tube
45 Braced fuselage mainframe
46 Front spar/fuselage attachment point
47 Pilot's seat (reinforced with 4-mm side and 8-mm rear armour)
48 Inter-cockpit bulkhead
49 Sliding canopy handgrip
50 External side armour
51 Pilot's back armour (8 mm)
52 Headrest
53 Aft-sliding cockpit canopy (shown part open)
54 Radio mast cut-out
55 Anti-crash hoop (magnesium casting)
56 Radio mast
57 Radio equipment (FuGe 16) compartment
58 Additional (internal) side armour

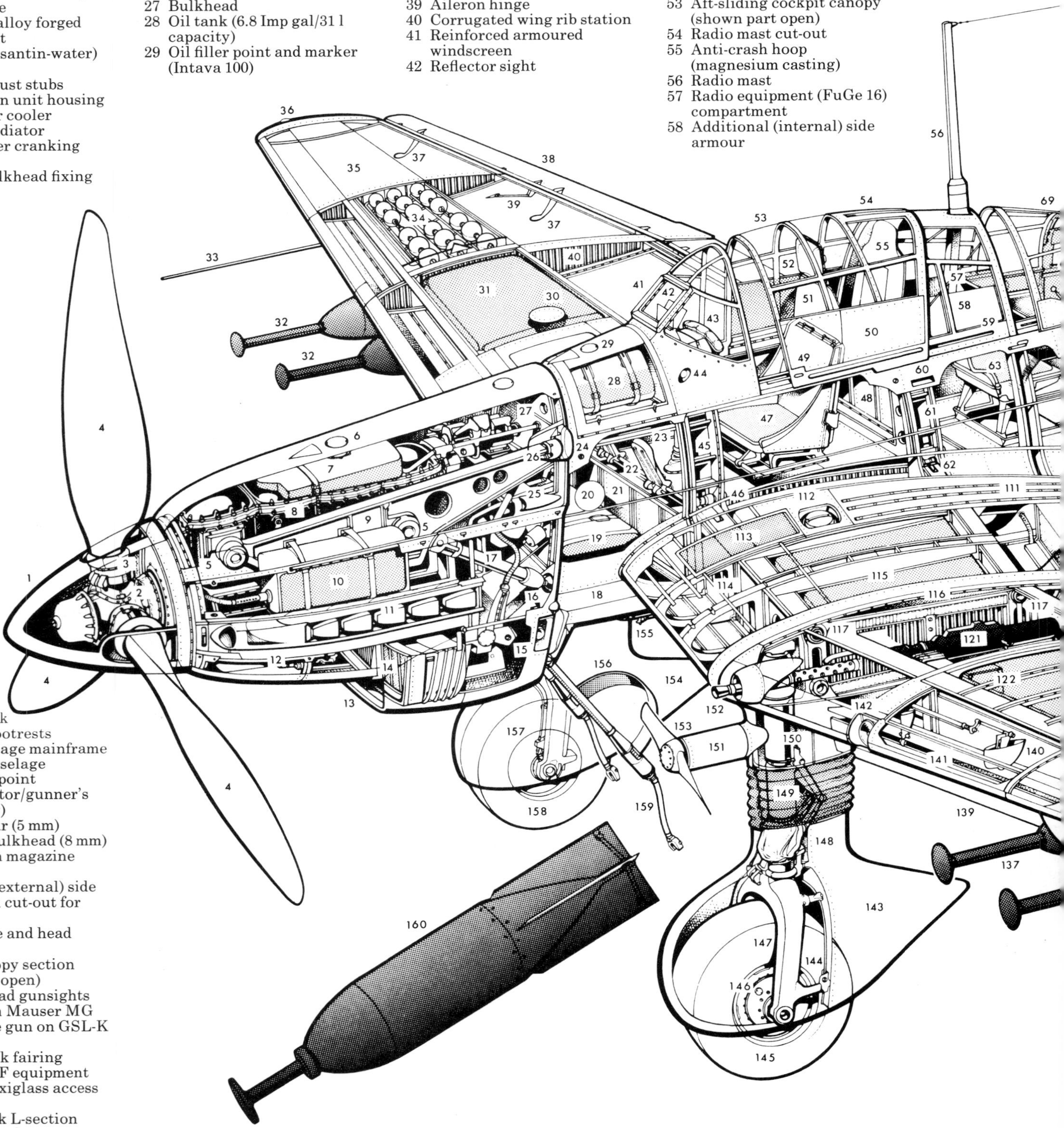

59 Canopy track
60 Handhold/footrests
61 Braced fuselage mainframe
62 Rear spar/fuselage attachment point
63 Radio-operator/gunner's seat (folding)
64 Floor armour (5 mm)
65 Armoured bulkhead (8 mm)
66 Ammunition magazine racks
67 Additional (external) side armour with cut-out for hand grip
68 Internal side and head armour
69 Sliding canopy section (shown part open)
70 Ring-and-bead gunsights
71 Twin 7.9-mm Mauser MG 81Z machine gun on GSL-K 81 mount
72 Canopy track fairing
73 Peil G IV D/F equipment
74 Circular plexiglass access panel
75 Back-to-back L-section stringers (fuselage horizontal break)
76 First-aid stowage
77 Z-section fuselage frames

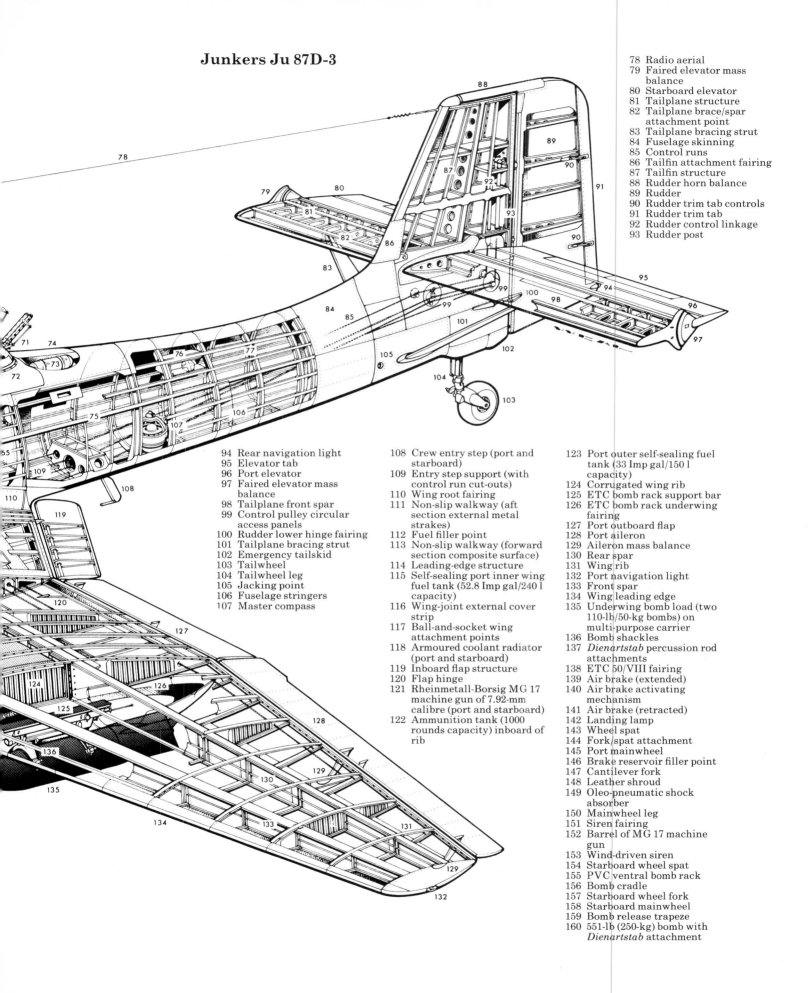

Junkers Ju 87D-3

78 Radio aerial
79 Faired elevator mass balance
80 Starboard elevator
81 Tailplane structure
82 Tailplane brace/spar attachment point
83 Tailplane bracing strut
84 Fuselage skinning
85 Control runs
86 Tailfin attachment fairing
87 Tailfin structure
88 Rudder horn balance
89 Rudder
90 Rudder trim tab controls
91 Rudder trim tab
92 Rudder control linkage
93 Rudder post

94 Rear navigation light
95 Elevator tab
96 Port elevator
97 Faired elevator mass balance
98 Tailplane front spar
99 Control pulley circular access panels
100 Rudder lower hinge fairing
101 Tailplane bracing strut
102 Emergency tailskid
103 Tailwheel
104 Tailwheel leg
105 Jacking point
106 Fuselage stringers
107 Master compass

108 Crew entry step (port and starboard)
109 Entry step support (with control run cut-outs)
110 Wing root fairing
111 Non-slip walkway (aft section external metal strakes)
112 Fuel filler point
113 Non-slip walkway (forward section composite surface)
114 Leading-edge structure
115 Self-sealing port inner wing fuel tank (52.8 Imp gal/240 l capacity)
116 Wing-joint external cover strip
117 Ball-and-socket wing attachment points
118 Armoured coolant radiator (port and starboard)
119 Inboard flap structure
120 Flap hinge
121 Rheinmetall-Borsig MG 17 machine gun of 7.92-mm calibre (port and starboard)
122 Ammunition tank (1000 rounds capacity) inboard of rib

123 Port outer self-sealing fuel tank (33 Imp gal/150 l capacity)
124 Corrugated wing rib
125 ETC bomb rack support bar
126 ETC bomb rack underwing fairing
127 Port outboard flap
128 Port aileron
129 Aileron mass balance
130 Rear spar
131 Wing rib
132 Port navigation light
133 Front spar
134 Wing leading edge
135 Underwing bomb load (two 110-lb/50-kg bombs) on multi-purpose carrier
136 Bomb shackles
137 *Dienartstab* percussion rod attachments
138 ETC 50/VIII fairing
139 Air brake (extended)
140 Air brake activating mechanism
141 Air brake (retracted)
142 Landing lamp
143 Wheel spat
144 Fork/spat attachment
145 Port mainwheel
146 Brake reservoir filler point
147 Cantilever fork
148 Leather shroud
149 Oleo-pneumatic shock absorber
150 Mainwheel leg
151 Siren fairing
152 Barrel of MG 17 machine gun
153 Wind-driven siren
154 Starboard wheel spat
155 PVC ventral bomb rack
156 Bomb cradle
157 Starboard wheel fork
158 Starboard mainwheel
159 Bomb release trapeze
160 551-lb (250-kg) bomb with *Dienartstab* attachment

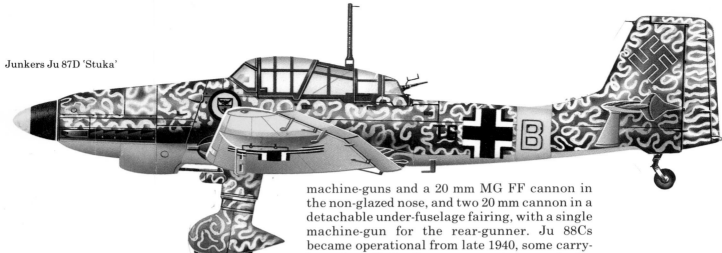

Junkers Ju 87D 'Stuka'

ground attack, torpedo-bomber or training roles.

Only pre-production B-series aircraft appeared, in 1940, followed much later in the war by the Ju 88S, an updated bomber with a smaller bomb load, high-rated BMW 801 engines, and a rounder and more aerodynamic nose, all to increase performance in the light of Allied aircraft development. Nearly two-thirds of all Ju 88 production centred on the bomber variants, but the type was adapted for a multitude of other tasks, which caused a lack of continuity of bomber development. The first of the non-bomber variants was the Ju 88C day and night fighter, armed initially with three 7.9mm MG-17

machine-guns and a 20 mm MG FF cannon in the non-glazed nose, and two 20 mm cannon in a detachable under-fuselage fairing, with a single machine-gun for the rear-gunner. Ju 88Cs became operational from late 1940, some carrying the distinctive nose antenna of the Lichtenstein night interception radar. Other Ju 88 versions included the 'D' long-range photographic-reconnaissance aircraft, 'G' improved night fighter, 'H' reconnaissance aircraft and heavy fighter (also used to carry a single-seat fighter on top of the fuselage as the Mistel composite aircraft – the Ju 88 being packed with explosive and used as a pilotless aircraft against ground forces from 1944, guided by the piloted fighter above), 'P' anti-tank aircraft (used mostly on the Eastern Front), 'R' heavy fighter and 'T' photographic-reconnaissance aircraft. Other tasks performed by Ju 88s included minelaying, making the aircraft one of the most versatile and valuable Nazi types. Total production was more than 15 000 aircraft.

Below Junkers Ju 88C-6b night fighter with Lichtenstein radar

Bottom Junkers Ju 88A-4

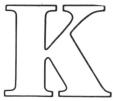

Kamov Ka-25 *USSR:* Known to NATO by the reporting name 'Hormone', the Ka-25 is a very important helicopter which operates on anti-submarine duties from many of the Soviet Navy's missile-armed ships, the helicopter cruisers *Moskva* and *Leningrad*, and the newest warships of all, the two Soviet carriers *Kiev* and *Minsk*.

First shown publicly in 1961, carrying two dummy air-to-surface missiles, this helicopter began soon afterwards to replace the older Mil Mi-4 in Navy service afloat and at shore bases. Although ungainly in appearance, the Ka-25 is highly efficient in its task, carrying a large search radar under its nose for submarine detection, and packing torpedoes, nuclear depth charges and other weapons in an internal bay. The Ka-25, like other Kamov helicopters, has two contra-rotating rotors, and the large main cabin can accommodate 12 passengers or assorted freight.

In addition to the anti-submarine version, there is the highly secret Hormone-B for special electronics work. About nine anti-submarine Ka-25s are operated by the Syrian Air Force.

A civil version of the helicopter has appeared as the Ka-25K, for use as a flying crane. It retains the internal passenger accommodation, but, in place of the radar/radome of the military version, has a gondola in which a pilot can face backwards and control the helicopter's flight while viewing directly the cargo attachment and handling below.

Kamov Ka-25 'Hormone-A' anti-submarine helicopter of the Soviet Navy

Leduc 0.10 *France:* Many have said that the heyday of aeronautical research was immediately after the Second World War, when the richer aeronautically-minded countries (like the United States) spent huge amounts on the development of military and civil aircraft, engines, electronics, etc. France did not have the same resources but among its more memorable efforts can be counted a series of unique monoplanes designed to test the theories of René Leduc concerning the use of athodyd or ramjet engines for aircraft propulsion.

Leduc, who had designed and built a small ramjet engine in 1935, decided after the war that he had developed the principle far enough to warrant building a full-size airplane. His basic concept entailed employing the complete outer fuselage shell of the aircraft as the annular duct of the ramjet, with the pilot's cockpit housed in the inner shell. Behind the pilot's cabin was mounted an auxiliary turbojet engine, to ignite the ramjet in the air, and then drive the ramjet's generator and fuel injection pumps, which in turn fed 500 burners. Although requiring to be air-launched, because a ramjet needs a flow of high-velocity air to be passed through the engine before it will work, the engine was expected to produce greater power than any turbojet engine in an aircraft of similar size.

The Leduc 0.10 was air-launched initially as a glider, in October 1947, to test its aerodynamic qualities. The first powered air-launching was on 21 April 1949. Having been released at 320 km/h (200 mph) the 0.10 attained 680 km/h (421 mph) while using about half of its potential power.

After these experiments, several more ramjet-powered aircraft were tested (such as the larger Leduc 0.21), but the planned Mach 2 military interceptor version was never built, and flying terminated in about 1957. Many experts believe, however, that future long-range airliners, with ramjet engines, will fly at 5500 km/h (3000 mph) or faster, using clean-burning liquid hydrogen fuel after the world's oil resources have been exhausted.

Lockheed C-5A Galaxy *USA:* The Galaxy is the world's largest airplane. Its wings span 67.88 m (over 222 ft) and its huge cargo hold is capable of accommodating either two M-60 main battle tanks; or 16 small lorries; or one M-60 tank, two Bell Iroquois helicopters, five personnel carriers and two lorries; or 36 cargo pallets; or ten Pershing battlefield missiles and associated vehicles. As a troop transport it can carry 345 equipped men on two decks. Heavy equipment is loaded via the upward-hinging ('visor' type) nose door of the

Opposite Lockheed C-5A Galaxy, the world's largest transport aircraft

Leduc 0.10 ramjet-powered aircraft being carried above its SE 161 carrier/launching aircraft

Lockheed L-1011 TriStar operated by Gulf Air

forces, including the Royal Air Force.

A medium to long-range aircraft, the Hercules can carry up to 92 troops, 64 para-troops, 74 stretchers and attendants, a 155 mm howitzer and tractor, other vehicles, large weapons or six big freight pallets. Many other cargo variations are possible. Loading is carried out via an hydraulically-operated main door and ramp at the rear of the fuselage, and the Hercules can employ normal unloading methods, air-drops or ground proximity extraction. In the latter technique the aircraft flies at about 1.5 m (5 ft) above the ground with its rear cargo ramp open. A hook attached to the cargo is trailed out of the aircraft, and when this engages on a cable stretched across the ground it pulls the freight out. Another method of extraction during a low-altitude flypast is by a trailing ribbon parachute.

The Hercules has also been adapted as a US Navy communications aircraft to relay emergency messages to strategic missile submarines, for electronic countermeasures, search and rescue and as a refuelling tanker for airplanes or helicopters. It can also undertake air recovery of cargoes on parachutes, including re-entering space satellites, aerial surveying and reconnaissance, drone recovery and weather reconnaissance, and can perform as an interdiction gunship.

Lockheed F-80 Shooting Star *USA:* On 8

aircraft.

First flown on 30 June 1968, the Galaxy was built to a United States Air Force requirement which dated back to 1963. The first of 81 production aircraft was delivered to Military Airlift Command in December 1969.

Lockheed C-130 Hercules *USA:* The Hercules is the most widely-operated Western-built heavy military transport aircraft. Designed originally to a specification from Tactical Air Command, United States Air Force, the first YC-130 made its maiden flight on 23 August 1954 and deliveries of the production C-130A began in December 1956. Since then over 1500 Hercules have been ordered, and the type is flown – primarily as a freighter – by many air

November 1950 Captain Russell Brown of the
51st Fighter-Interceptor Wing, United States
Air Force, was flying his Lockheed F-80C
Shooting Star fighter, with three others of his
Wing, near the border between North Korea
and China when he came across a number of
MiG-15s of the People's Republic of China.
Immediately the jets went into action, Captain
Russell quickly becoming involved in a dogfight
with one of the MiGs. After some minutes of
combat, Captain Russell shot down the MiG, in
what was the first victory by one jet fighter over
another.

The Shooting Star was the first jet-powered
fighter to become operational with the USAF,
when deliveries began in 1945. Unlike its
British and German counterparts, this aircraft
was too late to see active service during the
Second World War, and orders for 5000 aircraft
were cut immediately to just 677. Nevertheless,
as the air force continued its programme of
replacing piston-engined fighters, further
orders were placed until 1751 Shooting Stars
had been built.

United States aircraft based in the Far East
were the first jets to support the South Koreans
when the Korean War started in June 1950.
However, as better fighters began to replace the
Shooting Star, the airplane was gradually
sold off by the Air Force or joined Air National
Guard reserve units. This was by no means the
end of the design, for a two-seat trainer version
had been built as the T-33 'T-bird' and no less
than 5819 were eventually produced for the
United States services and numerous other
countries. Many T-33s are still operated today.

Lockheed SR-71A *USA:* The Lockheed SR-
71A, operated by the 9th Strategic Reconnaissance Wing of the United States Air Force
Strategic Air Command, is the world's fastest
production aircraft. It was developed from the
Lockheed A-11, an aircraft which was built in
great secrecy and was not publicly revealed
until 1964, nearly two years after the original
prototype had flown. The A-11 had been designed as a strategic reconnaissance aircraft, to
succeed the U-2 spyplane, capable of flying
higher and faster than any other known
operational aircraft, and so able to make
overflights through the airspace of a potential
enemy with little fear of interception.

Several A-11s were produced and three were
modified in 1964 into YF-12A prototype fighters,
each designed to carry eight Hughes air-to-air
missiles. The YF-12A did not go into production, but a version with a longer and very
flat fuselage entered limited production as the
SR-71A, for the original task of strategic
reconnaissance.

SR-71As became operational in 1966, and
about 27 were built, including trainer variants
with twin pilot's cockpits in tandem. Although
highly secret, an SR-71A was put on guarded
public display at the 1974 Farnborough Air
Show after it had set a New York to London

point-to-point record by flying the 5584 km (3470 miles) in 1 hour, 54 minutes and 56.4 seconds.

The SR-71A is packed with very sophisticated reconnaissance equipment and can photograph 259000 km² (100000 sq. miles) of terrain in one hour. On 27 July 1976 an SR-71A, or Blackbird as it is known, set several new world records by flying at 3367.221 km/h (2092 mph) around a 1000 km (621 mile) circuit and 3529.56 km/h (2193 mph) in a straight line. A new altitude record for sustained horizontal flight was also set up at 25 929 m (85 069 ft).

Lockheed F-104 Starfighter *USA :* No aircraft has ever been the centre of greater controversy than the Starfighter. Its concept goes back to 1952, when the Douglas company first flew a research aircraft designated the X-3. This had been designed to test, among other things, the efficiency of small-span double-wedge wings and a long slim fuselage at high speeds – and Lockheed decided to adopt this configuration for a new fighter. With huge United States Air Force contracts in mind, Lockheed produced a prototype which made its first flight on 7 February 1954. A developed version, known as the Starfighter, raised the world speed record to over 2250 km/h (1400 mph) in 1958, but the USAF, not over impressed, acquired only a small number of the F-104A/B/C/D versions which were deployed mainly for the air defence of North America and with tactical units.

Ex-USAF Starfighters were supplied to Pakistan and Taiwan, and the next version, the multi-mission F-104G, was adopted as a fighter and strike aircraft throughout NATO air forces in Europe. Despite publicity to the contrary, many defence ministries seem to have genuinely wanted these fighters and European assembly lines were set up in Germany, Holland, Italy and Belgium to provide over 1000

Starfighters, in addition to those supplied from Lockheed. Similar production lines were set up in Canada and Japan, and Starfighters were exported from the US and Canada to Denmark, Greece, Norway, Spain and Turkey. Further US production led to the two-seat F-104DJ for Japan, F-104F for Germany and a trainer version of the F-104G for European Starfighter operators.

The latest production version is the F-104S, built in Italy for the Italian and Turkish air forces. Deliveries began in 1969, to be completed in 1976. F-104Ss have nine stores attachment points on the wings and fuselage, for bombs, rockets, missiles and fuel tanks.

In service the Starfighter has seemed more accident-prone than other fighters, and has not been used widely in combat.

Lockheed TriStar (and McDonnell Douglas DC-10) *USA:* Between producing the L-188 Electra medium-range airliner in the late 1950s/early 1960s and delivery of the TriStar in 1972, Lockheed concentrated mainly on military aircraft and business jets like the JetStar. Yet, the lack of continuity did not put Lockheed behind its competitors, for its next airliner, the TriStar, was in the category of the world's most modern jet transports – the wide-bodies.

Design of the 256/400-passenger L-1011 TriStar began in 1966 and was heavily influenced by the requirements of domestic airline operators. The design changed from twin-engine to a triple-engined layout – the

engines chosen being Rolls-Royce RB.211s. It was the high development costs of these engines that led Rolls-Royce into financial troubles and delayed progress of the airliner. The first production TriStar started scheduled passenger services with Eastern Air Lines on 26 April 1972.

Four other versions have so far appeared; the longer-range L-1011-100, ordered by four of the 13 airlines that have chosen TriStars; the L-1011-200 increased-range version for operation to and from high-altitude and hot-climate airports; the L-1011-250 long-range version, usually with more room for freight and reduced passenger seating; and the L-1011-500 extended-

Lockheed P-38L Lightning of the USAAF, which remained in production as a long-range fighter for use in the Pacific theatre of war until VJ Day. This version flew at more than 425 mph and could carry a 4000 lb bomb load.

range version with a shortened fuselage. By
autumn 1976 a total of 136 TriStars had been
delivered.

The McDonnell Douglas DC-10 is also a
triple-engined wide-body airliner, with capacity
for between 270 and 380 passengers. Three
versions are currently available, the Series 10,
30 and 40, plus convertible-freighter versions,
Models 10CF/30CF. The DC-10 was designed for
economical flying over ranges varying from
only 480 km (300 miles) to 9815 km (6100 miles).
The first Series 10 flew initially on 29 August
1970, and American Airlines started scheduled
services with the type on 5 August 1971,
between Los Angeles and Chicago. Altogether,
36 airlines had ordered DC-10s by late 1976, by
which time 223 had been delivered.

Lockheed U-2 *USA:* Since before the First
World War, aerial reconnaissance has been
used to gather information on hostile or
potentially hostile forces, to reduce the possibility of surprise attack. No aircraft has ever
performed this task in such a cloak-and-dagger
way as the Lockheed U-2, which was developed
and built in secrecy in the US, and first flew in
1955.

Although the United States and the Soviet
Union had been allies, the end of the Second
World War heralded a political and military
split between these two countries. Both had
emerged as super powers, and there was soon

plenty of evidence of an arms race between
them. For the US, the surprise attack by the
north against the south in Korea, in 1950,
underlined the need for an all-out effort to keep
abreast of military development in the Soviet
Union and other countries. The 'open skies'
suggestion by President Eisenhower, to ensure
that any warlike preparation by either side
would be observed by aerial reconnaissance,
was rejected by the Soviet Union.

The U-2 was seen in the US as the answer
to the problem, and about 25 production
aircraft were built. The basic model was a jet-
powered aircraft of light construction, and
carried only a pilot. The long fuselage was
crammed full of electronic and photographic
equipment, and it could monitor radio and
radar transmissions from the ground. By far its
biggest attribute was that it had an extremely
long range, made possible by its huge-span
glider-type wings, which enabled the aircraft to
glide for periods of time with the engine
switched off and to fly at over 24 400 m (80 000 ft).
At that height no aircraft could then intercept
it.

Although some U-2s were flown for research
into clear-air turbulence and cosmic radiation,
the primary task was clandestine military
reconnaissance. All went well until 1 May 1960
when a U-2, flown by Gary Powers, was shot
down over Sverdlovsk in the Soviet Union by
a newly-produced Soviet missile. After this,

Lockheed U-2 'Spyplane' and reconnaissance aircraft

Eisenhower had to promise to end reconnaissance flights over the Soviet Union.

U-2s continued to be flown by the United States Air Force, in other areas, and in 1962 U-2s discovered Soviet nuclear missile bases in Cuba. Some U-2s remain operational with the USAF.

Lockheed Vega *USA:* Allan and Malcolm Lockheed built their first aircraft, a seaplane, in 1913, and in 1916 set up a small company to build airplanes for the US Navy. Early success encouraged the brothers to form the Lockheed Aircraft Company in 1926, using a garage in Hollywood as their first factory.

The Lockheed company's first product was the Vega, a high-wing monoplane with extremely fine aerodynamic lines, seating a pilot and six passengers. The first Vega was built for George Hearst, a US newspaper tycoon, and made its maiden flight on 4 July 1927. In the following month it was destroyed while taking part in an air race from California to Honolulu; but interest in the Vega was so great that the company moved to a new site in Burbank, California, in 1928 to make possible increased production.

Altogether, 131 Vegas were eventually built. As much as anything they established Lockheed as one of America's great aircraft manufacturers, because several achieved international fame at the hands of pilots like Polar explorer Hubert Wilkins, Amelia Earhart, James Mattern, and Wiley Post. This last pilot,

who had only one eye, began his flying career as a barnstormer at air displays. In 1930, Post was hired to pilot a Vega belonging to an oil magnate named F. C. Hall. This aircraft, named *Winnie Mae* after Hall's daughter, was used for duration flights and air races as well as business flying. On 23 June 1931 *Winnie Mae* made international headlines, when Post took off at the start of a flight which circumnavigated the world in 8 days, 15 hours and 51 minutes, starting and finishing at New York.

Two years later, Post and *Winnie Mae* made a further round-the-world flight in just 7 days, 18 hours and 49 minutes, from 15 July. In the same aircraft Wiley Post pioneered the pressure suit, flying at high altitude while wearing a fabric suit with a metal helmet containing a circular port-hole.

Wiley Post was killed in an air crash in 1935. *Winnie Mae* is preserved in the National Air and Space Museum, Washington, DC.

Opposite above Lockheed L-1011 TriStar of British Airways

Opposite below Lockheed Vega, restored as Wiley Post's famous *Winnie Mae*

151

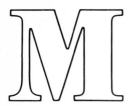

Martin Marietta X-24 *USA:* To acquire the skills and knowledge necessary to produce an aircraft able to orbit in space and then return to earth and land on an aerodrome runway, Martin Marietta began experiments with 'lifting body' designs in 1959. Following extensive theoretical research, the company built an unmanned lifting body vehicle, designated X-23A, which it flight tested to confirm that the concept of a wingless aircraft with a bulbous wedge-shaped body was practical.

With this initial success behind it, Martin Marietta was ready to go a stage further by building a manned vehicle, under contract to the United States Air Force. This vehicle was delivered to the USAF in July 1967, as the X-24A, and eventually completed a series of nine manned but unpowered flights during 1969.

On 19 March 1970 Major Jerauld Gentry of the USAF sat in the cockpit of the X-24A while it was carried to an altitude of about 13 700 m (45 000 ft) under the wing of a giant B-52 bomber 'mother-plane'. The X-24A was released from the B-52, and Major Gentry ignited the turbo-rocket engine to boost his speed and attain greater altitude. The flight lasted just $7\frac{1}{4}$ minutes, after which the X-24A was landed successfully on Rogers Dry Lake.

During the remainder of 1970 and part of 1971, 28 further flights were made before it was decided to take the X-24A apart and rebuild it as the higher-speed X-24B. When the aircraft re-appeared it was considerably longer, with a more pointed nose. The main difference, however, was that the X-24B was far less bulbous in shape, with a flatter undersurface and neatly curved top-decking. The programme restarted with an unpowered flight in August 1973, and 14 powered flights followed, the last being made in September 1975.

The culmination of this and other research can be seen in the incredible NASA Space Shuttle Orbitor which began its flight tests in 1977.

McDonnell XF-85 Goblin *USA:* Until long-range escort fighters became available in quantity, the United States Air Force in Europe experienced heavy casualties in bombing raids on Germany during the middle years of the Second World War. The United States was naturally anxious that its big post-war bombers, armed with nuclear weapons, should not risk a similar fate. The most difficult problem to overcome was that the new bombers, like the Consolidated-Vultee B-36, had far greater range than any fighter. To evaluate one possible answer, McDonnell was given a contract by the Air Force to develop a parasite fighter.

The result was the Goblin, a diminutive and dumpy jet fighter with a multitude of tail surfaces, that was to be carried in the forward bomb-bay of the B-36, and lowered out by a trapeze when needed for protection. To return to the bay, the Goblin was expected to fly under the lowered trapeze and hook onto it.

Two prototype Goblins were built, and the Air Force modified a B-29 bomber for flight tests. On 23 August 1948 a Goblin was released from the bomber for the first time, but when the pilot tried to hook-on again, the fighter smashed into the metal trapeze, breaking the canopy and knocking the helmet and oxygen mask off the pilot. Quickly the pilot put the damaged oxygen hose into his mouth and performed a successful emergency landing on the undercarriage skids, at 275 km/h (170 mph). Hook-ons were achieved eventually, but the whole parasite-fighter programme was then cancelled.

McDonnell Douglas A-4 Skyhawk *USA:* The Skyhawk has been operational with the United States Navy since 1956. Despite this, it is likely to continue as a front-line combat aircraft well into the 1980s.

Designed originally as a subsonic low-cost and lightweight attack aircraft for carrier operations with the US Navy, the prototype first flew on 22 June 1954. Other design considerations were small overall dimensions, enabling the aircraft to be stowed and brought up to the flight deck on a lift without folding wings, good low-speed flight characteristics, and a heavy weapon-carrying ability. The initial production version was designated A-4A, followed by the A-4B and A-4C, the latter with all-weather capability, terrain-clearance radar and other improvements. The A-4E version had a longer range and increased payload, and entered service in the early 1960s; by the end of its production run total output of Skyhawks had reached 1845 aircraft.

The A-4F represented a major update compared with earlier versions, with new lift-spoilers to shorten the landing run, better protection for the pilot, and updated electronics. The next versions were mostly two-seat trainers and export models for countries such as Israel (whose Skyhawks have seen combat), Australia, New Zealand, Kuwait, the Argentine and Singapore. However, the A-4M for the US Marine Corps differs in being known as the Skyhawk II, with a more powerful engine, a braking parachute as standard, increased ammunition and a larger cockpit canopy. The A-4Y (an A-4M with improved operational equipment) may enter production after existing A-4Ms have been modified to A-4Y standard.

McDonnell Douglas DC-9 *USA:* With the long-range DC-8 in service, Douglas (the company not then joined by McDonnell) set about the preliminary studies of a much smaller airliner for the short-to-medium-range market.

McDonnell Douglas DC-9
Series 40 of SAS

The first DC-9 made its maiden flight on 25 February 1965. By June four more aircraft had joined the test programme. As the DC-9 Series 10 Model 11, the aircraft went initially to Delta Air Lines, which made the first DC-9 passenger flight on 29 November 1965, followed by the first scheduled service on 8 December. A second version of the Series 10 appeared as the Model 15, with more powerful engines and additional fuel; 137 production examples of the two Series 10 models were built, plus DC-9 cargo versions (*see* below).

In an effort to gain more of the market, Douglas rapidly produced other versions of the DC-9, the first of which was the Series 30. This offers the potential operator a choice of engines of varying power, has a longer fuselage accommodating up to 115 passengers, greater wing span and new high-lift devices, like full-span leading-edge slats and double-slotted flaps to compensate for its heavier take-off weight. Scheduled services with Series 30 aircraft were started by Eastern Air Lines on 1 February 1967. This has become the most popular version

and by mid-1977 564 had been ordered.

Despite its model number, the Series 20 flew after both the Series 30 and 40, but only ten were produced for the airline SAS, each carrying up to 90 passengers under hot climate and high altitude conditions. The Series 40 holds up to 125 passengers, and the first of 67 aircraft ordered by mid-1977 were operated commercially by SAS in March 1968.

Apart from the DC-9F cargo, DC-9CF convertible and DC-9RC mixed passenger/cargo versions, and military variants (C-9A Nightingale, C-9B Skytrain II and VC-9C), the remaining version is the Series 50, of which 69 had been ordered by mid-1977. This has a stretched fuselage for up to 139 passengers and a 'new look' interior.

McDonnell Douglas F-4 Phantom II *USA:* Few military aircraft flying today have achieved the world-wide service or combat record of the Phantom II, an aircraft which was designed for naval service in the early 1950s. Still the backbone of NATO air forces, and

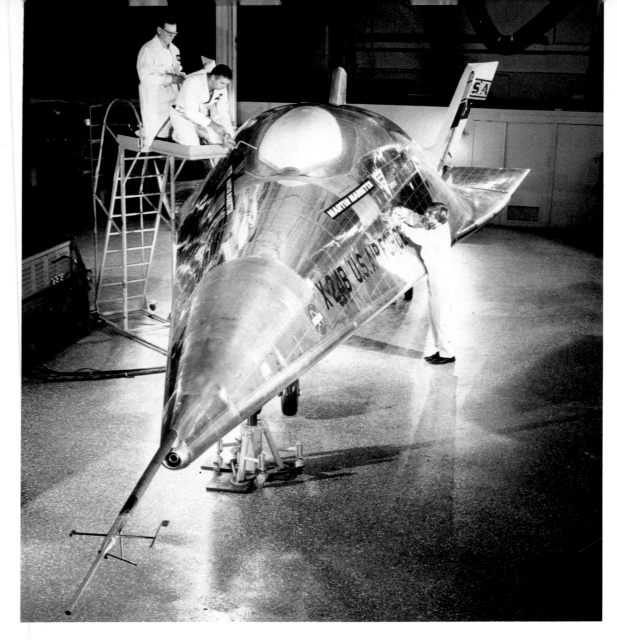

Opposite above McDonnell Douglas F-15B (originally TF-15A) Eagle of the USAF, here seen in special colours for the 1776–1976 bicentennial celebrations

Opposite below YC-14, built as Boeing's contender in the USAF's advanced medium STOL transport competition

Left Martin Marietta X-24B lifting-body research vehicle

Below McDonnell Douglas YC-15 STOL transport

those of other countries, Phantoms have been produced in some 19 variants, including a remotely-piloted highly manoeuvrable target drone version for the US Navy, designated QF-4B.

The Phantom II was ordered originally by the US Navy as a heavy attack fighter capable of flying at the then incredible speed of over Mach 2. Its role was changed to that of missile-armed fighter when Sparrow air-to-air missiles became available. The basic F-4A Phantom II was produced only in limited numbers, of which the first flew on 27 May 1958. The F-4B was the first major variant, of which 649 were built for the US Navy and Marine Corps as all-weather fighters.

Having test flown the F-4A, the United States Air Force became interested in the Phantom II and ordered its first series as F-4Cs; the total of 583 built included 36 for Spain. Some of the US F-4Cs were modified under the 'Wild Weasel' programme to carry electronic search equipment and homing missiles specially designed to attack early-warning and missile radar sites. These have been followed by improved F-4G 'Wild Weasels'.

Several reconnaissance and multi-role (air superiority/interdiction/attack) versions have also been produced, contributing to the total of more than 5000 built to date – other operators include the Royal Air Force (F-4M) and Royal Navy (F-4K) and the air forces of about nine other countries.

Phantom IIs have been used in action many times, notably during the Vietnam War and the Arab-Israeli conflicts.

McDonnell Douglas YC-15 (and Boeing YC-14) *USA:* Looking ahead to when it would need to replace its Hercules transport aircraft with a more modern type, the United States Air Force issued a requirement for a new Advanced Medium STOL Transport (AMST) in 1972. Five different aircraft were proposed to meet the requirement, of which two were funded to prototype stage. These were the McDonnell Douglas YC-15 and the Boeing YC-14.

The YC-15 was first flown in August 1975 and is powered by four turbofan engines. The secret of its very short take-off and landing distances is its high-lift blown flap system, which allows the aircraft to perform these manoeuvres well within the 610 m (2000 ft) specified by the USAF. The rival Boeing YC-14, which has a similar type of wide-body fuselage for carrying a great amount of bulky equipment, is powered by two very large General Electric CF6-50D turbofan engines of 23135 kg (51000 lb) each. The first prototype YC-14 made its maiden flight in August 1976, and its main features are its supercritical wing and the overwing positioning of the engines.

Lengthy evaluation trials of both transports were undertaken prior to the withdrawal of funds from the AMST programme. It is possible that the YC-15 and YC-14 might be converted into prototype commercial transport aircraft.

McDonnell Douglas F-15 Eagle *USA:* The Eagle is the newest, fastest and best fighter in the United States Air Force. It was designed primarily as an air superiority fighter, with the emphasis on rapid acceleration, high speed and manoeuvrability – if necessary, to the detriment of other applications such as ground attack. The first F-15A flew on 27 July 1972, followed a year later by the first F-15B two-seat trainer. After exhaustive trials, which proved beyond doubt that the Eagle was capable of its main task of countering the Soviet MiG-25 ('Foxbat') Mach 3 + fighter, production was begun.

By mid-1977 the USAF had 172 Eagles in operational status with Tactical Air Command. Orders are planned to total 749 aircraft for the USAF, to be delivered by 1981. Eagles are also being delivered to Israel, and Mitsubishi of Japan hopes to produce 117 under licence for the JASDF.

A novel feature of the Eagle is its optional use of 'Fast Packs' (Fuel And Sensor Tactical Packs). These are basically auxiliary fuel tanks, which attach to the sides of the engine air intakes and are designed to retain the aircraft's aerodynamic lines. With this extra fuel, an Eagle can be ferried 5560 km (3450 miles), making it independent of in-flight refuelling tankers. In addition to fuel, the tanks can also carry specialized reconnaissance equipment.

In January and February 1975, a specially prepared F-15A known as the *Streak Eagle* set up eight new time-to-height records, ranging from 27.57 seconds to an altitude of 3000 m to 3 minutes and 27.8 seconds to 30000 m. Two have since been bettered by the new E-266M (MiG-25).

Messerschmitt Bf 109 *Germany:* Bearing in mind that the Bf 109 was to become one of the Royal Air Force's major opponents in the Second World War, it is ironic that the prototype had a British Rolls-Royce Kestrel engine when it made its first flight in September 1935. The power plant was, however, soon changed. In any case, Rolls-Royce was using a German-built Heinkel He 70 to flight test some of its latest engines at about the same time.

The irony is, of course, far more apparent in retrospect. Hitler maintained to the end that he had never wanted to fight Britain. Nonetheless, the Germans were hard at work building up their armed forces to fight *somebody* in the mid-thirties, with special attention to the Luftwaffe. And what the Luftwaffe needed, it got. The first German fighters were, understandably, bi-planes. When first 'blooded' with the German Condor Legion in the Spanish Civil War, it became clear that they were inferior to fighters built in Italy and the Soviet Union. However, back at home Professor Willy Messerschmitt was already preparing the first production Bf 109s for dispatch to Spain.

Only a few Bf 109s operated in Spain, but they proved superior to all opposing fighters and showed that, with some refinement, the type was ideal for large-scale front-line operation. Simultaneously, specially prepared versions and developments of the Bf 109, fitted with greatly boosted engines, gained a series of world speed records, some of which were to remain unbeaten for 30 years.

On 1 September 1939 Germany attacked Poland, including in the aerial spearhead of its forces about 200 Bf 109s, which quickly destroyed the obsolescent Polish PZL fighters. The standard version of the German fighter at that time was the Bf 109E, which was still the major variant when the Battle of Britain began in August 1940. During this battle, which lasted many weeks, RAF Hurricane and Spitfire fighters were directed mainly against incoming German bombers, although escorting Bf 110 twin-engined fighters and Bf 109s were necessarily engaged. Fighter losses on both sides were comparable, but the battle ended in victory for the RAF, as it had prevented the achievement of German air superiority which might have heralded a sea invasion of Britain.

The fact that the Bf 109 had too limited a range to be fully effective as a bomber escort during this battle persuaded the German authorities to consider the type most useful as a defensive fighter in Europe. This was reflected in the more refined but relatively lightly-armed next production version of the fighter, the Bf 109F. Not until the arrival of the Bf 109G was faith in the type fully restored; and this version was then built in huge numbers for many varied roles. It was in a Bf 109G-14 that Major Erich Hartmann of the Luftwaffe reached his unrivalled total of 352 confirmed victories, although these were gained on the Eastern Front where German fighters easily outclassed the early Soviet fighters.

The Bf 109G remained the major version right up to the end of hostilities in May 1945; it is thought that some 35 000 Bf 109s of all versions were produced. Others were built in Czechoslovakia, and many went into Czech Air Force service after the war. Another post-war operator was Israel, while Bf 109s built by Hispano in Spain as HA-1109s and HA-1112s, were still active into the seventies. With the last of them the wheel turned full circle. Like the original prototype they were powered by a Rolls-Royce engine – this time the Merlin.

Messerschmitt Bf 110 *Germany:* The Messerschmitt Bf 110 was an aircraft of very mixed fortunes. It has often been criticized for its failure during the Battle of Britain, while its successes in other fields have been largely ignored. Yet, this aircraft that did not match up to Luftwaffe expectations managed to serve Germany throughout the Second World War in long-range escort fighter, fighter-bomber, reconnaissance, ground attack and night fighter roles.

Designed to a 1934 requirement for a long-range escort fighter, the first prototype Bf 110 made its initial flight on 12 May 1936. A key factor in the design was the use of two Daimler-Benz DB 600 engines; subsequent difficulty in obtaining enough of these to power development aircraft meant that the Bf 110 could not be tested during the Spanish Civil War. Nevertheless, one aircraft was tested at the Rechlin evaluation centre in 1937 and proved to be very fast, although not as manoeuvrable as hoped. Despite obvious shortcomings, the Bf 110 entered service in 1939 as the Bf 110C, powered by two 1100 hp DB 601A engines. Production was set up on a massive scale, and by the end of the year some 500 Bf 110s were flying operationally.

Against Poland and other European countries the aircraft fared well, but when used during the Battle of Britain to escort German bombers, Royal Air Force fighters dealt heavily with the aircraft, forcing the Luftwaffe to switch to short-range Bf 109s for escort duties. Although the Bf 110s had failed in this primary task, production continued at a high rate; by 1945 no fewer than 6150 had been built, ranging from Bf 110As to Gs. As later models became available, the early Bf 110Cs and Ds were transferred to the Middle East and Eastern Front.

When the 'improved' Messerschmitt Me 210 started to reach Luftwaffe units in 1941, manufacture of the Bf 110 was gradually run down, but it soon became clear that the Me 210 was not an improvement and production of the Bf 110 was again stepped up. The Bf 110Es were capable of carrying a respectable bomb load of 2000 kg (4410 lb) as fighter-bombers, while straight fighter and reconnaissance versions were also built. These, and later versions, were operated with a fair degree of success in many war zones. The Bf 110F was basically similar to the E, but two new variants were produced – the 110F-2 carrying rocket projectiles and the F-4 with two 30 mm cannon and an extra crew member for night fighting. The last version, the Bf 110G, was intended for use originally as a fighter-bomber but, in view of the success of the F-4 and the increasingly heavy attacks on Germany by Allied bombers, was employed mostly as a night fighter.

It was in a Bf 110 that Rudolf Hess, Deputy Führer of Germany, flew solo to Scotland on the night of 10 May 1941, in the hope of negotiating peace terms with Britain, without Hitler's knowledge.

Messerschmitt Me 163 Komet *Germany:* The extent of research and development in Germany during the Second World War was generally wider than that in any other country – although ultimately the finest aircraft and, of course, the atomic bomb, were produced by the Allies. Disregarding conventional aircraft, German scientists conducted advanced research into rocket-powered interceptors, flying bombs and artillery rockets (V2), as well as researching

Opposite above The
remarkable XF-85 Goblin
parasite jet-fighter

Opposite below An RAF
McDonnell Douglas F-4M
Phantom II investigating
a Soviet *Bear*

Right above McDonnell
Douglas A-4S Skyhawk
attack aircraft

Right centre Messerschmitt
Bf 109E-4 fighter of the
Luftwaffe

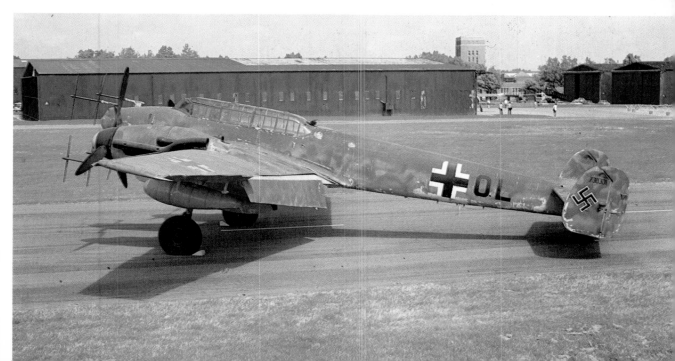

Right below Messerschmitt
Bf 110 night-fighter

jet-propelled aircraft with swept, delta, pivoting and swing wings, and many other aviation projects. It was, in fact, German scientists who started both America and Russia on their way into space after the war.

The Komet was a small swept-wing and tailless single-seat rocket-powered interceptor which became operational with the Luftwaffe in the summer of 1944. Although only one Jagdgeschwader (wing) became operational with Komets, they accounted for about 12 of the Allied aircraft shot down over Germany between 16 August 1944 and 7 May 1945.

Although the Komet did not become operational until 1944, the first powered flight by a prototype had been made in August 1941. Its development had been via the DFS 194, a test aircraft built to evaluate the whole concept of a rocket-powered fighting aircraft and itself the culmination of earlier experiments from 1928 with a rocket-powered glider. By the end of the war more than 350 Komets had been built, some

as Me 163A unpowered trainers, although by far the majority were Me 163B interceptors. The design concept was simple, for the aircraft had to be small and light, with sufficient speed to attack Allied bombers within minutes of being sighted. To achieve this, the engine burned fuel at such a rate that the Komet had an endurance of only some ten minutes, but could climb to 9150 m (30 000 ft) in two and a half minutes, and extend its endurance by periods of gliding. Its service ceiling was an incredible 16 500 m (54 000 ft), and maximum speed about 960 km/h (596 mph). Once within range, the enemy bomber was raked by the Komet's cannon.

Inevitably, such an advanced concept gave rise to problems especially in respect of crew safety. To save weight, the undercarriage was jettisoned at take-off, leaving the Komet to land on an underfuselage skid – the resulting bumpy, high-speed touchdown sometimes caused remnants of fuel to mix so that the aircraft exploded on landing. Komet pilots also suffered burns

Messerschmitt Me 163 Komet rocket-powered interceptor

from the fuel or back injuries caused by the bumping.

Messerschmitt Me 262 *Germany:* The brief story of Second World War German jet-powered fighters tells of both triumph and stupidity, mostly on Hitler's part. For although the story culminated in the operational Me 262, a fine fighter with a maximum speed of around 869 km/h (540 mph), months of arguing about its most useful role resulted in very limited operational use.

Before the war, German designers had produced two types of jet engine, and the Nazi leaders asked for prototype aircraft to be built around them. Both Heinkel and Messerschmitt built jet fighters, but the engines' thrust was too low to raise their speed greatly above that of contemporary piston-engined aircraft; this changed when the new Junkers Jumo jet engines became available.

Messerschmitt now produced the Me 262 with Jumo engines, and this combination proved successful. Although production could have got under way at once, other more conventional aircraft were given priority by Hitler, and so quantity production of the jet did not begin until late 1943. But, although the first Me 262s were planned as fighters, Hitler soon altered the production Me 262s to fighter-bombers, a role which reduced their performance greatly. The first Me 262s became operational with the Luftwaffe in October 1944.

By now the Allies were ploughing their way through Europe and, with German armies retreating, Hitler changed his mind again and ordered priority production of Me 262s as fighters. This meant that only about 15% of the Me 262s built were operational as fighters when needed. Indeed, no British Meteor jet ever met an Me 262 in combat, although 11 German pilots are reported to have gained between 5 and 16 victories while flying jets. Some Me 262s were destroyed by RAF piston-engined Tempests.

Messerschmitt Bf 109E of the
Swiss Air Force

Messerschmitt Bf 110G-4
night-fighter of the Luftwaffe

Right Messerschmitt Me 262
jet-fighter, preserved at the
Deutsches Museum, Munich

Right Messerschmitt Me 262
jet-fighter, preserved at the
Deutsches Museum, Munich

Below Mikoyan MiG-15 of
the Soviet Air Force, the
great rival of the American
Sabre

Mikoyan MiG-15 *USSR:* The first Soviet jet fighter to become operational was the Yakovlev Yak-15, which entered service in 1947. However, this was basically a much modified Yak-3 piston-engined monoplane, powered by a Soviet adaptation of the German Junkers Jumo jet engine. The Yak-15 was followed into service by the MiG-15, which was a completely different proposition.

Here was a real jet fighter, designed as such from the start, and built from 1948 in a quantity which has never been rivalled. More than 15 000 are thought to have been constructed for the Soviet Air Forces and those of other nations. The prototype had been test flown in 1947 and, like the production models, was powered by a Soviet adaptation of the Rolls-Royce Nene turbojet engine (Soviet designated RD-45 and VK-1). The MiG-15 possessed clean lines and swept wings, and had a very high performance for its time.

When the war in Korea started in 1950, MiG-15s of the North Korean Air Force, with others from China went into action against the south. The first-ever encounter between jet fighters was reported in November, between a MiG-15 and a Shooting Star (*see* Lockheed F-80 Shooting Star). The outcome in the Shooting Star's favour was due mainly to the experience and training of the American pilot, because in all respects the MiG was a superior combat plane. However, in the following month US F-86A Sabres first went into action, and on the first day a MiG was destroyed by a Sabre. Here was the classic situation of equally matched fighters, as the Sabre was a far more advanced aircraft than the Shooting Star. In the course of the war, the two opposing types were to meet regularly. Although the MiG was more heavily armed than the early Sabres and had better acceleration and rate of climb, the Sabre was more manoeuvrable, faster in a dive and had an edge with its more advanced gun/radar equipment. All in all, 807 MiGs were claimed as destroyed during the war, compared with 111 US jets – but it should be stressed again that experienced US pilots were generally fighting relatively inexperienced North Koreans.

MiG-15s are still operational today as trainers and fighters in many countries.

Mikoyan MiG-19 *USSR:* After the Second World War, the design bureau of Artem I Mikoyan became the principal source of Soviet fighter aircraft. The MiG-15 was its first really important fighter and a year after it entered service the improved MiG-17 made its first flight, becoming operational with the Air Force from 1952.

Only one more year was to pass before another Mikoyan fighter made its maiden flight, as the MiG-19. Its design had been authorized in 1951, and during trials the prototype achieved a maximum speed of Mach 1.1. This was all-important, as the MiG-19 was thus the first Soviet fighter capable of super-

Opposite Mikoyan MiG-19 of the Czech Air Force, known to NATO as 'Farmer-C'

sonic speed in level flight. Powered by two turbojets, side by side in the rear fuselage, early production aircraft were suitable for day operation only and were armed with three cannon. They became operational in 1955. The next version, known to NATO as 'Farmer-B', had underwing attachment points for air-to-surface rockets or bombs, in addition to the three cannon and had all-weather capability.

Important changes were introduced by the next two versions, the MiG-19PF and MiG-19PM (Farmer-Ds). The PM, in particular, could carry four 'Alkali' air-to-air missiles. Large numbers were built, and were supplied also to about a dozen air forces.

Before the political split between the Soviet Union and China, MiG-19s had been delivered to the Chinese Air Force – the design was subsequently copied and produced in China as the Shenyang F-6. The first F-6 flew in December

1961 and production continued into the mid-seventies, although Soviet production of the MiG-19 ended in the late 1950s. F-6s were also supplied to Pakistan and Tanzania. The Chinese Air Force is so satisfied with the basic MiG-19 that it has developed from it the faster, more powerful F-9.

Mikoyan MiG-21 *USSR:* This single-seat fighter remains one of the most widely used of all Soviet-built aircraft, although its design goes back to the mid-fifties. Vast numbers are flown by the Soviet air forces and those of about 23 other countries, and constant development and updating has produced some 16 variants, not including the few modified for record breaking and a special MiG-21, called 'Analogue', which was flown with scaled-down Tupolev Tu-144 supersonic transport delta wings to flight test them prior to the full-size

Below Mikoyan MiG-21 of the Czech Air Force, known to NATO as 'Fishbed'

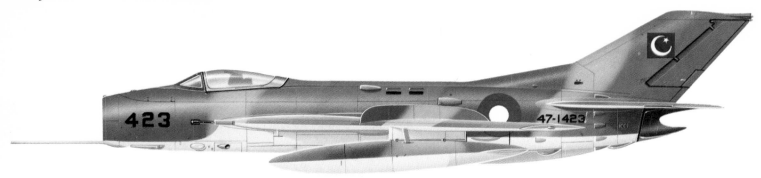

aircraft being built.

The prototype represented a major change of configuration compared with the earlier MiG-15, MiG-17 and MiG-19, being a carefully streamlined 'tailed delta' of small size and light weight. The initial production version was built in only small numbers, powered by a single turbojet engine of relatively low thrust. Armament was limited to two 30 mm cannon, and it could be flown only as a day and clear-weather fighter.

Meanwhile, the first Soviet air-to-air missiles were coming off the production lines and the first major production version of the MiG-21, known to NATO as 'Fishbed-C', had underwing pylons for two of these Atoll missiles, or rocket pods, in addition to a single cannon. The engine was also of increased power. A further major leap in the MiG-21's overall performance was initiated with the MiG-21 (NATO Fishbed-D) which had more advanced search-and-track radar to give it an all-weather capability. From this point, constant improvements were made to enhance performance, increase weapon load and make possible operation of the aircraft as a multi-role fighter.

MiG-21s have been built also in Czechoslovakia and China, the latter licence agreement being signed before the political split. The Chinese version is known as the F-8, but it is thought that only a limited number have been produced.

MiG-21s have been used in combat on many occasions during the Vietnam War and the Indo-Pakistan and Arab-Israeli conflicts. To compare the type with Western fighters is difficult but it is recognized that the MiG-21 is generally a good lightweight fighter with fine all-round performance.

Mikoyan MiG-23 and MiG-27 *USSR:* The MiG-23 and MiG-27 are basically similar variable-geometry (swing-wing) aircraft, and are known to NATO as 'Flogger'. The MiG-23 is an interceptor fighter that has been operational with the Soviet Air Force since 1971 – while the MiG-27 has a redesigned forward fuselage, an uprated engine and other changes which suit it for its main role of ground attack. Both MiGs operate with a laser rangefinder mounted in the nose. It is believed that well over 850 had been delivered by early 1977, of which a substantial

Mikoyan MiG-23 'Flogger-F'
of the Soviet Air Force

Soviet Mikoyan MiG-25 'Foxbat-A' interceptors, the fastest aircraft of their type in the world

WSK-Swidnik Mi-2, built in Poland

operational trainer version, designated MiG-23U or Flogger-C.

There seem to be two ground attack models (presuming that the MiG-23U is used also as the MiG-27 trainer and that a new trainer has not yet been identified by NATO). Most important is the MiG-27 (Flogger-D) Soviet Air Force version, which is specially configured to fly at high subsonic speed at low altitude, and has five weapon attachment points for a variety of stores, including tactical nuclear weapons. This Soviet version is fitted with an under-fuselage six-barrel Gatling-type gun, instead of the non-rotating, twin-barrel type on the MiG-23 interceptors, and carries a laser rangefinder and marked target seeker. The export ground attack model (Flogger-F) is basically a MiG-23 with the nose shape of a MiG-27.

Mikoyan MiG-25 *USSR:* Better known in the West under its NATO reporting name 'Foxbat', this is the fastest combat aircraft in service anywhere in the world. It has been produced in the Soviet Union in several versions for fighter-interceptor, reconnaissance and twin-cockpit training duties.

The existence of Foxbat was first announced to the West in 1965, when an example designated E-266 set up a speed record of 2320 km/h (1441.5 mph) over a 1000 km closed circuit while carrying a 2000 kg payload. Many other speed, height and time-to-height records were set up subsequently.

It was thought that well over 400 Foxbats were operational from bases in the Soviet Union, East Germany, Poland and Syria by mid-1976. Reconnaissance Foxbats have made flights across the Sinai Peninsula and off the coast of Israel (Israeli Phantoms failing to make contact), over Iran and parts of Western Europe.

The Foxbat has a maximum speed of Mach 3.2 without any external stores, or Mach 2.8 with external missiles, but little else was known until a Foxbat-A interceptor was flown to Japan by a defecting Soviet pilot in September 1976. Construction proved to be almost entirely of steel, with very advanced structural fuel tanks, the most powerful radar fitted to any interceptor, four attachments for air-to-air missiles, and electronic countermeasures equipment of unexpected efficiency.

Mil Mi-1, Mi-2 and Mi-4 *USSR:* Remarkably, the Mil Mi-1 is still flown in many countries around the world, despite the fact that it was the first helicopter to be mass produced in the Soviet Union. It made its first flight in September 1948, and both military and civil versions appeared in Russia before production was transferred to Poland in 1955. With basic accommodation for four passengers, Mi-1s were and still are flown as agricultural spraying helicopters, freight carriers, ambulance helicopters, personnel transports, military transports, and dual-control trainers.

number are based in East Germany.

The prototype MiG-23 was first shown publicly at the 1967 Aviation Day air display in Moscow, but a great many changes were made to the design before production went ahead. Not including the prototype, which NATO called Flogger-A, there are three operational versions of the MiG-23 flying at this time. The MiG-23S (or Flogger-E) for export is equipped to a lower standard than the Soviet Air Force's Flogger-B and has been supplied to Middle East countries. There is also a tandem two-seat

The Mi-2 represented a larger and twin-turboshaft-engined development of the earlier helicopter, and the prototype first flew in 1962. However, although it is designated Mi-2, the second Soviet production helicopter was the Mil Mi-4, which entered production in 1952 and resembles in some respects the earlier US Sikorsky S-55. The Mi-4 was built in thousands and was exported to many countries.

The Mi-2 was itself designed in the Soviet Union, where the prototypes were built and flown. However, development and production were undertaken in Poland from 1965 by WSK-Swidnik, the last version appearing as recently as 1975. Mi-2s are produced for both civil and military use, with standard accommodation for nine. In addition to performing the same roles as the Mi-1 (although able to carry over twice the load), the Mi-2 is operated as an aerial camera-carrying helicopter for outside broadcasts and as an attack helicopter carrying air-to-ground rockets.

Mil Mi-6 and Mi-10 *USSR:* When the Mi-6 first appeared in public in 1957 it took many observers by surprise, as it was much larger than any other helicopter built in the Soviet Union up to that time. Though dwarfed by the later Mi-12, it remained the world's largest helicopter for more than ten years, and over 500 have been built for military and civil duties in the Soviet Union and for export. Following some 35 prototype and pre-production Mi-6s, production models went first to the Soviet Air Force as assault transports, able to carry 65 troops, missiles and associated ground equipment, or up to 12000 kg (26450 lb) of cargo. A machine-gun is carried in the nose. Small wings help to increase cruising speed.

In a civil configuration, the Mi-6 has been

flown by Aeroflot for many years, as a transport for passengers or freight, an ambulance with accommodation for 41 stretchers and medical attendants, and as a water-bomber for aerial fire-fighting.

The Mi-10 is a flying-crane version of the Mi-6. Its overall length is unchanged, but the fuselage has been made shallower to give a long flat undersurface. This, combined with very long and wide-track undercarriage legs, enables bulky items to be carried externally, including prefabricated buildings and road vehicles. Up to 28 passengers or internal freight can also be accommodated. This version does not have fixed wings. The Mi-10K is similar, but has a shorter undercarriage and an undernose gondola for a second pilot (*see* Kamov Ka-25K).

Mil Mi-12 (V-12) *USSR:* The late 1960s brought many surprises for the aviation industries of the West, as news came that the Soviet Union had not only flown the first supersonic transport aircraft and put into service the fastest combat aircraft in the world, but had built and flown the largest helicopter by far.

Development of the Mi-12 had begun in 1965,

when a requirement was issued for a vertical take-off and landing aircraft able to carry military loads as wide and tall as those carried by the huge Antonov An-22 freight-plane. The design team led by Mikhail Mil decided that the helicopter should have twin rotors mounted on outriggers on each side of the fuselage rather than the more conventional tandem layout. This configuration would, it was claimed, give the helicopter greater stability; and it was not untried, as a series of similarly-configured experimental helicopters had been built in the early 1940s. The big advantage of the Mil design was that they were able to fit two of the complete rotor/power plant 'packages' already used singly in the Mi-6, almost without change.

The resulting prototype Mi-12 set up several load-to-altitude records in 1969 but crashed soon afterwards, due to engine failure. Other prototypes were flying by 1971, and it was expected that refined production examples would appear without too much delay. It is possible that the first production Mi-12s went to the Soviet Air Force, which could explain why there has been little recent news of the type. Others are expected to be used by Aeroflot for

transporting 50 passengers and freight on domestic routes, for supporting oil and gas exploration, and for carrying heavy cargo and geophysical equipment in remote areas of the Soviet Union.

Mil Mi-24 *USSR:* When the existence of this Soviet assault helicopter first became known in the West, in about 1972, it became a matter of high priority to discover as much about it as possible. Not until 1974 did the first photographs become available to the Press, and these showed two large single-rotor helicopters, one obviously an early example and the other a developed production version. The latter (NATO reporting name 'Hind-A') appears to be designed for two main tasks. The primary task is assault, with accommodation for about eight fully-armed troops in the rear cabin. The second task is attack, for which the helicopter's fuselage-mounted stub wings carry rocket pods and anti-tank missiles, while a machine-gun is flexibly mounted in the nose.

Hind-A's ability to beat down opposition in a drop-zone while delivering a squad of assault troops gave the Warsaw Pact nations a completely new attack capability, and nobody was surprised when large numbers were observed near the borders between Eastern and Western forces in Europe. The force became stronger still when Hind-D was revealed. This version has a completely new gunship-type front fuselage, with tandem cockpits for a weapons operator and pilot, and an undernose pack containing a four-barrel rapid-fire machine-gun with sensors – probably low light-level TV and infra-red – for increased efficiency in poor weather conditions or at night. At the same time, Hind-C replaced Hind-A, without nose gun or wingtip missiles. With an estimated speed of around 320 km/h (200 mph), Hind must clearly be treated with the greatest respect.

Mitsubishi A5M *Japan:* The Japanese pioneered the change from biplanes to monoplane fighters for naval carrier operations. In February 1935 a new Mitsubishi prototype, powered by a 785 hp Nakajima Kotobuki 41 radial engine, reached a creditable speed for the period of 452 km/h (281 mph). During development of this and the further five Ka-14 prototypes, split flaps were introduced for the first time on a Japanese aircraft, while the original 'cranked' wing was discarded in favour of a straight centre-section with marked dihedral on the outer panels. A spatted undercarriage was fitted, and the open cockpit layout was retained at the insistence of Navy pilots, although a small number of the A5M2a versions had canopies fitted. 'Claude', as the fighter was known to the Allies, had minimal armament of two machine-guns, but was an extremely nimble dogfighter.

The A5M2 equipped the 14th and 15th Kokutais (air corps) fighting the Chinese around Shanghai in 1937. The sturdiness of

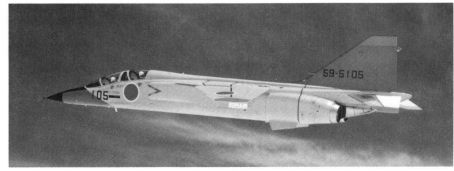

Mitsubishi T-2 two-seat supersonic jet trainer

the type was indicated when, after fighting in the Shanghai/Nanking area, Petty Officer Kashimura brought his machine back with the whole outer section of one wing shot away.

The final production version, the A5M4, served in the carriers *Ryujo*, *Zuiho* and *Hosho* during the invasion of the Philippines in December 1941. The A5Ms were called upon only to support the landing in the extreme south around Davao, since land-based 'Zeros', operating at extreme range, met all the needs of the High Command.

By the close of production 982 A5M fighters had been built, plus 103 A5M4-K two-seat trainers.

Mitsubishi A6M Zero-Sen *Japan:* The supremacy of the 'Zero', or Mitsubishi Type 0, in the Far East during 1941 and 1942 is illustrated by the story of just one engagement, on 11 April 1942. Flying out of Lae airstrip in eastern New Guinea, Japanese Navy 'ace' pilot Saburo Sakae, section leader in a nine-plane formation of A6M2 fighters ('Reisen' to the Japanese), crossed the Owen Stanley range at 4875 m (16000 ft) and made for Port Moresby airfield, held by the Allies. There the formation encountered four United States Army Air Force Bell P-39D Airacobras, which were left to Sakae and his wingmen. Opening up with his 20 mm cannon before the Americans could take evasive action, Sakae dived on the two rear-most fighters and sent them both down in flames. His wingmen bagged one apiece. Within minutes the battle was over, with the Zeros hardly scathed.

Designed by Jiro Horikoshi to achieve the highest possible speed and manoeuvrability from a Nakajima Sakae 12 engine of only 950 hp, the Zero had a light structure and powerful armament. It was an aggressive weapon, designed to perform well in a dogfight, and against Allied aircraft of 1941–2 vintage it did just that. It mastered all opposing fighters, irrespective of whether it flew from carriers, as at Pearl Harbor, or had to operate over long distances from land bases. Even the Philippines did not escape the Zeros' scourge, as the Japanese fighter used a jettisonable fuel tank to help cover the hundreds of miles of sea between those islands and its bases on Formosa.

The tables were turned when the A6M5 version of 'Zeke', as the Type 0 was known to the Allies, came up against a new generation of US

Opposite above The largest helicopter in the world, the Mil Mi-12 (V-12)

Opposite below Mitsubishi Ki-46

Navy and Army fighters, with powerful engines and heavy protection for their pilot and fuel tanks. Against them the Zero – still basically the design which had flown first on 1 April 1939 – offered minimal protection for either pilot or fuel. From 1943 the Zeros fell like flies, due in part to the newly-found confidence of Allied pilots, who were by now better trained, and with improved morale after the Coral Sea and Midway victories.

Zero production totalled more than 10930 (over 80% of all Navy single-seat output). Some were also the first aircraft used intentionally as suicide attack planes (*see* Yokosuka Ohka).

Mitsubishi G3M and G4M *Japan:* Two days after the Japanese attack on Pearl Harbor, HMS *Prince of Wales* and HMS *Repulse*, with destroyer escort but without air cover, set out from Singapore naval base and sailed north along the eastern coast of Malaya. The two capital ships had not anticipated serious air attack, since it was known that no Japanese aircraft carriers were within striking distance.

The Genzan and Minoro Kokutais (Air Corps) of the Imperial Japanese Navy Air Force had, however, moved into French Indo-China (now Vietnam) two months earlier. A total of 60 Mitsubishi G3M2 Type 96 Model 22 twin-engined bombers and 26 G4M1 Type 1 Model 11s took off and flew towards the ships, which had been spotted by a submarine and reconnaissance aircraft. The British ships were pinpointed and the bombers attacked on the morning of 10 December. After two hours of pounding with torpedoes and bombs, both of the big ships went down, taking nearly a thousand officers and men with them. This triumph was the high point in the careers of the Mitsubishi bombers.

A total of about 1100 G3Ms ('Nells' to the Allies and 'Chukohs' to the Japanese) were built between 1935 and 1943. But, from 1942 onwards many were converted to transports. The G4M ('Betty') had first gone into service in 1941, and by the time production ceased in 1945, about 2480 had been built. The G4M's long and streamlined fuselage earned it the nickname of 'Hamaki' ('Cigar') in Japan. By the spring of 1942, the type equipped the 1st, 4th, Kanoya and Takao Kokutais, and was deployed throughout the Dutch East Indies (Indonesia), New Guinea, Papua and New Britain. Air raids on Port Darwin in northern Australia in 1943 hit the headlines – but the G4Ms had considerable losses.

Then, on 18 April 1943, two G4M1s carrying Admiral Yamamoto, the naval C-in-C, and his staff were shot down over the Solomons by US Lockheed P-38F Lightning fighters, which ambushed the Japanese aircraft after intercepting radio details of the flight. This event had tragic consequences for the Japanese, and heralded the demise of Bettys. Outnumbered, with inadequate escort, the G4Ms were shot down in large numbers everywhere they were encountered. Their unprotected fuel tanks, and consequent tendency to catch fire easily, earned them the universal nickname of 'Flying Lighter'.

The greatly improved G4M2 version, with two 1800 hp radials and increased armament, was one of the chief victims of the 'Marianas Turkey Shoot' of June 1944, when US Navy fighters despatched Japanese aircraft in droves.

Finally, the G4M2e version was developed to carry the Ohka Model 11 rocket-propelled, single-seat suicide attacker in its bomb-bay. Few succeeded in approaching to within the proper launching distance from target before interception. Nevertheless, the battleship USS *West Virginia* was severely damaged by an

A captured Mitsubishi G4M 'Betty' medium bomber

Ohka on 1 April 1945 and, among other successes, a US destroyer was sunk 11 days later.

Numerically Betty and Nell were the Japanese Navy's main bombers of the war.

Mitsubishi Ki-46 *Japan:* During 1941 six Independent Chutais (squadrons) and one Sentai (wing) of the Imperial Japanese Army Air Force were equipped with a high-performance, twin-engined, beautifully streamlined aircraft known as the Mitsubishi Ki-46 or Type 100 command reconnaissance aircraft. When the Japanese launched their great offensive against the Allied powers across the full span of the Pacific in December 1941, small sections of Type 100s were deployed to reconnoitre ahead over Allied territory. At that time the maximum speed of the Type 100 was sufficiently in excess of the opposing fighters to make it virtually immune from interception. Only later, with aircraft like the P-38F Lightning, could the Type 100 be caught.

A total of 1742 were manufactured up to the time of the final Japanese collapse, including 611 Model 3 aircraft which went into production from 1943 onwards. The Model 3, capable of nearly 640 km/h (400 mph), performed regular missions over the United States Army Air Force Boeing B-29 Superfortress bases in the Marianas, and gave the Japanese High Command a continuously updated picture of the disposition of US units and aircraft. The Model 3 incorporated many improvements on earlier versions, and differed externally in having a continuous upper fuselage contour, thanks to an unstepped pilot's windscreen.

The Type 100 (known as 'Dinah' to the Allies), can lay claim to having been one of the finest long-range reconnaissance aircraft used by either side during the Second World War.

Attracted by its high performance, Air Headquarters developed an interceptor version of the Model 3. Armament comprised two forward-firing 20 mm Ho-5 cannon and an obliquely-mounted, forward-firing 37 mm Ho-203 cannon in the top of the fuselage. The new fighter was not a success, but despite this a ground attack variant was also produced.

Mitsubishi T-2 *Japan:* The T-2 is a very neat, high-performance jet trainer, built by Mitsubishi for the Japanese Air Self-Defence Force. It was the first supersonic aircraft designed and built in Japan, and has been produced as an advanced trainer and as a combat trainer. A further version, originally designated the FS-T2-KAI and now known as the F-1, is entering service as a single-seat close support fighter to replace Japan's existing North American F-86F Sabres.

The prototype T-2 first flew in July 1971 and reached supersonic speed initially in November of the same year. Delivery of the first 20 production T-2s had taken place by March 1976 with further aircraft on order.

Far larger than the new generation of European jet trainers, the T-2 looks somewhat like a SEPECAT Jaguar two-seater. Its very high speed for its role, of Mach 1.6, combined with an armament of one 20mm cannon and attachment points for air-to-air missiles and bombs (or other stores) on the combat trainer version, gives it a useful operational capability.

Mitsubishi Ki-46-IV, known to the Allies as 'Dinah'

Nakajima Ki-43 *Japan:* The first prototype Nakajima Ki-43 single-seat fighter flew in December 1938 and received the popular name 'Hayabusa' (Peregrine Falcon). Extensive development proved necessary, and when Japan attacked in the Far East in December 1941, only two Sentais (wings) were operational with the Imperial Japanese Army Air Force. The British fliers who first encountered 'Oscar' (its Allied reporting name) acknowledged it as a tough and manoeuvrable opponent in a dogfight.

The Ki-43 had been the first Japanese Army fighter with a retractable undercarriage to reach operational units. As more Oscars became available, they took over the role of principal Army single-seater from the obsolete Nakajima Ki-27 'Nate'. A total of about 5900 Ki-43s were built up to September 1944 – a number matched by no other Japanese Army fighter.

Oscar appeared on every front where Japanese ground troops were committed, and finally over the homeland itself, mainly on suicide missions. When confronted with Allied types in service in 1941 and 1942, the initial version, Ki-43-I, did well. Brewster Buffaloes, Curtiss Mohawks and early Warhawks fell to its guns. When later planes appeared, however, the absence of pilot armour and self-sealing fuel tanks led to heavy losses. These omissions were rectified in the Ki-43-II, which entered service in 1943. This version also had a more powerful engine, giving better performance; but the armament remained poor, although twin 12.7 mm machine-guns replaced the pitiful twin 7.7 mm weapons of the Ki-43-I.

Navy-Curtiss NC-4 *USA:* Glenn Curtiss began experiments with seaplanes in the USA in 1908. Although his earliest trials on water were unsuccessful, continued work led to the first entirely practical seaplanes and flying-boats, followed by development of the Curtiss *America* flying-boat in 1914 (*see* Felixstowe F.2A).

When the United States declared war on Germany in April 1917, it was an army force that was sent initially to France, the first Air Service units not leaving until August. A few days after the aviation units had set sail, Rear Admiral D. W. Taylor of the United States Navy decided that there was a need for a flying-boat that could attack German submarines, preferably with sufficient range to cross the Atlantic and so avoid delivery problems. Glenn Curtiss and Navy officers met and agreed the parameters of the design.

The first Navy-Curtiss or NC flying-boat, as it was named, made its maiden flight on 4 October 1918, just over a month before the war ended. However, the NC design was not to be wasted. Construction continued until four of the aircraft had been built. The intention was to use them not for war but for an attempt at the first transatlantic crossing by air, in stages.

Each aircraft was allocated a crew of five or six, but NC-2 was subsequently dismantled to provide spare parts for the others. On 8 May 1919, the three remaining NCs set off from Rockaway, New York, led by Commander J. H. Towers. Flying via Newfoundland, the Azores, and Portugal, the only aircraft to complete the journey was NC-4, commanded by Lieutenant-Commander A. C. Read. It covered 6315 km (3925 miles) in a little over 57 hours of flying time, reaching Plymouth, England, on 31 May. Both NC-1 and NC-3 had come down in the sea during the flight, the former sinking.

North American B-25 Mitchell *USA:* The Mitchell became one of the finest medium bombers of the Second World War, and one of the most heavily armed in certain versions.

The first Mitchells were ordered at about the time that war broke out in Europe, the construction of prototypes being waived in favour of immediate production. The first of the original batch of 24 flew on 19 August 1940, and all of these aircraft, plus 40 B-25As, were operational when the US was attacked by Japan.

As the war progressed, many thousands of Mitchells served as bombers with the United States Army Air Force, the Royal Air Force, and the air forces of Russia, the Netherlands, Canada and Brazil, while the US Navy operated some as PBJ-1s for anti-submarine work. Some B-25Cs and Ds were also modified for anti-shipping missions. The bomber versions culminated in the B-25J, of which 4318 were built from 1943, but Mitchells also proved outstanding as ground attack aircraft. The B-25G introduced a 75 mm cannon mounted in a non-glazed nose, while the B-25H also had provision for 14 machine-guns, up to 3200 lb of bombs or a torpedo. Some B-25Js were modified to carry

North American B-25J-32 Mitchell of the USAAF

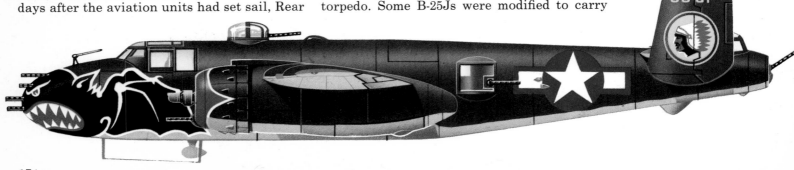

eight machine-guns in a similar non-glazed nose.

Operating mainly in the European, Pacific and Eastern Front arenas, B-25s carried out many spectacular raids, but perhaps the most famous was that made by 16 Mitchells of the USAAF against Tokyo during daylight hours on 18 April 1942. The aircraft, led by the famous Lt. Col. Jimmy Doolittle, flew from the US aircraft carrier USS *Hornet* and, although causing little actual damage, had an incalculable psychological effect on the Japanese people.

By the end of the war, Mitchells were still giving good service, although ever-growing numbers were being withdrawn for training duties. An unfortunate event involving a Mitchell is also well remembered, as one flew into the 79th floor of New York's mighty Empire State building during fog on 28 July 1945, killing or injuring 45 people. After the war the Mitchell continued for a while with the USAF as a bomber, then as a transport and trainer, finally being withdrawn completely in 1960.

North American F-86 Sabre *USA:* The introduction of the Sabre had as great an impact in raising the capabilities of the United States Air Force as did the arrival of the McDonnell Douglas F-4 Phantom II 14 years later.

The Sabre was conceived in 1945, originally with straight wings. Having studied captured German material relating to the advantages offered by swept wings, North American promptly adapted their design. The first XP-86 made its maiden flight on 1 October 1947, with swept wings and tail unit, and exceeded Mach 1 in a dive six months later.

Production F-86As had already been ordered in 1946 and were delivered from February 1949. In all, 544 F-86As with J47-GE-1, -7 or -13 engines were built. As well as setting new world speed records, F-86As were sent to Korea in late 1950, and first went into combat on 17 December. One aircraft of the 336th Squadron, USAF, shot down a MiG-15 on that day with its guns, marking the beginning of a period of fierce rivalry between the US and Soviet-built fighters.

The F-86A was followed by the F-86D, the first all-weather version of the Sabre, of which production eventually totalled over 2500 aircraft. The prototype made its maiden flight in December 1949 and represented a major change in design. Fitted with a J47-GE-17 or -33 engine, with afterburner, the F-86D had a nose-mounted radar and was armed with 24 Mighty Mouse rockets in a retractable underfuselage pack, in place of the usual guns. At the peak of their career, F-86Ds equipped 20 wings of Air Defence Command, based in the United States, Western Europe and the Far East. Many others were supplied to foreign air forces. The later F-86L was a modernized version of the D with advanced electronics.

The next two fighter versions built for day flying only were the F-86E and F, the latter having initially a more powerful J47-GE-27 engine and receiving equipment changes and modified wings during its production run. Many were delivered abroad and some were licence-built in Japan. Both the F-86E and F could carry underwing stores. The F-86H was also a fighter-bomber, but was powered by a J79-GE-3 engine. Fixed armament for about three-quarters of the 475 built was four 20 mm cannon.

The last version of the Sabre was the F-86K, intended specifically for NATO countries in Europe and armed with four 20 mm cannon. Many were assembled in Italy, by Fiat, and air forces equipped with Ks included Italy, France, Norway, the Netherlands and West Germany. Some went later to Turkey and Thailand.

In Australia, the Commonwealth Aircraft Corporation licence-built the Avon-Sabre, powered by a Rolls-Royce Avon RA.7 engine. Armed with two 30 mm Aden cannon, the Avon-Sabre was basically an F-86F, although the new engine and other modifications made it the fastest of all versions, with a top speed in level flight of 1126 km/h (700 mph). In the 1960s Sidewinder air-to-air missiles were fitted to Avon-Sabres to supplement underwing rockets or bombs. The type remained operational with the Royal Australian Air Force into the late sixties, until replaced by Dassault Mirage IIIs. Large-scale Sabre production was also undertaken in Canada for the RCAF and other air forces, including the RAF, which flew Sabres from 1953 to 1956.

Sabres remain operational as fighters and fighter-bombers to this day with air forces of many countries, including Japan and Pakistan. Commonwealth Sabres are first-line equipment in Malaysia and Indonesia.

North American P-51 Mustang *USA:* The North American Mustang – one of the most famous fighters of the Second World War – was originally designed to a requirement of the British Purchasing Commission who, in 1940, were trying to buy effective combat aircraft from America to supplement those built in Britain.

The North American Company thus designed a single-seat fighter designated NA-73, which first flew on 26 October 1940. Test flying showed that the aircraft had excellent range and speed, although it performed best at lower altitudes, and an initial order of 320 aircraft for the RAF was soon agreed. In RAF service the early production aircraft were known as Mustang Is. Like most single-seat fighters of the time, they had a panelled-glass cockpit canopy, flush with a raised and faired rear fuselage. Because their Allison engine lost power at height, they were allocated to Army co-operation duties.

As production continued, for Britain and later the USA, the better-remembered bubble canopy and lowered rear upper fuselage became standard. More important, higher overall performance, especially at height, resulted from the fitting of a Packard-built version of the British Merlin engine.

During and after the Second World War over 14 800 Mustangs were built, in many versions, including a dive-bomber variant that began to enter service in late 1942. However, the Merlin-engined Mustang, or P-51 as it was designated in the United States, is best known as a long-range escort fighter, together with its contemporaries the Republic Thunderbolt and Lockheed Lightning.

Before the advent of these aircraft, fighter escort for bombers raiding enemy territory was limited by the fighters' comparatively short range, leaving the bombers to defend themselves at periods when help was most needed to stave off intercepting fighters. When long-range fighters appeared which could fly with the bombers all the way to distant targets, the

Left North American X-15 rocket-powered research aircraft, the fastest manned airplane ever flown

Below North American Mustang in the operational colours of the Dominican Republic Air Force

Northrop F-5E Tiger II
lightweight fighter of an
American 'Aggressor'
Squadron

attrition rate for bombers fell dramatically. Reichsmarschall Hermann Goering is said to have commented that he knew Germany had lost the war when he first saw Mustangs escorting B-17s over Berlin.

After the war the Mustang was still rated as an excellent fighter-bomber, despite the introduction of jet fighters. Even when the Korean War started, Mustangs were still being operated as ground-attack fighters.

A small number of P-82 Twin Mustangs had appeared during the Second World War, and production continued afterwards. These were basically two Mustangs joined together by common centre wing and centre tail surfaces. They became standard long-range escort aircraft in Korea, and the first three aircraft of the North Korean Air Force to be destroyed in the air, Russian-built Yak-9s, fell to five Twin Mustangs of the USAF two days after the war started.

North American X-15 *USA:* In one of the most spectacular research programmes ever carried out in the United States, three X-15 aircraft achieved such extremes of speed and altitude that the unofficial records they set have never

been beaten by a manned aircraft. In fact, the heights attained enabled some of their pilots to be termed astronauts.

The research programme started in 1955 when the United States Air Force and Navy, together with the NACA, gave North American a contract to build three aircraft capable of flying at Mach 7 and an altitude of 80500 m (264 000 ft). The idea was not simply to build fast aircraft, but to gain vital information on structural heating, control and stability problems at hypersonic speeds during entry into, and return from, the upper atmosphere. For this the aircraft had to be built mainly of titanium and stainless steel, with an armoured skin covering to withstand very high and very low temperatures.

As the X-15s were rocket powered, they were designed to be air-launched from a B-52 bomber 'motherplane', although conventional landing was necessary. The first X-15 became airborne in March 1959, but was not released, the flight being basically to explore the aerodynamics. The next step came in June of the same year when an X-15 was released, although the flight was made with the engine switched off. On 17 September 1959, the first powered flight was

179

Early North American P-51
Mustang long-range fighters
of the USAAF

made, although speeds were kept low for initial testing.

In May 1960 an X-15 achieved a speed of Mach 3.19, raised to Mach 4.90 in May 1961 and over Mach 6 by the end of the year. Finally, on 3 October 1967, an X-15 achieved Mach 6.72, or 7297 km/h (4534 mph). The highest altitude achieved was 107 960 m (354 200 ft) attained in August 1963. There had been accidents along the way: the second X-15 had been damaged in November 1962 and was rebuilt in even better form; the third was destroyed in November 1967. In all, 199 flights had been made by the X-15s by the time the programme was terminated in November 1968.

Northrop F-5 and Tiger II *USA:* In July 1959 the first flight took place of a Mach 1.4 lightweight tactical fighter known as the Northrop N-156C. From this prototype were developed the F-5A single-seat fighter, F-5B two-seat fighter-trainer and RF-5A reconnaissance aircraft. Examples were supplied to many air forces under a US aid programme and others were purchased by countries such as the Netherlands, Canada, Norway and Spain. Many were also built under licence.

In March 1969 Northrop flew the prototype of a new version of the F-5, later to be known as the Tiger II. This prototype was basically an F-5B fitted with two General Electric YJ85-GE-21

engines instead of the J85-GE-13 engines of 1850 kg (4080 lb)st that had powered the original versions. Flight trials indicated a maximum speed of over Mach 1.6, and the new aircraft was entered for a US competition for a new International Fighter Aircraft, which it won, and initial orders were placed. A high degree of manoeuvrability was considered paramount for the International Fighter; thus the Tiger II is fitted with manoeuvring flaps, based on those fitted earlier to the Netherlands' NF-5A/Bs. Full-span leading-edge flaps are fitted, in addition to trailing-edge flaps, working together to ensure optimum manoeuvrability. Other improvements include a two-position nose-wheel, which can increase the angle of attack of the wing, thus giving improved take-off performance.

The first production F-5E Tiger II made its maiden flight on 11 August 1972, and deliveries began to the United States Air Force in early 1973. Export deliveries (including two-seat F-5Fs) began later that year, the recipients including the air forces of Jordan, South Korea, Saudi Arabia and Switzerland. The F-5E is licence-built in Taiwan.

F-5Es are also operated by the US Navy Fighter Weapons School and the USAF Aggressor squadrons. They are used to simulate enemy fighters and often engage US Air Force and Navy fighter squadrons in simulated combat.

P

Panavia Tornado *West Germany/Italy/Great Britain:* The importance of the Panavia Tornado cannot be over emphasized, for it will form the backbone of the Royal Air Force, German Luftwaffe and Naval Air Arm, and Italian Air Force when it becomes operational. Although the Phantom has been replacing British Lightning and German Starfighter aircraft for interceptor duties in the past few years, it is a 20-year-old design and most other major air forces have already begun to operate new technologically-advanced combat planes.

The Tornado, known originally as the MRCA or multi-role combat aircraft, is the result of international collaboration between the three countries that will receive the type, and certain components of the aircraft are being built in each country. It is a two-seater, fitted with swing-wings to ensure optimum flying characteristics throughout the speed range, up to about Mach 2, and has been designed to fulfil the roles of close support and battlefield interdiction, counter air strike, air superiority, interception, maritime strike and reconnaissance. The air defence variant will have a longer fuselage, increased fuel and new radar. Armament will include four Sky Flash and two Sidewinder missiles.

The RAF plans to purchase 385 Tornados, to replace a wide range of older combat aircraft such as Lightnings, Buccaneers, Canberras, Vulcans and, eventually, Phantoms. Two-thirds of all RAF front-line aircraft will be Tornados, the first due to enter service in 1979.

Nine prototype Tornados have been built, the first flying on 14 August 1974. In 1977 six pre-production Tornados were also completed, prior to production proper.

Piper Cub *USA:* The Cub is remarkable in two ways – firstly because its success in the light aircraft field has led to more than 40 000 Cubs and Super Cubs being built since 1931, and secondly because it gave the new Piper Aircraft company the basis on which to expand and so produce other familiar aircraft, like the Aztec, Comanche, Cherokee, Navajo and Cheyenne.

The Cub originated in the design office of the Taylor Aircraft Company, of which a man named William T. Piper was secretary and treasurer. When the Taylor company moved to Ohio in 1936, Piper bought the old factory at Bradford, Pennsylvania, and began to manufacture the Cub under his own name. By 1938 an improved version of the aircraft was flying as the J3 Cub, and this was soon in mass production for both civil and military use, heralding the start of the Piper company's rapid growth. Production of the basic Cub lasted until 1950, including many thousands of wartime observation and liaison models, after which refinements gave rise to new versions. Even with updated materials used in the construc-

Piper Cub which has been in production, latterly as the Super Cub 150, since 1931

tion, and new equipment added, tne original Cub and the latest models remain basically similar in appearance, but the more powerful engine fitted to the Super Cub makes the old 35 hp Continental-powered version, which achieved 129 km/h (80 mph) maximum speed, seem a little slow.

Piper Pawnee *USA:* The Pawnee is typical of the specialist aircraft that have been designed in various parts of the world for agricultural duties.

Aerial spraying of crops and hillside grasslands has always been a dangerous business. To ensure an even but adequate distribution of chemicals over the land, the pilot has to fly at very low level, often pulling up only when confronted by trees or other obstacles that mark the end of the field. However, the benefits of spraying chemicals by air are so numerous that the risks are accepted, although minimized by careful design of the aircraft.

The Pawnee exemplifies the high degree of attention that has been paid to pilot safety by manufacturers. The main items of equipment for such an aircraft are its spraying appliances, consisting of a large tank or hopper for dry or liquid chemicals, and either a spreader for dust or spraybars which extend along the wings. The pilot himself sits high in the small cockpit so that he has good all-round vision, and is protected by roll-bars which prevent the canopy from crushing him if the aircraft turns over. This type of accident is among the most common, as telephone or electrical cables and other obstacles, unseen until too late, are sometimes struck by the fixed undercarriage, causing the aircraft to end up on its back. If the pilot simply flies too low, knocks off the wheels and ends up with the aircraft on its belly, he is protected by the extra-strong safety harness, collapsing forward fuselage, rounded instrument panel, and the hollow floor, which takes the impact of a belly-landing.

Pitts Special *USA:* Internationally renowned

as an aerobatic aircraft, the Pitts Special was until recently the standard mount of the United States and British world aerobatic championship teams. It is flown also by individual world class aerobatic pilots, with great success, and remains the workhorse of the highly acclaimed Rothmans Aerobatic team. Yet, despite its current attraction and ability, its origins go back to the time of the Second World War, when the original Pitts Special was designed and built by Mr Curtis Pitts and first flown in September 1944.

Its career began in earnest a couple of years after the war when an example named *Little Stinker* was built for the then-famous woman aerobatic pilot, Betty Skelton. From that time, constant uprating of its engine has kept it in the forefront of its contemporaries. The greatest year for the Pitts was 1972, when the US aerobatic team won the World Aerobatic Championship held in France, and also carried off both the men's and women's individual

Above Panavia Tornado 'swing-wing' multi-role combat aircraft, Britain's, West Germany's and Italy's newest attack and fighter aircraft

Opposite Pitts S-2A Specials of the Rothmans Aerobatic Team

Below Piper Pawnee agricultural aircraft, photographed while crop-spraying

Panavia Tornado

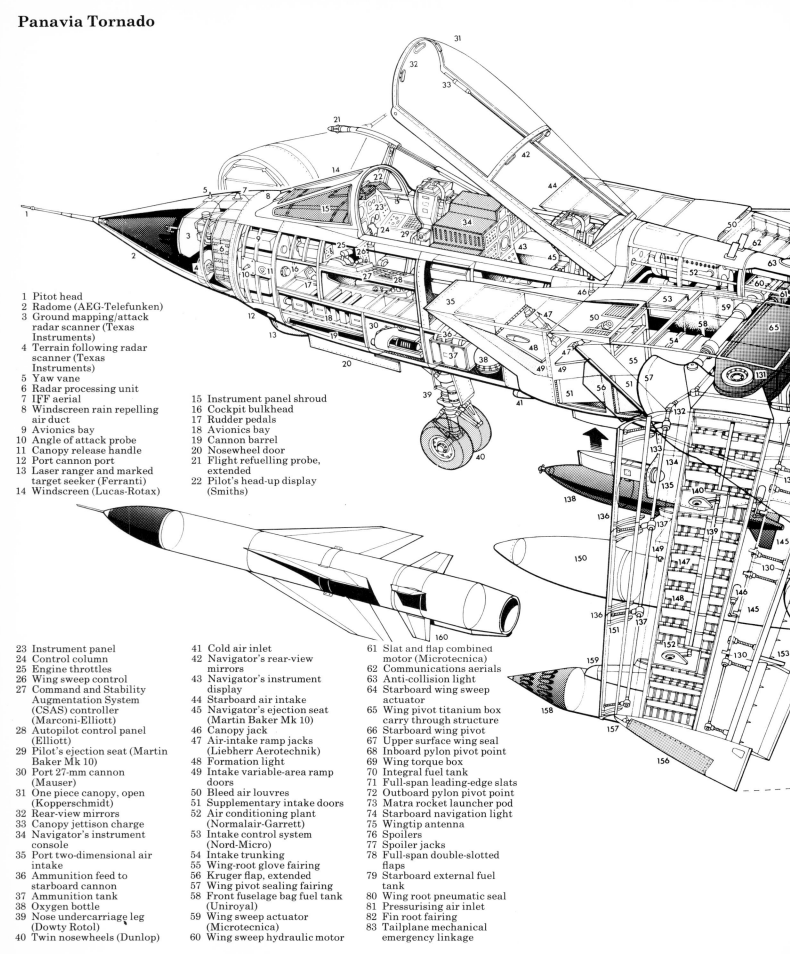

1 Pitot head
2 Radome (AEG-Telefunken)
3 Ground mapping/attack radar scanner (Texas Instruments)
4 Terrain following radar scanner (Texas Instruments)
5 Yaw vane
6 Radar processing unit
7 IFF aerial
8 Windscreen rain repelling air duct
9 Avionics bay
10 Angle of attack probe
11 Canopy release handle
12 Port cannon port
13 Laser ranger and marked target seeker (Ferranti)
14 Windscreen (Lucas-Rotax)

15 Instrument panel shroud
16 Cockpit bulkhead
17 Rudder pedals
18 Avionics bay
19 Cannon barrel
20 Nosewheel door
21 Flight refuelling probe, extended
22 Pilot's head-up display (Smiths)

23 Instrument panel
24 Control column
25 Engine throttles
26 Wing sweep control
27 Command and Stability Augmentation System (CSAS) controller (Marconi-Elliott)
28 Autopilot control panel (Elliott)
29 Pilot's ejection seat (Martin Baker Mk 10)
30 Port 27-mm cannon (Mauser)
31 One piece canopy, open (Kopperschmidt)
32 Rear-view mirrors
33 Canopy jettison charge
34 Navigator's instrument console
35 Port two-dimensional air intake
36 Ammunition feed to starboard cannon
37 Ammunition tank
38 Oxygen bottle
39 Nose undercarriage leg (Dowty Rotol)
40 Twin nosewheels (Dunlop)

41 Cold air inlet
42 Navigator's rear-view mirrors
43 Navigator's instrument display
44 Starboard air intake
45 Navigator's ejection seat (Martin Baker Mk 10)
46 Canopy jack
47 Air-intake ramp jacks (Liebherr Aerotechnik)
48 Formation light
49 Intake variable-area ramp doors
50 Bleed air louvres
51 Supplementary intake doors
52 Air conditioning plant (Normalair-Garrett)
53 Intake control system (Nord-Micro)
54 Intake trunking
55 Wing-root glove fairing
56 Kruger flap, extended
57 Wing pivot sealing fairing
58 Front fuselage bag fuel tank (Uniroyal)
59 Wing sweep actuator (Microtecnica)
60 Wing sweep hydraulic motor

61 Slat and flap combined motor (Microtecnica)
62 Communications aerials
63 Anti-collision light
64 Starboard wing sweep actuator
65 Wing pivot titanium box carry through structure
66 Starboard wing pivot
67 Upper surface wing seal
68 Inboard pylon pivot point
69 Wing torque box
70 Integral fuel tank
71 Full-span leading-edge slats
72 Outboard pylon pivot point
73 Matra rocket launcher pod
74 Starboard navigation light
75 Wingtip antenna
76 Spoilers
77 Spoiler jacks
78 Full-span double-slotted flaps
79 Starboard external fuel tank
80 Wing root pneumatic seal
81 Pressurising air inlet
82 Fin root fairing
83 Tailplane mechanical emergency linkage

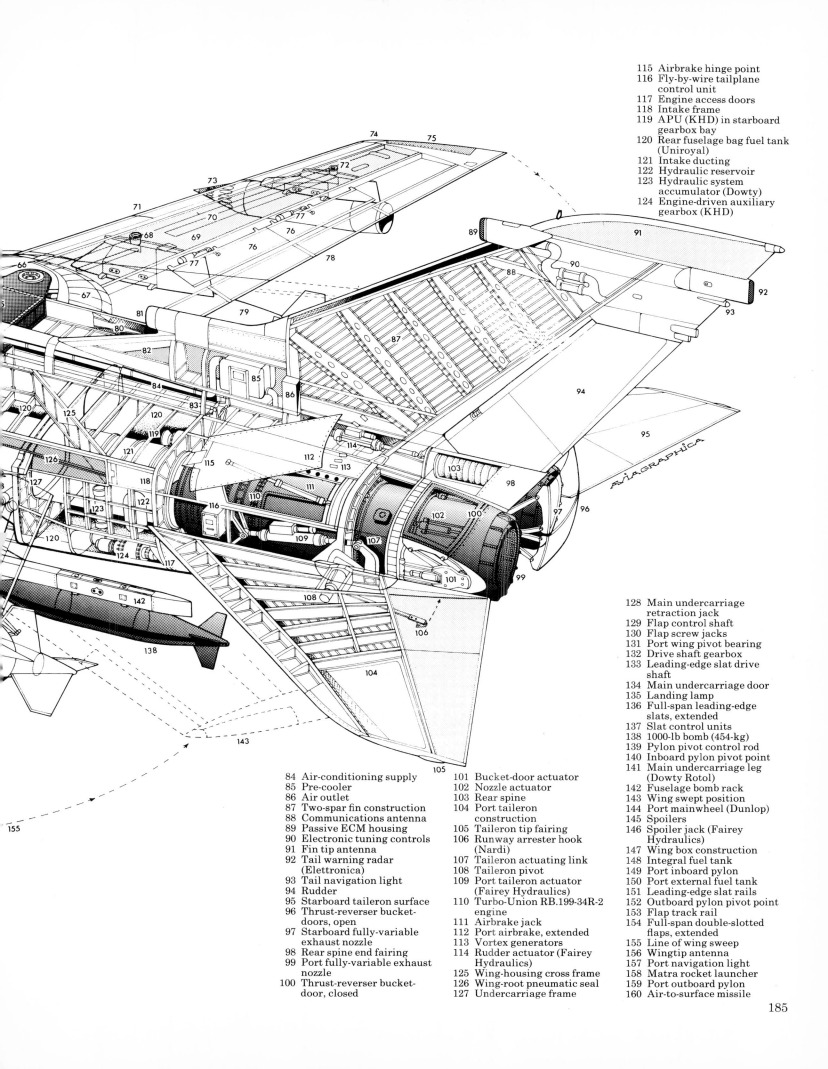

115 Airbrake hinge point
116 Fly-by-wire tailplane control unit
117 Engine access doors
118 Intake frame
119 APU (KHD) in starboard gearbox bay
120 Rear fuselage bag fuel tank (Uniroyal)
121 Intake ducting
122 Hydraulic reservoir
123 Hydraulic system accumulator (Dowty)
124 Engine-driven auxiliary gearbox (KHD)

128 Main undercarriage retraction jack
129 Flap control shaft
130 Flap screw jacks
131 Port wing pivot bearing
132 Drive shaft gearbox
133 Leading-edge slat drive shaft
134 Main undercarriage door
135 Landing lamp
136 Full-span leading-edge slats, extended
137 Slat control units
138 1000-lb bomb (454-kg)
139 Pylon pivot control rod
140 Inboard pylon pivot point
141 Main undercarriage leg (Dowty Rotol)
142 Fuselage bomb rack
143 Wing swept position
144 Port mainwheel (Dunlop)
145 Spoilers
146 Spoiler jack (Fairey Hydraulics)
147 Wing box construction
148 Integral fuel tank
149 Port inboard pylon
150 Port external fuel tank
151 Leading-edge slat rails
152 Outboard pylon pivot point
153 Flap track rail
154 Full-span double-slotted flaps, extended
155 Line of wing sweep
156 Wingtip antenna
157 Port navigation light
158 Matra rocket launcher
159 Port outboard pylon
160 Air-to-surface missile

84 Air-conditioning supply
85 Pre-cooler
86 Air outlet
87 Two-spar fin construction
88 Communications antenna
89 Passive ECM housing
90 Electronic tuning controls
91 Fin tip antenna
92 Tail warning radar (Elettronica)
93 Tail navigation light
94 Rudder
95 Starboard taileron surface
96 Thrust-reverser bucket-doors, open
97 Starboard fully-variable exhaust nozzle
98 Rear spine end fairing
99 Port fully-variable exhaust nozzle
100 Thrust-reverser bucket-door, closed

101 Bucket-door actuator
102 Nozzle actuator
103 Rear spine
104 Port taileron construction
105 Taileron tip fairing
106 Runway arrester hook (Nardi)
107 Taileron actuating link
108 Taileron pivot
109 Port taileron actuator (Fairey Hydraulics)
110 Turbo-Union RB.199-34R-2 engine
111 Airbrake jack
112 Port airbrake, extended
113 Vortex generators
114 Rudder actuator (Fairey Hydraulics)
125 Wing-housing cross frame
126 Wing-root pneumatic seal
127 Undercarriage frame

185

championships.

Three main versions are currently available – the standard Pitts S-1S Special, which is a single-seater that can be purchased ready-built or in kit form; the S-1D Special which is solely for home construction; and the two-seat factory-built S-2A Special. It is the S-2A which is used by the Rothmans Team, the idea being to fly the version most easily viewed by spectators on the ground. This also enables the team to take up with them passengers, who can take air-to-air photographs during manoeuvres in close formation.

Polikarpov I-15 *USSR:* Whether Soviet Air Force officials still·believed there was a place for the biplane fighter, or whether it was meant as insurance against failure of the revolutionary I-16 monoplane, the I-15 first flew in 1933 and was produced alongside the I-16. It could never match the overall speed of the monoplane, but was highly manoeuvrable, with a devastating four-gun fire power. Mass production began in 1934 and, with the outbreak of the civil war in Spain, many were shipped to aid the Republican forces. In all, about 550 I-15 and I-15*bis* fighters were supplied to Spain and, although the first ones arrived after the initial batch of I-16s, they beat the latter into combat by one day, flying a mission over Madrid on 4 November 1936.

At first the I-15s were opposed by German Heinkel He 51 fighters of the Nationalist forces and soon proved themselves superior in every respect. This, more than anything else, caused the He 51s to be relegated to ground attack duties, leaving subsequent fighting to Fiat C.R.32s and Messerschmitt Bf 109s. These soon took control, and it is thought likely that over 400 of the I-15s were eventually destroyed.

Other I-15s were used during the war between China and Japan, and in 1939 against the Japanese in Mongolia. Although development led to moderate improvements in overall performance, the I-15 was well outdated by the beginning of the Second World War and gradually faded out of front-line service from 1941. However, it is believed that some I-15s were still flying in 1944.

Polikarpov I-16 *USSR:* The Polikarpov I-16 was a Soviet fighter which first flew in prototype form in 1933. Although not among the best remembered aircraft of the thirties, it was nevertheless a very able and rugged machine and featured prominently in the events of the time.

When it first appeared, it was powered by a radial engine which developed a modest 450 hp. Even with this it achieved a creditable 376 km/h (234 mph) and, as the world's first single-seat fighter to have low monoplane wings, an enclosed cockpit (on some versions) and a retractable undercarriage, it was immediately put into mass production alongside the Polikarpov I-15 biplane fighter. Development led eventually to one version of the I-16

reaching over 520km/h (325 mph), with an engine of about two-and-a-half times the original power.

At this point the I-16 might well have faded into obscurity but for the outbreak of the Spanish Civil War in July 1936. This war drew support from all over the world. The Nationalists, supported mainly by German and Italian forces, were the better equipped. Britain, France, the United States, the Netherlands, Czechoslovakia and Turkey all sent an assortment of aircraft to the Republican forces, directly or indirectly. But by far the major supporter of the Republicans was the Soviet Union, which supplied 1409 of the 1947 aircraft contributed by other countries. Of these 475 were Polikarpov I-16s.

They first entered combat in Spain in November 1936. Flown in many cases by Soviet pilots, they proved more than a match for German He 51 fighters, but met their equals in the Italian C.R.32 biplanes and were overpowered by Messerschmitt Bf 109s. From March 1937, all remaining I-16s were concentrated into Fighter Group 31, and this was by far the most successful of all Soviet-equipped units.

Meanwhile, I-16s were fighting also in China, and in 1939 were operated against the Japanese in Mongolia. Their final fling came during the

Polikarpov I-15 biplane fighter in Spanish markings

Polikarpov I-16 monoplane fighter

PZL P-11C of the Polish Air Force

PZL P-11 interceptors of the Polish Air Force, which faced the might of the German Luftwaffe in September 1939

early part of the Second World War, but by then they were overshadowed by more advanced foreign types. Suffering the brunt of the German invasion, those remaining were replaced by more modern fighters in 1942–3.

PZL P-7 and P-11 *Poland:* In 1929, the Polish PZL company flew a small monoplane fighter which was to influence subsequent Polish fighter design until the war. This aircraft, the P-1, was unusual for a monoplane in that it had 'gull' wings, which meant basically that the straight high-mounted wings suddenly dropped to meet the fuselage top-decking at the centre, to give the pilot a clear upward view. This configuration became famous as the 'Pulawski

wing', named after its designer.

With a maximum speed of 305 km/h (190 mph), the P-1 was fast – so it was decided to clean up the design still further to put into production a new fighter for the Polish Air Force. The new aircraft was designated the P-7. It retained the same wings, but had a neat oval-section fuselage and a large radial engine. Maximum speed was marginally increased by the modifications, and it went into Polish service from 1932. With its P-7s, the Polish Air Force could claim to be the first with all-metal monoplane fighters equipping all its front-line squadrons.

Even before the P-7s began to be delivered to the air force, a further development of the concept had brought the P-11. Although designed on the same basic lines, it gave the pilot an improved forward view and greater fire power, with four machine-guns, and maximum speed was increased to over 385 km/h (240 mph).

Unfortunately, although all production P-7s and P-11s had been delivered by 1936, when Germany invaded Poland in 1939 about 30 P-7s were still operated as first-line fighters, together with 128 P-11s. They constituted the bulk of the Polish fighter force and had to fight against modern low-wing fighters, including 200 Messerschmitt Bf 109s. The courage of the pilots was not enough, and by the end of the German campaign few PZL fighters remained intact, most having been destroyed in just two weeks from 1 September.

When Russia invaded Poland from the east the hopeless battle was clearly over, and the pilots of the few remaining airworthy PZL fighters escaped to Hungary and Romania, after which some of them flew with other Allied air forces.

Republic P-47 Thunderbolt *USA:* The big and powerful Thunderbolt was one of the best fighters built in the United States during the Second World War. It shared with the Mustang the unenviable task of escorting large bomber formations during their assault on German targets from 1943, meeting well organized German fighter and later jet-fighter opposition.

The prototype Thunderbolt first took to the air on 6 May 1941. It was by far the largest and heaviest single-engined fighter that had been built, and was powered by a massive 2000 hp Pratt and Whitney Double Wasp piston-engine. Production began with the P-47B, which entered United States Army Air Force service in November 1942, first becoming operational with the Eighth Air Force stationed in the UK on 8 April 1943. The P-47B's range was not really good enough for escort duties, and its manoeuvrability was poor, but at least it offered a measure of real protection to the Allied bombers which had previously suffered very heavy losses.

By mid-1943 improved P-47Cs were becoming available, with external fuel tanks to increase range and a longer fuselage to improve manoeuvrability. Next came the major production version, the P-47D, and then P-47Gs, and P-47Ms with more powerful engines, giving a maximum speed of 756 km/h (470 mph). They were used for anti-V1 flying bomb duties; while the final version, the P-47N, was built primarily for use against the Japanese.

In service also with the Royal Air Force, and with the Soviet Union on the Eastern Front (plus a few with France after liberation), the Thunderbolt was able to outfly most German fighter opposition until the advent of the Messerschmitt Me 262 jet. Thunderbolts served also in the Mediterranean and in the epic Burma offensive, often carrying a heavy load of bombs or rockets for ground attack missions. The aircraft's exceptionally strong construction resulted in a very low attrition rate. More than 15 600 were built.

Rockwell International B-1 *USA:* Designed as a successor to the long-serving Boeing B-52 Stratofortress strategic bomber, the B-1 was originally scheduled to become operational with the United States Air Force in 1978. It was not the first aircraft built as a B-52 replacement – there was the North American XB-70 Valkyrie Mach 3 delta-wing bomber, cancelled in 1963. History repeated itself in June 1977 when, in turn, the B-1 production programme was cancelled, although the four aircraft that had been ordered by then will continue to be used for research and development.

The B-1 features huge variable-geometry wings, to give it the best possible flight characteristics. Again it is not first, as swing wings have already been fitted to a large strategic bomber, the operational Soviet Tupolev 'Backfire'. However, the B-1 was designed to carry a heavier weapon load, of up to 52160 kg (115000 lb) of nuclear or conventional bombs and missiles.

Despite continual cut-backs in defence spending, the first B-1 flew on 23 December 1974. By the middle of July 1976, three B-1s had logged a total of more than 200 flight hours, during which a maximum speed of Mach 2.1 had been attained. Production of the B-1 was then planned to total 244 aircraft.

Carrying equipment to allow it to attack its designated targets at very low altitude at near-sonic speed, or in a high-altitude supersonic dash, the B-1 would have raised the offensive potential of the USAF to an unprecedented level, thought by many essential to match and elude the modern high-technology aircraft now flying in the East.

Royal Aircraft Factory B.E.2 *Great Britain:* The B.E.2 reconnaissance aircraft had a very mixed career with the Royal Flying Corps and Royal Air Force, but served from before the First World War until the Armistice in 1918. Why it was allowed to be flown and to remain in production for such a long time is a mystery. For although aircraft lost on the Western Front and elsewhere had to be replaced, several better aircraft were available in the later war years.

The B.E.2 was the brainchild of Geoffrey de Havilland and first appeared in 1912. For that time it was an extremely neat aircraft with a good turn of speed, stable in flight, and accommodating a crew of two in tandem. The first production version was the B.E.2a, an unarmed machine with which two squadrons were sent to France on 13 August 1914 as part of the British Expeditionary Force. Only six days later, a B.E.2, in company with a Blériot monoplane, made the first reconnaissance flight over the German lines. B.E.2s were also used very early in the war as light bombers.

By April 1915 the first armed version was in service in France, as the B.E.2c. This replaced both the B.E.2a and 2b and featured a larger engine, staggered wings with dihedral, and a machine-gun. Unfortunately, the B.E.2c had two major faults. The machine-gun had been placed in the front cockpit, so limiting the field of fire, and the aircraft had been made even more stable in flight. This caused high losses in combat as B.E.2c pilots could not manoeuvre out of the way of an attacking German aircraft. The newly introduced Fokker Eindecker fighter of 1915 tore the B.E.2cs to shreds and caused very high British losses. The lesson was clear yet not heeded, as B.E.2cs were again among the worst hit British aircraft in 'Bloody April' 1917, when German Albatros fighters rampaged over the Western Front.

Opposite
Above Royal Aircraft Factory B.E.2a of No 2 Squadron, RFC. This was the first British aircraft to land in France at the beginning of the First World War.

Centre Royal Aircraft Factory F.E.2b two-seat fighter of the RFC

Below Royal Aircraft Factory S.E.5a with Albert Ball in the cockpit

Overleaf
Above left Republic P-47 Thunderbolt long-range fighter, preserved today in the United States

Below left One of the prototype Rockwell International B-1 'swing-wing' strategic bombers·

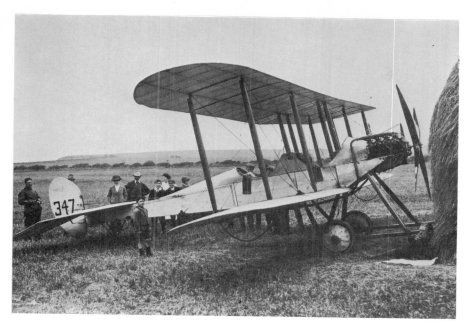

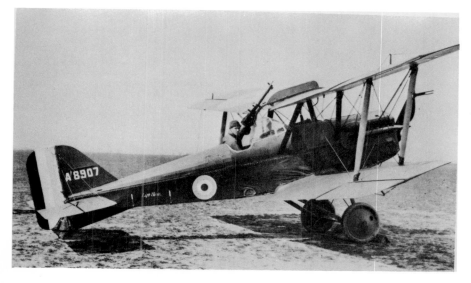

At home in Britain, early B.E.2s were operating as trainers, while some B.E.2cs found success as night fighters against Zeppelin airships. Next in production came the B.E.2d, in which the pilot occupied the front seat and a forward-firing machine-gun was added. Amazingly, in the last version, the B.E.2e, the crew seats were again reversed to the old layout and this version was produced in the greatest numbers, at a time when the design was thoroughly obsolete.

Although it did some very useful work over the Western Front, in North Africa, and elsewhere, especially in the early war years, the B.E.2 series should have been withdrawn from front-line service in 1916 at the latest.

Royal Aircraft Factory F.E.2b and d *Great Britain:* Like the de Havilland D.H.2, the F.E.2a was also a pusher fighter. Unlike the former, however, it carried a crew of two, pilot at the rear and observer/gunner in front, and was armed with a movable forward gun which the observer fired. Only a very small number of F.E.2as were built.

The following and major production version of the aircraft type was the F.E.2b, of which 1939 were delivered. These were powered by either the 120 hp or 160 hp Beardmore engines and in most cases added a rearward firing machine-gun to the armament, which the observer again fired – standing up!

The F.E.2b was seen in France from the winter of 1915 and, among its later duties, took on reconnaissance, ground attack and night bombing. Thus, F.E.2bs were the mounts of No 100 Squadron, Royal Flying Corps, which was the first British squadron formed for night bombing, making its first raid on the night of 5/6 April 1917 against Douai Airfield, the base of Richthofen's own squadron. There was perhaps a measure of justice in this, as Richthofen's personal first official victory was gained over an F.E.2b of No 11 Squadron in September 1916. An F.E.2b of No 25 Squadron had earlier been responsible for shooting down Germany's first great 'ace', Lt. Max Immelmann, in June 1916.

After just two F.E.2cs had been built, the F.E.2d appeared, in July 1916, powered by a much more powerful 250 hp Rolls-Royce Eagle I engine. Armament was also revised, with the additional installation of a gun or guns fired by the pilot. Despite these improvements, the latest Albatros and other tractor German fighters outclassed the F.E.2s, although they remained operational in one role or another until the end of the war. One of the type's last major tasks was that of home defence fighter, to counter the Zeppelins and Gotha bombers that by mid-1917 were raiding England in numbers. For this task an 0.45 in Maxim gun was fitted, although some aircraft, flown as single-seaters, had two fixed Vickers guns.

Royal Aircraft Factory S.E.5 and S.E.5a *Great Britain:* These were the last Royal

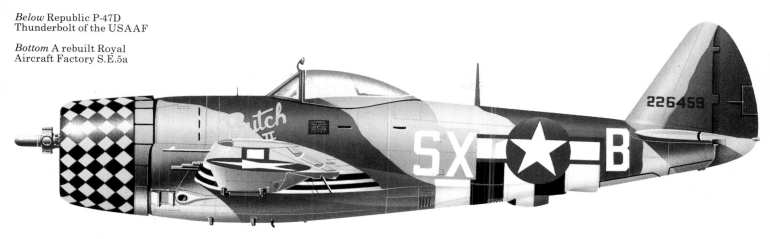

Below Republic P-47D Thunderbolt of the USAAF

Bottom A rebuilt Royal Aircraft Factory S.E.5a

Aircraft Factory designs to go into large-scale production during the First World War and were by far its most successful. At the beginning of the war the Factory had been producing very stable aircraft like the B.E.2 for reconnaissance and light bombing duties. When fighter aircraft were needed, the Factory produced the pusher F.E.2 series, and in 1916 the B.E.12, the latter being basically a fighter adaption of the B.E.2.

By 1916 real fighters were urgently required on the Western Front – fast, manoeuvrable, tractor-engined and with deadly fire power. Sopwith was first to really take up the gauntlet, but soon afterwards the Factory produced its S.E.5 single-seat fighter. Special attention had been given to making the S.E.5 easy to fly, as the 1916 pilot attrition rate was so high that near-novice pilots were becoming operational. In particular, the use of a 150 hp Hispano-Suiza in-line engine avoided the high torque of the Sopwith fighters.

S.E.5s were first delivered to No 56 Squadron, Royal Flying Corps, in April 1917 and quickly stamped their presence on opposing German aircraft. Leading No 56 Squadron at that time was a young man named Albert Ball, a brilliant pilot who was Britain's first great air 'ace'. Unfortunately, he was killed in May. In July another pilot, named James T.B. McCudden, flew an S.E.5 with No 56 Squadron for the first time. As the unit's commander, he became subsequently the fourth-ranking British and Empire 'ace' with 57 victories. Yet another pilot, Edward 'Mick' Mannock, Britain's top 'ace' of the war, gained most of his 73 victories while flying S.E.5/5as.

In June 1917 the first of the improved S.E.5as became available and, as production continued throughout the rest of the war, various engines

were fitted, including 200–240 hp Hispano-Suizas and Wolseley Vipers. The S.E.5a was one of the fastest First World War fighters and was second only to the Camel as the most successful British fighter of the war. Production of the S.E.5/5a series eventually totalled more than 5200 aircraft, some of which were flown by pilots of the American Expeditionary Force.

Ryan NYP monoplane *Spirit of St Louis*

USA: In 1925 Ryan Airlines began the pre-liminary design of a twin-open-cockpit aircraft with a high-mounted monoplane wing. Known as the M-1 parasol monoplane, it first flew on 14 February 1926, at the hands of T. Claude Ryan himself, and was the first monoplane to enter production in the USA. A year later Charles Lindbergh visited the Ryan works, test flew an M-1, and asked if a modified version could be built for him.

Through the efforts of 20 Ryan workers, the NYP monoplane was produced in two months, and was first flown on 28 April 1927. The pilot sat to the rear of the cabin, allowing a huge auxiliary fuel tank to be carried in the forward fuselage, filling the cabin completely from floor to roof. The only way in which the pilot could see forward was through a per-iscope.

The scene was set for the first non-stop crossing of the Atlantic by a solo pilot, between New York and Paris. Lindberg achieved this in the NYP, named *Spirit of St Louis*, on 20/21 May 1927, in a flying time of 33 hours 39 minutes. The distance covered was 5810 km (3610 miles). This epic flight won for Lindbergh a $25 000 prize, offered by a US hotelier, Raymond Orteig, and instant fame as one of the great navigators of history.

S

Saab 37 Viggen *Sweden:* The Saab company of Sweden has been supplying the Swedish Air Force (and others) with major combat aircraft since the early 1950s – including the Lansen attack-fighter, Draken fighter and reconnaissance aircraft, and Saab 105 light attack and training aircraft. Its latest product is the Viggen, which began replacing A32A Lansens from mid-1971.

The Viggen is a single-seat aircraft with excellent manoeuvrability, acceleration and the ability to take off and land on runways only 500 m (1640 ft) in length (or from major public roads in a dispersal or emergency situation). A multi-mission type, the basic airframe is used for all-weather attack (AJ37), interceptor (JA37), all-weather armed photographic-reconnaissance (SF37) or all-weather maritime-reconnaissance (SH37) roles, while a two-seat training version with attack capabilities is also produced as the SK37.

Powered by a Swedish version of a US Pratt and Whitney JT8D turbofan engine, fitted with a Swedish afterburner, the Viggen features rear-mounted main delta wings and canard delta foreplanes, with trailing-edge flaps.

Armament is carried externally. For attack duties this comprises Saab-Scania RB04E missiles for use against naval targets, RB05A missiles for use against ground, sea or some airborne targets, rockets, bombs, mines or 30 mm Aden gun pods. A 30 mm Oerlikon KCA long-range cannon and air-to-air missiles, including Sidewinders or Falcons are carried for interceptor missions; two air-to-air missiles are standard on reconnaissance versions of the Viggen.

Santos-Dumont 14-*bis* *France/Brazil:* Alberto Santos-Dumont was the son of a wealthy Brazilian plantation owner, and from his earliest years was keenly interested in mechanical vehicles. At the age of 24 he made his first balloon ascent and this started him on his aviation career, as a dirigible (airship) designer and pilot. On 19 October 1901 he won a 100 000 franc prize for making the first airship flight around the Eiffel Tower in Paris, and became famous for the nonchalant way in which he sometimes tethered his little airship to nearby railings while lunching in a Parisian restaurant.

By the early nineteen-hundreds, heavier-than-air flight was in vogue – so Santos-Dumont set about the design of an airplane. The Wright brothers had proved the possibility of powered and controlled flight in the United States, while in Europe Germany's Carl Jatho had also made a 'hop' flight in 1903. The way was still open for the first officially-accredited, sustained, powered flight in Europe.

By way of a starter, Santos-Dumont flew his strange-looking 14-*bis* biplane 7 m (23 ft) on 13 September 1906, the hop ending in an accident. After rebuilding the 14-*bis*, with an engine of nearly double the power of the original, Santos-Dumont made a flight of nearly 65 m (200 ft) on 23 October, so winning the 3000 franc Archdeacon prize for the first observed and sustained flight of more than 25 m. The big moment came on 12 November, when he flew the same aircraft for 21 seconds, covering 220 m

Below Santos-Dumont's 14-*bis*, photographed while making the first officially recognized powered flight in Europe on 12 November 1906

Bottom The ultra-light Santos-Dumont Demoiselle No 19

(722 ft), to gain the distinction of making the first officially recognized sustained and powered flight in Europe.

The 14-*bis* was a large tail-first aircraft with a covered fuselage and wheeled undercarriage. Power was provided by a 50hp Antoinette engine, driving a two-blade pusher propeller mounted at the extreme rear of the airplane, just behind the box-kite type biplane wings. The whole aircraft appeared to be flying backwards, with the box-like 'tail' control surfaces fitted in the foremost position. The smartly-hatted Santos-Dumont wore a body harness attached to primitive ailerons, and leaned from side to side to pull on this and so achieve lateral control.

Santos-Dumont Demoiselle *France/Brazil.* Alberto Santos-Dumont was designer, builder and pilot of the first low-cost, 'do-it-yourself' aircraft for the would-be pilot. Known later as the Demoiselle, the aircraft first appeared as the Santos-Dumont No 19 in 1907.

With a wing span of only 5m (16ft 5in), it was made of bamboo and was powered by a 20 hp Dutheil-Chalmers engine. The pilot sat on a small seat below the monoplane wing and engine, controlling via steel wires the all-moving cruciform tail unit which was attached to the forward section of the aircraft by a single bamboo pole. Lateral control was achieved by

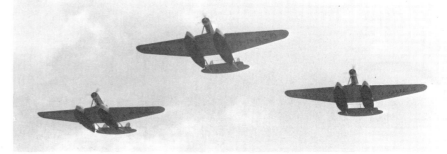

the pilot rocking his body either left or right.

No 19 achieved a few modest hops in 1907. Subsequent development brought about several changes to the design, culminating in a 1909-model Demoiselle (No 20) with a 30 hp engine, a three-bamboo-pole fuselage, twin-wheel undercarriage and tail skid. Several aircraft of this configuration were flown successfully by other early pilots. However, the Demoiselle had been designed with small overall dimensions because of the diminutive size and weight of Santos-Dumont himself. As a result only the smallest of men were normally able to get airborne. The high landing speed of the Demoiselle also put off a number of would-be owners.

Savoia-Marchetti S-55 *Italy:* The inter-war years were marked by a thrilling succession of

Top Saab AJ37 Viggen of the Swedish Air Force

Above Three Savoia-Marchetti S-55 flying-boats photographed during the 1933 transatlantic flight

194

Savoia-Marchetti SM.79-II Sparviero, rated one of the best torpedo-bombers of the Second World War

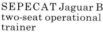

SEPECAT Jaguar B two-seat operational trainer

hulls; each hull seated from four to six passengers. The crew sat in a usually open cockpit above the wing. Civil S-55s of Societa Aerea Mediterranea were flown on a passenger service between Brindisi and Constantinople in 1925, and one was operated in the United States of America. The military version was intended for use as a torpedo-bomber, the torpedo or bombs being carried between the hulls. The aircraft used for the formation flight to Chicago were S-55Xs, the ultimate development of the type.

historic long-distance flights, by both civilian and military pilots. The civilian flights (such as that made by Amy Johnson from Britain to Australia) were performed by single aircraft; long-distance flights by the military were often accomplished by several aircraft flying in formation to 'show the flag' overseas.

The most spectacular formation flight of this period was that achieved by 24 Italian Savoia-Marchetti S-55 flying-boats which, between 1 July and 15 July 1933, flew from Orbetello in Italy to the 'Century of Progress Exposition' being held in Chicago, USA, via Iceland, Greenland and Labrador. The flight was led by General Italo Balbo, who had also led an earlier formation flight across the South Atlantic.

The S-55 flying-boat had first appeared in 1924 and was subsequently produced in both military and civil forms. The latter was basically similar to the military version, except for deletion of the gun emplacements in the noses of the twin

Savoia-Marchetti SM.79 Sparviero *Italy:* In the summer of 1942, Allied efforts to relieve beleaguered Malta culminated in 'Operation Pedestal', when 14 merchantmen with heavy Royal Navy escort left Gibraltar on 10 August. Among the enemy aircraft sent against them were 74 Sparvieri (Sparrow Hawks), a number of which had already scored hits on the battleship HMS *Malaya* and the carrier HMS *Argus*. 'Pedestal' eventually got through to Malta, but at the cost of one carrier, two cruisers, a destroyer and nine merchant ships, many of them having been hit by torpedoes from the S.M.79s.

The prototype SM.79 had flown on 2 September 1935, powered by three 750 hp Alfa-Romeo 125 RC.34 engines, and so following the Regia Aeronautica's preferred tri-motor formula. About 1300 production models were built over a nine year period. They had internal provision for 1250 kg (2750 lb) of bombs, supplemented by underfuselage racks for a pair

Short Skyvan of Olympic
Airways, Greece

of heavy bombs, or two torpedoes in the case of the SM.79-II and SM.79-III.

The SM.79-I served with the Italian Aviazione Legionaria in support of Franco in the Spanish Civil War. The more powerful SM.79-II served in North Africa, the Balkans, and Mediterranean during the Second World War. When the Italians surrendered on 8 September 1943, it did not end the combat record of the SM.79, and a new version, the SM.79-III torpedo-bomber, was placed in production by the RSI, the fascist government in northern Italy.

The SM.79 had a distinctive 'hump' on the upper forward fuselage, which housed both the fixed forward-firing heavy machine-gun and the dorsal gunner's position. Its appearance earned the aircraft the nickname 'Gobbo Maleditto' ('Damned Hunchback').

SM.79s served widely in the normal bombing role; but it is as a land-based torpedo-bomber that the type deserves its place in military aviation history, being regarded by many as one of the finest torpedo-bombers of the war. Surviving SM.79s were converted into transports during the last phases of the war, serving in that role until the early 1950s.

SEPECAT Jaguar *Great Britain/France:* The Jaguar is a lightweight single-seat tactical support aircraft or two-seat operational and advanced trainer, developed by the British Aircraft Corporation and Dassault/Breguet of France, and produced by a joint company known as SEPECAT. The first prototype, a two-seater for French service, made its maiden flight on 8 September 1968 – the first British service prototype flew initially on 12 October 1969 as a single-seat support aircraft.

Five versions of the Jaguar have so far been produced. The Jaguar A is the French Air Force single-seat tactical support model, with which the first operational unit equipped in mid-1973. A total of 160 As were ordered, to equip eight squadrons. Armament includes two 30 mm DEFA cannon mounted in the fuselage and up to 4535 kg (10 000 lb) of external weapons carried on five attachment points. Loads can include the AN 52 tactical nuclear weapon, Martel AS. 37 all-weather anti-radar missile, R.550 Magic air-to-air missiles, etc. The Jaguar B and E are the Royal Air Force and French Air Force two-seat models respectively. The Jaguar S is the British tactical support single-seater. Basically similar to the French Jaguar A, the S has an advanced inertial navigation and weapon aiming system. The first RAF unit to form with Jaguar Ss did so in March 1974, with some of the first of 165 production aircraft ordered as Jaguar GR Mk 1s. In all, the RAF planned to equip eight squadrons, four of which were operational in Germany as early as the spring of 1976, one as a reconnaissance unit. Armament is similar to that of the French aircraft, except that Aden cannon are fitted and British aircraft do not carry the AN 52. Air-to-air missiles can be carried at the wingtips.

The fifth version is the Jaguar International, an export model with more powerful Adour engines, which has proved to have better all-round performance and acceleration in the lower speed range. First orders for the International came from Oman and Ecuador.

Shin Meiwa PS-1 *Japan:* In 1966 the Shin Meiwa company of Japan was given a contract to develop a new anti-submarine flying-boat for use by the Japanese Maritime Self-Defence Force. In view of the advanced technology involved in building a flying-boat of the required size, Shin Meiwa undertook first the rebuilding of a Grumman Albatross amphibian.

Shin Meiwa then built the large SS-2, known as the PS-1 by the military. The initial prototype flew on 5 October 1967 and was delivered to the JMSDF in July 1968 for testing. It was soon joined by a second aircraft. Key factors in the design of the PS-1 are its use of a boundary layer control system, and large flaps to deflect the slipstream of the propellers, to allow a landing speed of only 76 km/h (47 mph) and similarly low take-off speed. This means that the PS-1 needs a run of only 250 m (820 ft) to take off from water.

Two basic production versions have so far been delivered to the JMSDF. The PS-1 flying-boat, for anti-submarine duties, carries sophisticated electronic equipment and is armed with four 330 lb bombs internally, four homing torpedoes carried in two underwing pods, and six 5-inch air-to-surface rockets on wingtip launchers. The US-1 (originally known as the PS-1 Mod) search and rescue amphibian has an added retractable undercarriage, and accommodation for 69 passengers, 36 stretchers or mixed loads. In co-operation with the National Fire Agency, Shin Meiwa is also testing a water-bomber version.

Short C Class flying-boat *Great Britain:* By 1935 Imperial Airways of Britain had set up many routes to countries then in the British Empire using, among other types of aircraft, Short biplane flying-boats. At this time, Shorts produced drawings of a completely new four-engined monoplane flying-boat which was larger than its predecessors and offered a new standard of passenger comfort that was virtually unrivalled among its landplane contemporaries. In what represented a huge vote of confidence in the Short design team, Imperial Airways ordered 28 of these aircraft (which became known as C Class Empire flying-boats) before even a prototype had been built.

At a cost of nearly two million pounds, this really was a gamble – but it paid off. The first C Class flying-boat to fly was named *Canopus*. It took to the air in July 1936, and three months later, on 30 October, scheduled services with the C Class aircraft began between Alexandria and Brindisi.

Below Short C Class flying-boat *Clare*

Bottom Short Stirling III four-engined heavy bomber of the RAF

Shin Meiwa PS-1 maritime patrol amphibian of the Japan Maritime Self-Defence Force

Despite the fact that eight C Class flying-boats were lost within the first two years of operation, the type was an outstanding success and regular services were rapidly built up to India, Australia, Egypt, East Africa, South Africa and Malaya. Following experimental route-proving flights across the Atlantic between Southampton and New York by two specially modified flying-boats, and a series of trials with in-flight refuelled aircraft, trans-atlantic mail services were introduced, although not on a scheduled basis until 5 August 1939. To make this possible, four Handley Page Harrow bombers were modified into tankers. The outbreak of war quickly halted the service.

Short Skyvan *Great Britain:* One of the most remarkable small transport aircraft flying today, the Skyvan combines simplicity and versatility with STOL (short take-off and landing). It is the Skyvan's unique cargo cabin that makes it such a useful aircraft. It is not only of large, uncluttered, completely square cross-section, but is long enough to accommodate vehicles of various civil and military types, 19 passengers, 22 troops, 16 paratroopers and a despatcher, 12 stretcher cases and attendants, or about 2 tons of freight. The rear loading door enables the aircraft to be used for supply dropping – essential for some military roles and for relief work where natural disasters have occurred far from a suitable landing strip.

The prototype Skyvan first flew in January 1963, the design originating as a private venture. Today, Skyvans are flying in both civil and military roles all over the world. Several versions have appeared, the current main variants being the Series 3, 3A and Skyliner (all passenger) civil transports, and the Series 3M military aircraft.

Short Stirling *Great Britain:* The Stirling was the first four-engined bomber to become operational with the Royal Air Force during the Second World War. It was one of the mainstays of Bomber Command when it began its massive night offensive against German targets in Europe, after the Battle of Britain had been won.

Despite its extensive use, the Stirling had a number of shortcomings, some resulting from the Air Ministry specification to which it was developed. Two major design faults were that the bomb-bay was divided into quite small sections, so preventing the carriage of bombs of more than 4000 lb in weight, and that the high wing position made necessary long and complicated, retractable main undercarriage legs. At the Air Ministry's door must be laid blame for demanding that the aircraft should fit into existing RAF hangers, resulting in shorter-span wings of greater chord than would otherwise have been fitted. This restricted the height at which the aircraft could fly through hostile skies, leading to unnecessary losses.

After flight trials had been made with a half-scale replica, the first Stirling prototype made its maiden flight in May 1939. Production Stirling Mk Is were given more powerful engines and entered RAF service in August 1940. On 10 February 1941 three Stirlings opened the aircraft's operational career with a raid on oil storage tanks in Rotterdam. A few spectacular daylight missions were made, but before long Stirlings operated mainly at night.

After a few Mk IIs had been built with Wright Cyclone engines, the Mk III entered production.

Short Stirling Mk I of the RAF

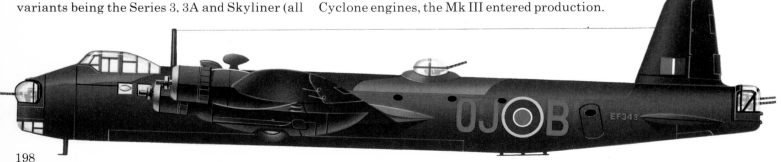

Short Sunderland GR Mk V flying over destroyers during an exercise in the Mediterranean

This was the major version in terms of numbers built, and was powered by 1650 hp Bristol Hercules XVI engines. Another improvement was the installation of a new dorsal gun turret. However, by the time operations with Mk IIIs really got underway, in 1943, the Stirling was becoming outdated. It was used less and less for bombing from 1944, but was produced in two more forms, the Mk IV transport and Horsa glider tug, and Mk V unarmed transport. In all, Stirling production totalled 2375 aircraft, of which 1630 were bombers.

Short Sunderland *Great Britain:* Side by side with the Consolidated Catalina, purchased from the United States, the Short Sunderland was the Royal Air Force's main patrol and reconnaissance flying-boat during the Second World War, performing equally well as a rescue

or transport aircraft when the situation demanded this. It was, generally speaking, a military adaptation of the Empire or C Class flying-boat, differing mainly in the type of engines fitted, cockpit and forward hull redesign, and the installation of gun positions. As production continued through versions from the Mk I to Mk V, armament increased to a point where the Sunderland became known to the Germans as the 'Flying Porcupine'.

The prototype Sunderland first flew in October 1937 and production aircraft became operational in mid-1938, replacing Singapore III biplanes. Three squadrons were equipped with Sunderlands by September 1939 and went into action immediately. The type claimed its first U-boat (German submarine) destroyed in January 1940 and performed excellent work throughout the war. This made it a prime target for German

Above Focke-Wulf Fw 61, the first completely successful helicopter in the world.

Opposite Sikorsky VS-300 helicopter with twin tail rotors

Opposite A model of Igor Sikorsky's huge four-engined aircraft *Le Grand*

long-range fighters, but even when individual Sunderlands were attacked by formations of German Ju 88s they managed to give a good account of themselves.

After the war, Sunderlands remained operational with the RAF until 1959, having served in Korea and Malaysia. The French Navy also flew a small number after the war, as did the Royal New Zealand Air Force until 1966.

Sikorsky R-4 *USA:* The R-4 has a place in history mainly by virtue of being the first US helicopter put into series production. It was basically a two-seat development of the earlier, experimental Sikorsky VS-300, and the prototype, designated XR-4, first flew on 13 January 1942.

Following the prototype, three development aircraft were ordered as YR-4As, and these were used extensively in trials which took place during 1943. Satisfied that the helicopter was suitable for military service, the United States Army Air Force ordered an initial batch of 27 YR-4Bs, followed by 100 R-4Bs. These entered Air Force and Navy service for experimental observation and air rescue duties, and gave them their first real taste of helicopter operations.

Britain received a few R-4s in early 1945. They were known to the Royal Air Force as Hoverfly Is and served at the Helicopter Training School at Andover.

Sikorsky S-55 and S-58 *USA: see* Westland Wessex.

Sikorsky S-61 series *USA:* The S-61 is a twin-engined, multi-purpose helicopter that has been produced in many military and civil versions. The operator with the largest number of S-61s is the United States Navy. The prototype, built to US Navy contract, flew for the first time on 11 March 1959, and deliveries of production models began in September 1961.

The initial Navy version was the HSS-2, later redesignated SH-3A Sea King, an amphibious anti-submarine helicopter which was also selected for service with the Japanese Maritime Self-Defence Force. Subsequent US Navy versions have included the S-61A amphibious transport for 26 troops or 15 stretchers, HH-3A for search and rescue, RH-3A for mine counter-measures, SH-3D Sea King which superseded the SH-3A as the Navy's standard anti-submarine helicopter, SH-3G utility helicopter and SH-3H multi-purpose helicopter to support fleet defence operations against submarines and low-flying missiles. Further military versions include VH-3D VIP transports, and the CH-3B, operated by the USAF for missile site support and drone recovery. The considerably modified British Westland Sea King anti-submarine, search and rescue, and general-purpose helicopter, and the Commando tactical helicopter are both built under a licence agreement. S-61s are licence-built in Italy and Japan, and are operated by the armed forces of ten other countries.

The military versions listed above are covered by the manufacturer's designations of S-61A, B and F. The designation S-61R applies to a series of amphibious helicopters built for the USAF as CH-3C and E transports, HH-3E Jolly Green Giants for the Aerospace Rescue and Recovery Service, and HH-3F Pelican search and rescue helicopters for the US Coast Guard.

Commercial versions are the non-amphibious S-61L, amphibious S-61N and Payloader. The prototype S-61L made its first flight on 6 December 1960 and by 1977 a total of 88 civil S-61s had been delivered. The Payloader is a lightweight version of the N for heavy-lift duties.

Sikorsky S-64 Skycrane *USA:* The Skycrane has proved one of the most successful specialist helicopters ever built. It is made up basically of a very shallow and flat-bottomed fuselage which carries two engines and a rotor system, a tail unit and a forward cabin for the crew. Tall and wide-track undercarriage legs ensure that a large space is left beneath the helicopter when it is on the ground, so that all kinds of different and bulky cargoes can be attached to the underside of the fuselage, or slung on a cable beneath it.

Although large vehicles and weapons or other heavy or outsized loads can be carried beneath the helicopter, or on a special platform, the main payload for the United States Army is the Universal Military Pod. This is a detachable metal container that can be clamped into position to act as a conventional cabin. Different pods can be equipped to carry 45 fully-armed troops or 24 stretchers and attendants, or fitted out as hospitals, workshops, communications or command posts. In Vietnam, one helicopter lifted a record 90 people in a detachable pod of an early type, while over 380 damaged aircraft were retrieved by cable and hook, slung from Skycranes, during the war.

The Skycrane was designed originally for military use, but examples have also been delivered to civil operators for use in support of oil drilling operations in remote areas, construction work, general heavy lifting, logging, etc. The first prototype made its maiden flight on 9 May 1962, and deliveries to the US Army began in late 1964. The Army operates two versions, the CH-54A and B Tarhe, the B with more powerful engines and other improvements to increase its capabilities. Civil versions are designated S-64, S-64E and S-64F.

Sikorsky S-67 Blackhawk *USA:* The Sikorsky Blackhawk holds the world speed record for helicopters, at 355.485 km/h (220.888 mph), which it achieved over a 15/25 km straight line course on 19 December 1970.

Intended originally as a second-generation high-speed attack helicopter, the Blackhawk prototype was built as a private venture. It proved highly successful, with outstanding manoeuvrability. Unfortunately, during a display at the 1974 Farnborough Air Show, the prototype was destroyed in a fatal accident. It retained the concept of a very slim fuselage, making it a difficult target to hit from the ground. Many new and advanced design features contributed to its high performance, and it could be rolled or looped like a fixed-wing airplane. (The S-67 should not be confused with the new Sikorsky UH-60A Black Hawk assault helicopter, which seats a crew of 3 and 11 passengers.)

Sikorsky VS-300 *USA:* Born in Czarist Russia, Igor Sikorsky began experiments with helicopters in 1909, when he built his first full-size experimental machine. This had two rotors which turned in opposite directions to eliminate the problem of torque.

Sikorsky R-4, the first helicopter in the world to go into series production

Sikorsky HH-3F Pelican of the US Coast Guard on a rescue mission

Sikorsky S-16N amphibious helicopter of Bristow Helicopters, Great Britain

Sikorsky S-64E Skycrane demonstrating its flying-crane lifting capability

machines in that it had a single main rotor and one or more small tail rotors to counter the inevitable torque forces. Designated VS-300, the helicopter had full cyclic-pitch control, and made a number of manned but tethered flights from 14 September 1939. Modifications followed, and on 13 May 1940 the first successful free flight was made. Further modifications brought some refinement of the VS-300 and a year later it set up an endurance record for helicopters of 1 hour, 32 minutes and 26 seconds. The old record had been set by the German Fw 61, which had been the first completely successful helicopter in the world, but because of its heavy twin-rotor design it could carry very little payload.

Sikorsky had produced the first successful single-rotor helicopter in the VS-300, which formed the starting point for the whole Sikorsky family of later types.

Not satisfied with such poor results, he changed to fixed-wing designs and eventually completed the four-engined Le Grand and the famous Ilya Mourometz bombers. Even after going as an emigré to the USA after the Revolution, Sikorsky restarted his career with a large landplane transport. After a while, feeling in a mood for a further change of direction, Sikorsky began to develop amphibians and flying-boats, which culminated in the famous *Clipper* series for Pan American in the 1930s.

This move must have been inspired by the many overwater routes, linking continents, that were being opened up at that time.

However, Sikorsky never forgot his early longing to build a practical helicopter. Finally, in the late thirties, he decided that the time had come to test his new theories with a prototype helicopter. This differed greatly from his earlier

Sikorsky Le Grand *Russia:* Having abandoned his helicopter experiments temporarily, the Russian (although later to become a United States citizen) Igor Sikorsky began to design a multi-engined biplane which incorporated several then-novel features. Against all advice, his aircraft not only had an enclosed cabin for four passengers, but the two pilots' seats were also enclosed in the tram-like fuselage. He persuaded his employers, the Russo-Baltic Wagon Works, to find the necessary finance to build his airplane in the autumn of 1912, and began construction immediately.

When it was completed, in early 1913, it was by far the largest airplane ever built, and the first with four engines. Its biplane wings spanned over 28 m (91 ft 11 in), and it was 20 m (65 ft 8 in) in length. The cabin was just

Sikorsky S-67 Blackhawk

about high enough for a man to stand inside, and the whole aircraft rested on a sixteen-wheel undercarriage. Flight testing began on 13 May, with Sikorsky himself at the controls. This first flight, carrying two other crew, lasted nearly ten minutes. One crew member stood on the open nose 'balcony' and the second in the passenger cabin. The latter had been ordered to move forward or aft if the aircraft pitched up at the nose or tail, to help stabilize it.

All went well, and in August the aircraft completed a flight lasting 1 hour 54 minutes with no fewer than eight passengers on board. Flying continued, and a total of 54 flights had been logged when disaster struck. An aircraft passing over the stationary Le Grand broke up and its engine hit and damaged the biplane so badly that it was decided to dis-mantle Sikorsky's giant.

This was by no means the end of the Russian-built, four-engined Sikorskys. In January 1914 a more refined aircraft flew, named the Ilya Mourometz, which was the forerunner of about 70 big bombers of the same name which operated with great success during the First World War.

Sopwith 1½-Strutter *Great Britain:* Sopwith was the greatest British manufacturer of fighter aircraft during the First World War. Paradoxically, Tabloids, the first Sopwith aircraft used in action, carried out the first successful *bombing* raids against German targets.

The Royal Flying Corps and the Royal Naval Air Service managed to hold their own against German aircraft until late 1915. The 'Fokker

Sopwith Camel 2F.1, the most successful fighter of the First World War

during and after the war, with the normal wheeled undercarriage replaced by twin skids, running along rails fixed to the ship's deck.

Sopwith Camel *Great Britain:* Most successful British fighter of the First World War, the Camel was a development of the earlier Pup, with a much larger rotary engine. This not only gave higher overall performance but produced high torque, so conferring the ability to turn extremely rapidly to the right, making the Camel highly manoeuvrable. When confronted with a Camel for the first time, some pilots thought it too manoeuvrable, and several were killed while trying to master the very 'vices' which might have saved them in a dogfight.

Camels reached the Western Front in mid-1917, shortly before the Germans received Fokker Dr. I triplanes, and the Royal Flying Corps and Royal Naval Air Service began equipping simultaneously. The Sopwiths soon proved far superior to all German types, as dogfighters, until the introduction of the Fokker D.VII in 1918, and were credited with 1294 enemy aircraft destroyed by the Armistice. Camels were also heavily committed to strafing and bombing German infantry trenches. Other Camels were based in England for intercepting attacking Gotha bombers and Zeppelins.

Of the many historic actions undertaken by Camels, including more than one occasion when a British pilot gained six victories in a single day, the most noteworthy must be when a Camel of No 209 Squadron, piloted by Captain A. Roy Brown, shot down the top 'ace' of the First World War, Manfred von Richthofen, on 21 April 1918. There has in fact been great speculation as to whether Richthofen was shot down by Brown or hit by ground fire. However, all that is known positively is that Richthofen uncharacteristically chased an inexperienced British pilot over the Allied lines at low level, eventually to be caught and attacked by Brown.

No account of the Camel could be complete without reference to its aircraft-carrier and associated activities. The sea-going version of

scourge' which then started almost drove the Allied air forces from the skies. Britain's answers appeared over the Western Front in early 1916, in the form of the de Havilland D.H.2 single-seat pusher fighter and the Sopwith 1½-Strutter. The latter was a two-seater, armed with the usual rear flexibly-mounted Lewis machine-gun, but, more importantly, having also a forward-firing Vickers machine-gun which fired between the blades of the tractor propeller. First British fighters designed and built with a synchronized gun, 1½-Strutters (officially designated Type 9700 but so nicknamed because of their interplane strut arrangement) were used also as single-seat and two-seat light bombers by the British air services. In addition, a vast number were built in France for the French Air Force, and later for the American Expeditionary Force. Of 5720 1½-Strutters built, well over 4000 were of French manufacture, although French units did not receive them until they had been made obsolete by newer enemy types in 1917.

The most unusual roles for which 1½-Strutters were used must have been with the RNAS. Many operated from short platforms built over the gun turrets of warships. Others flew from the earliest British aircraft carriers

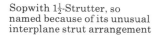

Sopwith 1½-Strutter, so named because of its unusual interplane strut arrangement

Sopwith Camel 1F.1

Sopwith Pup *Great Britain:* The pendulum-like process by which air superiority passed from Allied to German fighters, and vice versa, in 1916/17 makes it difficult to sort out the progress of the air war. By early 1916 the Sopwith 1½-Strutter was coming on to the scene, and was being matched by German Halberstadt fighters, soon to be followed by superb Albatros D.Is and IIs. Shortly before these last German aircraft became operational on the Western Front, the Royal Flying Corps began to receive its first Sopwith Pups.

The Pup got its name unofficially as the imagined offspring of the 1½-Strutter, and was a single-seat fighter armed with one forward-firing or forward-and-upward-firing machine-gun. A few Pups also carried Le Prieur firework-type rockets on anti-Zeppelin patrols, launched from the interplane struts. They were 'pilots' airplanes' – easy to fly although underpowered, with excellent manoeuvrability due partly to the torque of the rotary engine.

Pups began to be seen over France in the late summer of 1916, the first German aircraft to fall to the type being an LVG two-seat armed reconnaissance biplane on 24 September. In the

the Camel was designated 2F.1 and was operated principally in the North Sea from gun-turret platforms on warships, and from towed lighters (barges) and aircraft carriers. When the first attempt to fly from a towed lighter was made in July 1918, the pilot crashed into the water, but was saved. Experiments continued, and on 1 August a successful take-off was achieved. Flt. Sub-Lt. Stuart Culley repeated the feat ten days later, and shot down Zeppelin L.53 with incendiary ammunition. This was the last Zeppelin to be brought down during the war, the one survivor jumping from the burning airship at 6500 m (19 000 ft) over water.

Altogether, 5490 Camels were built, and were flown by US, Belgian, Canadian and Greek pilots, as well as by the RFC/RAF and RNAS.

Sopwith Pup powered by an 80 hp Le Rhone engine

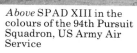

Above SPAD XIII in the
colours of the 94th Pursuit
Squadron, US Army Air
Service

Sukhoi Su-7BM of the
Egyptian Air Force

same year the Royal Naval Air Service also received the fighter. Pups were the great rivals of the Albatros, and the two types were in constant bitter conflict during the battles of Ypres, Messines and Cambrai, each trying to gain air control so that friendly reconnaissance aircraft could bring back vital information on infantry and artillery movements. Pups were also flown as home defence fighters.

Pups were joined from mid-1917 by the S.E.5 and 5a, but one of their most important roles was still to unfold. The RNAS had been involved in carrying aircraft on naval vessels since the start of the war, beginning with seaplanes on HMS *Ark Royal*. Next came HMS *Furious*, the first real aircraft carrier, and it was on this ship that the first landing of an aircraft on a moving vessel took place. This particular Pup was flown by Sqn. Cdr. E. H. Dunning, on 2 August 1917. As no proper method of stopping the aircraft after it landed had been devised, straps were fitted to the Pup so that the deck crew could grab them and pull the aircraft to a stop. All went well first time. During a repeat performance five days later, Dunning was killed when his aircraft went over the side of the carrier. He had, nevertheless, pointed the way to future carrier operations. Pups went on to help develop fully-effective deck-landing techniques, including the use of arrester gear. Meanwhile, on 21 August 1917, another Pup, launched from a platform built over a gun turret on HMS *Yarmouth*, intercepted and shot down Zeppelin L.23.

SPAD XIII *France:* With the German Fokker Eindecker fighter out of the way, and the Allied air forces in command of the skies over the Western Front, the time was right for an offensive – and after much planning, the Battle of the Somme started in July 1916. Very quickly tens of thousands of soldiers were killed and, although it became obvious that the preceding artillery bombardment had failed to crush

Sukhoi Su-7M landing with drag parachutes to help decrease speed

German opposition, the battle raged until November. Luckily, the Royal Flying Corps retained its superiority in the air, but with the arrival of the new German Albatros D.I fighter in late 1916 things again began to change.

Quickly, however, the pendulum swung once more in the Allies' favour, with the arrival of numbers of British Sopwith Pups and French SPAD VIIs. This time, the enemy was not again to overtake Allied aircraft development, and by April 1917 a new SPAD fighter was being flown in prototype form. This, the SPAD XIII, possessed the then-incredible speed of 222 km/h (138 mph), thanks to its more powerful engine and aerodynamic changes, incorporated to increase speed, manoeuvrability and control. It was armed with two Vickers machine-guns.

By the end of May the first SPAD XIIIs were entering French service, and production continued until the end of the war, later examples being fitted with supercharged Hispano engines. In all 8472 were produced, of which most equipped 81 French squadrons. The next largest user was the American Expeditionary Force, which acquired 893. The Americans flew these fighters to great effect and, although operational over German lines only from March 1918, Captain Eddie Rickenbacker and Lt. Frank Luke managed to score 26 and 21 victories respectively before the Armistice.

Although the SPAD VII had been used in numbers by the RFC, only two British squadrons flew the SPAD XIII, preferring the new

Supermarine Seafire IB taking off from the aircraft-carrier HMS *Indomitable*

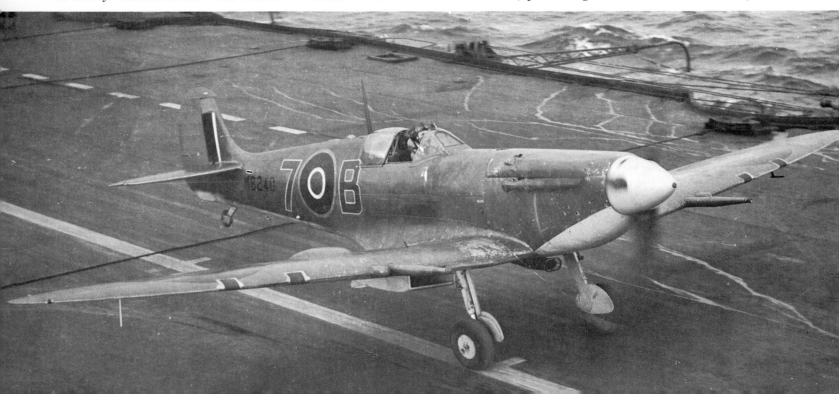

Sopwith types. Others were flown by Italian and Belgian squadrons. After the war only the air forces of France and Belgium continued to fly SPAD XIIIs, although others were exported to Czechoslovakia, Japan and Poland.

Perhaps the SPAD XIII is best remembered as the mount of the French 'ace' Capitaine Georges Guynemer who, with 54 victories, was his country's second ranking pilot. He occupied an unrivalled position in wartime France as a young hero of the air, although he was in truth pale, weak and shy. Refusing to be grounded, he was shot down seven times and finally failed to return from a patrol over Belgian territory, in September 1917.

Sukhoi Su-7 *USSR:* With the possible exception of the MiG-15 and MiG-21 fighters, the Sukhoi Su-7 (NATO reporting name 'Fitter') has seen more action in war than any other Soviet jet aircraft. Unlike the other two, it is a ground attack fighter, and usually carries rocket packs or bombs under its wings, supplemented by a pair of 30 mm cannon in the wing-roots.

Using a similar basic fuselage and tail unit to those of the Sukhoi Su-11 ('Fishpot') single-seat all-weather fighters, the Su-7 prototype was first seen publicly at the 1956 Aviation Day display. By the early 1960s production Su-7Bs were in service with the Soviet Air Force, and quickly became its standard fighter-bomber. About 500 still remain on its strength despite the fact that later types like the single-seat Su-17 and the very fast and advanced two-seat Su-19 attack-fighters (both with variable-geometry wings), have become operational.

Many Su-7Bs were also supplied to other countries, including Czechoslovakia, East Germany, Hungary, Poland, Cuba, Egypt, India, Iraq, Syria and North Vietnam. Those in India and the Middle East have been used in action.

A two-seat version of the aircraft was first seen in 1967 and has the NATO reporting name 'Moujik'. Designated Su-7U, it is basically similar to the single-seat version but has two cockpits in tandem under a larger and higher canopy.

Supermarine Spitfire *Great Britain:* The Schneider Trophy contests for seaplanes, inaugurated before the First World War, were resumed almost as soon as hostilities ended. Although Britain had won the second contest in 1914, and gained a further victory in 1922, America had won the 1923 contest and could have won the 1924 contest, had it not sportingly cancelled it. When it began to look as if the United States might eventually win the Trophy outright, the Supermarine company produced the S.4 to represent Britain in the 1925 contest. This was a small monoplane designed by R. J. Mitchell and, although it crashed, it set the pattern for the S.5, S.6 and S.6B with which Royal Air Force pilots won three contests in a

row and so kept the Trophy for good. The date of the final contest was 1931, and the S.6B won at an average speed of 548.5 km/h (340.8 mph). Later in the same year an RAF pilot set a new world absolute speed record of 654.9 km/h (406.94 mph) with the S.6B.

At about that time, the Air Ministry issued specification F.7/30 for a new fighter to replace the biplanes in service with the RAF. To meet the requirement, Mitchell designed a 'cranked-wing' monoplane with a fixed undercarriage which proved to have a very disappointing overall performance. While the Air Ministry looked elsewhere for its new fighter, Mitchell designed a completely new aircraft embodying his own ideas on what a fighter ought to be like, rather than what the Air Ministry wanted. He used all the experience gained with his Schneider racers and the Supermarine company agreed to finance a prototype as a private venture. It was originally to be called the Shrew, but ended up as the Spitfire.

The prototype flew on 5 March 1936, powered by the new and highly promising Rolls-Royce Merlin engine. The combination was tremendous. Flying at nearly 565 km/h (350 mph), the prototype showed the Air Ministry just how a modern fighter should perform, and orders for a large number of Spitfires were placed. Unfortunately, production was slower than hoped, as the design was more complicated than that of earlier fighters, or even the contemporary Hurricane. It was, therefore, 1938 before deliveries started, and even then the Mark I aircraft had only four machine-guns instead of the planned eight. The shortcomings were gradually remedied, and by the outbreak of war the RAF had nine squadrons of Spitfires. By the start of the Battle of Britain, in 1940, Spitfires and Hurricanes made up the major part of the nation's defence force. After many hard-fought weeks, the Luftwaffe was left in no doubt of who had won.

Production of some 40 different variants of the Spitfire took place throughout the war and after. They served in every combat area, operating as fighters, fighter-bombers, reconnaissance aircraft and carrier-based fighters with the Royal Navy. Griffon engines replaced Merlins after a time, and the Spitfire XIX reconnaissance version became the fastest of all the wartime Spitfires with a speed of nearly 748 km/h (460 mph). The last Spitfire was built in 1947. As a fighter at all altitudes it had proved superb, while continuous edges gained firstly by German Bf 109s and Focke Wulf Fw 190s and then by different versions of the Spitfire led to closely-matched battles throughout the war.

Ironically, after the war the RAF found itself flying Spitfires on frontier patrols along the Egyptian/Israeli border, and on 7 January 1949 four reconnaissance Spitfires were shot down by Israeli Messerschmitt Bf 109s. Nor was this the last incident, by a long way. The final Spitfire operations by the RAF did not take place until April 1954 in Malaya.

T

Tupolev TB-3 *USSR:* Between the two world wars, the Soviet Union built up a very large air force, and was able to send large numbers of fighters and bombers to Spain to aid the Republican forces during the civil war. Most were soon outclassed, although a few modern types did appear, such as the twin-engined Tupolev SB-2 monoplane medium bomber which had a speed of 402 km/h (250 mph).

Typical of most inter-war types was, however, the huge, angular and lumbering TB-3 heavy bomber, first seen in 1930. Powered by four engines, mounted on the leading-edge of wide-chord monoplane wings, it carried a crew of six in open cockpits, ten defensive machine-guns and more than 2200 kg (4850 lb) of bombs – but the clumsy multi-wheel fixed undercarriage helped to restrict its maximum speed which, after many years of development, only reached 290 km/h (180 mph) with M-34RNF engines. In 1934, more than 250 TB-3s flew in mass formations over Moscow during a May Day flypast, and production eventually totalled 800 aircraft.

TB-3s were operated against Finland and Poland with some success, but were clearly no match for the Luftwaffe in 1941 and were soon relegated to paratroop and general transport duties.

During their heyday, TB-3s made several memorable long-distance flights, and are remembered particularly for their work in support of Arctic expeditions. They were also used widely for experiments involving the carriage of parasite fighters. One TB-3 flew with two Polikarpov I-15 biplane fighters carried above its wings and two I-16 monoplanes beneath – all four parasites being released successfully in flight.

Tupolev Tu-16 *USSR:* Known to NATO as 'Badger', this medium bomber and maritime attack and reconnaissance aircraft was the Soviet Union's first operational jet aircraft in these categories. The Tu-16 in its original form began to be seen in numbers by the mid-1950s, at Aviation Day displays in Moscow. It is thought that about 2000 were produced, of which nearly half remain operational with Soviet strategic bomber units and the naval air force.

Seven versions of the Tu-16 were produced, all except one of which remain in service. The original version, Badger-A, is the basic bomber, carrying its weapons internally, and has seven cannon for its own defence. It was followed by Badger-B and then Badger-C, the latter carrying a large stand-off or antishipping missile. ('Kipper'). The last version, Badger-G, carries two long-range rocket-powered missiles ('Kelt') of more advanced type. Badger-D is a maritime reconnaissance version, with several under-fuselage fairings for electronic equipment, while Badger-E has cameras in the bomb bay. Badger-F is basically similar to the E but has electronic intelligence pods under the wings. It is the F that is most often detected flying around the coasts of other countries, especially NATO countries, and over NATO naval forces at sea.

Several Badger-As were supplied to Iraq and about 20 to Egypt. The latter were operational during the 1967 Six Day War, but were destroyed by Israeli forces. Replacement Badger-Gs were delivered to Egypt, and these launched missile attacks against Israeli targets during the Yom Kippur War of 1973. About 60 aircraft similar to Badger-As were built in China as Shenyang Tu-16s.

Tupolev Tu-22 *USSR:* This aircraft was unknown to the West until it appeared in the 1961 Aviation Day flypast over Moscow. Nine of the Tu-22s seen on that occasion were configured as reconnaissance-bombers, while the tenth carried an air-to-surface winged missile, semi-submerged under its fuselage.

The Tu-22 was the Soviet Union's first supersonic bomber, and began flying in the late fifties. About 250 are thought to remain in operational service with the Soviet long-range bomber force and the Navy – 12 have been seen in Libya.

Designated 'Blinder' under the NATO reporting system, four versions are known to have been built. The first was the basic reconnaissance-bomber, followed by the version equipped with an air-to-surface stand-off missile, then a maritime-reconnaissance version, and finally a training variant with two stepped tandem cockpits. It is thought that some Tu-22s are equipped for electronic countermeasures and electronic reconnaissance duties.

Although the Tu-22 remains in use, it was not really a successful design, as it had been built originally as a long-range strategic bomber. Tests soon showed that the aircraft did not possess an adequate range for such a role and

Opposite above Full-size replica of the Supermarine S.5 seaplane built by Leisure Sport of Egham, Surrey. The original S.5 was built by Supermarine to take part in the 1927 Schneider Trophy races, which it went on to win. From it was developed the similar S.6 racer and subsequently the Spitfire fighter.

Opposite below Supermarine Spitfire Mk LF XVI (foreground)

Huge Tupolev TB-3 heavy bombers of the inter-war Soviet Air Force

Supermarine Spitfire VB

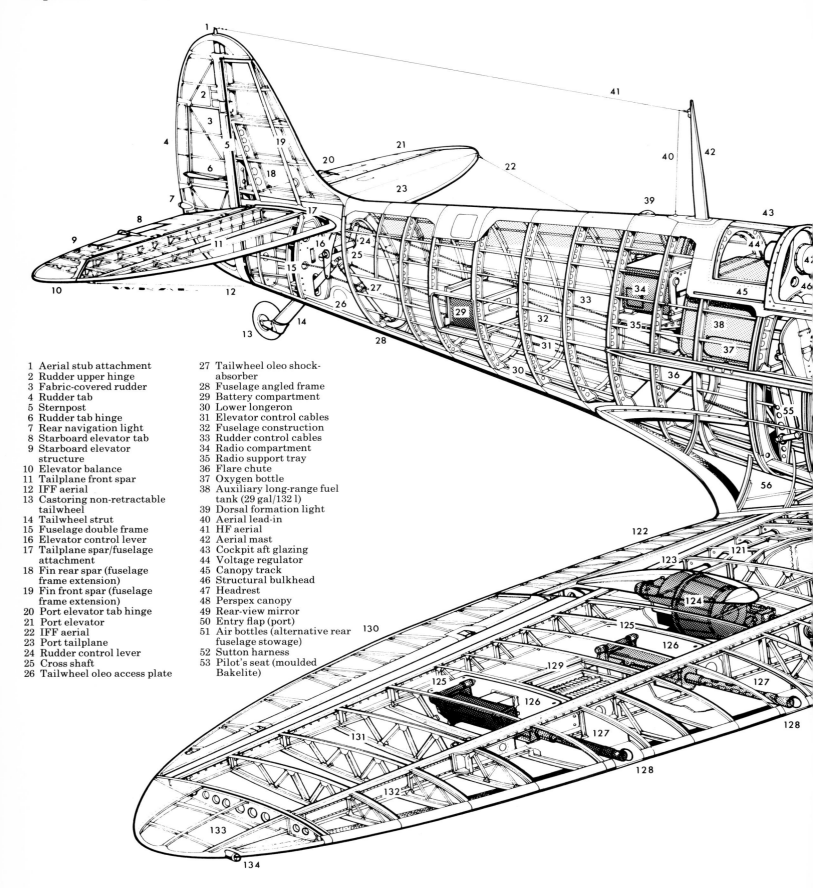

1 Aerial stub attachment
2 Rudder upper hinge
3 Fabric-covered rudder
4 Rudder tab
5 Sternpost
6 Rudder tab hinge
7 Rear navigation light
8 Starboard elevator tab
9 Starboard elevator structure
10 Elevator balance
11 Tailplane front spar
12 IFF aerial
13 Castoring non-retractable tailwheel
14 Tailwheel strut
15 Fuselage double frame
16 Elevator control lever
17 Tailplane spar/fuselage attachment
18 Fin rear spar (fuselage frame extension)
19 Fin front spar (fuselage frame extension)
20 Port elevator tab hinge
21 Port elevator
22 IFF aerial
23 Port tailplane
24 Rudder control lever
25 Cross shaft
26 Tailwheel oleo access plate

27 Tailwheel oleo shock-absorber
28 Fuselage angled frame
29 Battery compartment
30 Lower longeron
31 Elevator control cables
32 Fuselage construction
33 Rudder control cables
34 Radio compartment
35 Radio support tray
36 Flare chute
37 Oxygen bottle
38 Auxiliary long-range fuel tank (29 gal/132 l)
39 Dorsal formation light
40 Aerial lead-in
41 HF aerial
42 Aerial mast
43 Cockpit aft glazing
44 Voltage regulator
45 Canopy track
46 Structural bulkhead
47 Headrest
48 Perspex canopy
49 Rear-view mirror
50 Entry flap (port)
51 Air bottles (alternative rear fuselage stowage)
52 Sutton harness
53 Pilot's seat (moulded Bakelite)

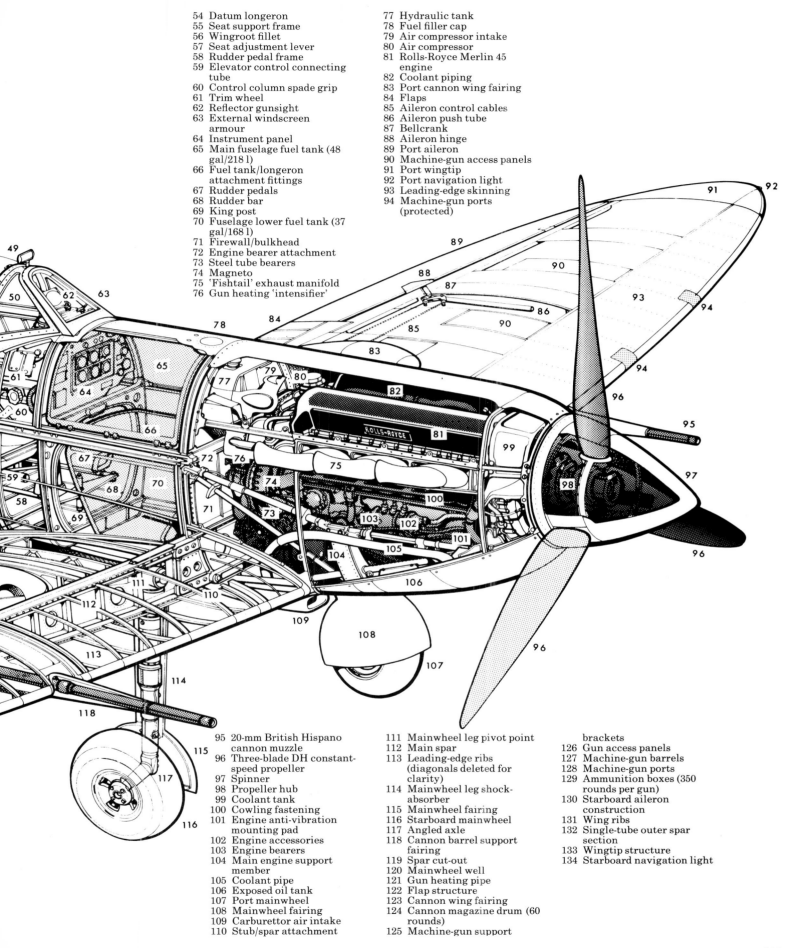

54 Datum longeron
55 Seat support frame
56 Wingroot fillet
57 Seat adjustment lever
58 Rudder pedal frame
59 Elevator control connecting tube
60 Control column spade grip
61 Trim wheel
62 Reflector gunsight
63 External windscreen armour
64 Instrument panel
65 Main fuselage fuel tank (48 gal/218 l)
66 Fuel tank/longeron attachment fittings
67 Rudder pedals
68 Rudder bar
69 King post
70 Fuselage lower fuel tank (37 gal/168 l)
71 Firewall/bulkhead
72 Engine bearer attachment
73 Steel tube bearers
74 Magneto
75 'Fishtail' exhaust manifold
76 Gun heating 'intensifier'

77 Hydraulic tank
78 Fuel filler cap
79 Air compressor intake
80 Air compressor
81 Rolls-Royce Merlin 45 engine
82 Coolant piping
83 Port cannon wing fairing
84 Flaps
85 Aileron control cables
86 Aileron push tube
87 Bellcrank
88 Aileron hinge
89 Port aileron
90 Machine-gun access panels
91 Port wingtip
92 Port navigation light
93 Leading-edge skinning
94 Machine-gun ports (protected)

95 20-mm British Hispano cannon muzzle
96 Three-blade DH constant-speed propeller
97 Spinner
98 Propeller hub
99 Coolant tank
100 Cowling fastening
101 Engine anti-vibration mounting pad
102 Engine accessories
103 Engine bearers
104 Main engine support member
105 Coolant pipe
106 Exposed oil tank
107 Port mainwheel
108 Mainwheel fairing
109 Carburettor air intake
110 Stub/spar attachment

111 Mainwheel leg pivot point
112 Main spar
113 Leading-edge ribs (diagonals deleted for clarity)
114 Mainwheel leg shock-absorber
115 Mainwheel fairing
116 Starboard mainwheel
117 Angled axle
118 Cannon barrel support fairing
119 Spar cut-out
120 Mainwheel well
121 Gun heating pipe
122 Flap structure
123 Cannon wing fairing
124 Cannon magazine drum (60 rounds)
125 Machine-gun support

brackets
126 Gun access panels
127 Machine-gun barrels
128 Machine-gun ports
129 Ammunition boxes (350 rounds per gun)
130 Starboard aileron construction
131 Wing ribs
132 Single-tube outer spar section
133 Wingtip structure
134 Starboard navigation light

other duties were found for it. Now that the Soviet Union has a new strategic bomber in service, in the form of the Tupolev 'Backfire', the Tu-22's maritime reconnaissance role is also being taken over. However, it is unlikely that the Tu-22 will disappear from active service for several years, as there are reports of Tu-22s being modified and used operationally as long-range interceptors.

Tupolev Tu-26 *USSR:* 'Backfire' is a reporting name given by NATO to the latest and most formidable Soviet bomber – a second-generation, long-range supersonic strategic bomber designed to fulfil the role left vacant by the relatively unsuccessful Tupolev Tu-22.

Its existence in prototype form has been known to the West since 1969, when the prototypes were about to be joined by a dozen or so pre-production aircraft. The first Soviet Air Force unit to operate the early version of Backfire formed in 1974, followed by a second unit with a developed version, having a greater wing span, modified undercarriage and other changes to increase range. Other units have since formed, including some for Naval Aviation duties. The Soviet forces are expected to operate eventually about 400 Backfires.

Able to reach targets throughout Europe with internal fuel, and targets in the USA using refuelling tankers, Backfire would prove to be a most difficult target for interceptors as it is capable of high- or low-level penetration and possesses an over-the-target speed of Mach 2.25–2.5. It carries a good deal of sophisticated equipment to make its detection more difficult, and can deliver free-fall weapons or very high-speed, accurate nuclear attack missiles. These increase its likelihood of success, bearing in mind that many of the surface-to-air long-range anti-aircraft missiles that were in Western service a few years ago have been deactivated under defence spending cuts.

Like many of the latest European, US and Soviet military aircraft, Backfire has been

designed with variable-geometry wings to give it a swept configuration for high-speed flight and straighter wings for low-speed flying, take-off and landing.

With production of the United States' B-1 strategic bomber cancelled at the time of writing, it seems probable that 'Backfire' will remain the only large supersonic bomber in service for many years to come.

Tupolev Tu-95 *USSR:* Better known in the West under its NATO reporting name of 'Bear', the Tu-95 is a long-range bomber with the Soviet Air Force and a maritime-reconnaissance aircraft with the Soviet Navy. Roughly in the class of the Boeing B-52, though smaller and lighter, and of about the same age, the Tu-95 features four very large turboprop engines, each of which drives two contra-rotating reversible-pitch propellers.

First flown in the summer of 1954, the Tu-95 has since been built in several versions, from Bear-A to Bear-F, differing mainly in defensive armament and equipment carried. Bear-A is the standard strategic bomber, carrying 11 340 kg (25 000 lb) of bombs and armed with three pairs

Above Soviet Tupolev Tu-16 'Badger' reconnaissance-bomber

Opposite above Tupolev Tu-104 of Aeroflot, the Soviet national airline

Opposite below Tupolev Tu-134 of Aeroflot

Below Tupolev 'Backfire' supersonic 'swing-wing' strategic bomber of the Soviet Air Force

of 23 mm guns. Bear-B was the first version to carry the long-range strategic nuclear air-to-surface missile known as 'Kangaroo', and was first seen by Western observers at the 1961 Soviet Aviation Day flypast. Bear-Bs remaining operational are used mainly as maritime patrol aircraft, and Bear-Cs are generally similar. Bear-D is one of the most important versions and has a multitude of fairings, blisters and antennae, under the fuselage, for special radar and other sophisticated equipment. One of its main functions is to locate and then transmit information on targets to distant missile-launching ships or airplanes, so that an attack can be launched before the latter see the targets for themselves. Bear-E carries reconnaissance cameras in the bomb bay, while Bear-F has some similar features to the Bear-D but retains only a tail gun turret for defence.

Bears are often flown by Soviet pilots over United States' warships at sea and are usually escorted away from the area by US Navy carrier-borne fighters. Similarly, Bears located over the North Sea are intercepted by Royal Air Force or Royal Navy Lightnings or Phantoms.

Tupolev Tu-104 *USSR:* When it was learned by Western nations that the Soviet Union had designed and built its first turbojet-powered airliner, it was with mixed feelings of surprise and curiosity that everyone waited for a first glimpse of the aircraft. The opportunity for inspection came on 22 March 1956, when a prototype Tu-104 flew into London's Heathrow Airport on a special visit. Internally, it offered the strange sight of string-mesh luggage racks, lace antimacassars on the seats, and glass cabinets containing porcelain ornaments between cabins. Externally, it was impressively modern.

The prototype Tu-104, embodying the wings, engine installation, tail unit and landing gear of the Tupolev Tu-16 medium bomber, had made its maiden flight in Russia on 17 June 1955. The original version of the airliner was designated

simply Tu-104, and had accommodation for 50 passengers. It is believed that anything from 20 to 50 of this version were produced, mainly for development, training and inauguration of scheduled services, the first of which was operated on 15 September 1956, between Moscow and Irkutsk. The first international routes, to Prague and Peking, were opened in the same year.

Although the British Comet had been the first jet-powered passenger airliner to start scheduled services, way back in 1952, accidents had necessitated its temporary withdrawal from flying in 1954. So, for a period, the Tu-104 was the only jet airliner in scheduled service in the world. The original version was followed rapidly by the improved Tu-104A, fitted with higher-powered engines and with seating for an additional 20 passengers. About 100 were produced, six going for export to the Czechoslovakian airline CSA. The last major production version, of which a similar number

Tupolev Tu-22, the Soviet Union's first supersonic bomber

Tupolev Tu-95 'Bear-D' long-range maritime reconnaissance-bomber of the Soviet Navy, seen flying over NATO ships on exercise

Tupolev Tu-144 supersonic airliner

were built, was the Tu-104B, which appeared in 1958 with still more powerful engines. Later modifications led to 80/85-seat Tu-104Ds and 100-seat Tu-104Vs.

As the Tu-104 is still in service with the Soviet state airline Aeroflot, it is the longest-serving turbojet airliner yet produced.

Tupolev Tu-134 *USSR:* As with all Soviet aircraft the Tu-134 was allocated a NATO reporting name – in the case of this rather pleasant-looking medium-range airliner, the choice of 'Crusty' seems a little undignified.

Third jet-powered airliner designed by the Tupolev team to go into quantity production, and the first with rear-mounted engines, the Tu-134 has been in continuous production since the mid-1960s and is in much the same class as the BAC One-Eleven. It was probably the first of the Tupolev jet airliners to be fully economical to operate, as its design did not have to utilize component parts from military bombers, as did the Tu-104 and the Tu-124. It first entered service with Aeroflot on 9 September 1967, between Moscow and Sochi on the Black Sea. Soon the 64/72-passenger airliner was operational on many domestic routes and on international services in Europe. Export Tu-134s went into service with Aviogenex of Yugoslavia, Interflug of East Germany, Balkan Bulgarian Airlines, LOT of Poland, Malev of Hungary, and Iraqi Airways.

In 1968 the improved Tu-134A appeared, having a longer fuselage to accommodate 80 passengers and many other modifications and refinements. This version also entered service with Aeroflot, some of the airlines already listed, plus CSA of Czechoslovakia and Egypt-Air.

Tupolev Tu-144 *USSR:* The Tupolev Tu-144 is the Soviet counterpart of the Anglo-French Concorde and became the first supersonic transport aircraft to fly when, on the last day of 1968, the prototype took to the air near Moscow. A little larger overall than Concorde, and powered by four higher-thrust engines, its accommodation for 100 to 140 passengers is roughly similar to that of the Anglo-French aircraft.

It was confirmed as early as 1965 that the Soviet Union was developing a supersonic transport aircraft. As development progressed, the Tu-144 was considerably modified. It became the first commercial transport aircraft to fly faster than the speed of sound, on 5 June 1969, and on 26 May 1970 the first to fly at twice the speed of sound, five days after it had been put on public display for the first time in Moscow.

No pre-production aircraft were produced; instead, early production Tu-144s began to come on the scene in 1973, fitted with retractable foreplanes to improve take-off and landing characteristics. One aircraft, exhibited that year at the Paris Air Show, crashed during a demonstration flight, but enquiries showed that it was not caused by a design fault and production continued. Domestic route-proving flights began in 1974, between Moscow and Vladivostock, with the aircraft carrying mail and some cargo on occasions. Despite the lead the Tu-144 seemed to have over its Anglo-French counterpart throughout its development, it was Concorde that started the first scheduled passenger flights by a supersonic airliner in 1976.

While national and international problems still hang over Concorde operations in the West, the Soviets are able to press on with their development programme. This does not necessarily guarantee a bright future for the Tu-144, which has proved to have a shorter-than-expected range due to the need to employ engine afterburning continuously in order to achieve a speed of around Mach 2 in cruising flight.

Vickers F.B.5 Gunbus *Great Britain:* Despite the fact that guns had been fired and bombs dropped from airplanes as early as 1911, it was near-freakish for an airplane to be seen mounting any sort of armament before the First World War. The Olympia aero show of 1913 exhibited the prototype of a two-seat military aircraft called the Destroyer, which mounted a heavy Maxim machine-gun. Built by Vickers, the Destroyer prototype was quickly followed by four developed versions, culminating in the Experimental Fighting Biplane No 5 (E.F.B.5) of 1914 which carried a more compact Lewis machine-gun on a front cockpit mounting.

Perhaps foreseeing Germany's aggressive intentions, Vickers decided to take a gamble and began the manufacture of 50 F.B.5s as a private venture in anticipation of Royal Flying Corps orders. The type was officially accepted for military service in the summer of 1914, and the first examples began reaching France in February 1915. They were used initially to escort reconnaissance aircraft, as the first RFC fighter squadron of F.B.5s did not form until July.

As with the other first-generation fighters of the RFC and Royal Naval Air Service, the F.B.5 had one serious drawback: it was powered by a 'pusher' engine, because no method of firing a machine-gun forward between the blades of a rotating tractor propeller had been developed. This gave the F.B.5 serious short-comings in terms of performance. Although it had been reasonably successful in combat initially, the advent of the German Fokker Eindecker on the Western Front in late 1915 soon made the F.B.5 obsolete as a fighter-scout. Although better British fighters eventually appeared to cope with the Eindecker, the F.B.5 continued to be flown on artillery-spotting and reconnaissance missions until mid-1916, making excellent 'Fokker-bait'.

Vickers themselves had not been slow to see the impending obsolescence of the F.B.5 and tried to interest officials in a new and faster version, designated F.B.9. Luckily for potential RFC crews this was not adopted as a fighter, though a small number saw limited service as trainers.

Vickers Vernon, Victoria and Valentia *Great Britain:* After the First World War a new type of aircraft entered the Royal Air Force inventory – the purpose-built troop and general-transport biplane. Three different types became, in turn, the Air Force's main transports in the Middle East and India, where the RAF did most of its flying between the wars. They were the Vernon, Victoria and Valentia, which served successively from 1922 until as late as 1943, although latterly in reduced numbers.

All were based on two bombers, the Vimy for the Vernon and the Virginia for the other two. All three had the same rotund appearance, with a rounded nose and open cockpit for the two pilots, who sat high up in the nose, and inside the fuselage sat 12 troops in the Vernon and 22

Vickers F.B.5 Gunbus

Vickers Victoria III troop
transport of the 1920s

in the Victoria and Valentia (all probably
wishing they were somewhere else). If necessary, bombs could be carried for attack duties.

The Vernon was the first to enter RAF
service, in 1922, serving with two squadrons in
Iraq and on the Cairo to Baghdad air mail route.
Next came the Victoria, which first became
operational in 1926. Eight took part in the
famous Kabul airlift when, between December
1928 and February 1929, some 586 people and
over 24000 lb of baggage were airlifted out
of the city during a rebellion, over 3050 m
(10000 ft) mountains, in some of the worst
weather on record. Among the evacuees was
King Inyatullah of Afghanistan himself.

The last of the trio was the Valentia, to which
standard many Victorias were converted, becoming operational in 1934.

Vickers Vimy *Great Britain:* The Vimy heavy
bomber was designed in 1917 to supplement the
Handley Page O/400 in the strategic bombing
campaign being waged against German industrial centres.

In general layout, the two aircraft were
basically similar, although the Vimy was
marginally faster and carried a heavier bomb
load. Whereas the O/400 had become operational with the Independent Force, Royal Air
Force, during the last year of the war, the Vimy
was not ready before the Armistice.

The Vimy entered service proper in July 1919,
with No 58 Squadron stationed in Egypt, and
latterly with No 216 Squadron, serving until
mid-1926, on the Cairo to Baghdad air-mail
route. In England, only a single flight was

equipped with Vimy aircraft – representing for
a time the RAF's entire home-based, twin-
engined bomber force. Strength built up gradually from 1924, when RAF bomber units began
to equip with Virginias, but enough Vimys for
one squadron served in Northern Ireland until
1929.

With no real combat record, the Vimy could
easily have been forgotten by historians had it
not been for two men, Captain John Alcock and
Lt. Arthur Whitten Brown. On 14/15 June 1919
these men flew a Vimy from Newfoundland to
Ireland (where they crash-landed in a bog),
becoming the first airmen to cross the Atlantic
non-stop. For this achievement the men received a £10000 prize from the London *Daily
Mail* newspaper and knighthoods from King
George V. Unfortunately, Alcock was killed in
an air crash in France later that year. Before
Christmas, another Vimy, flown by the
Australian Smith brothers, began the first
successful flight from Britain to Australia.

The Vimy also founded Vickers' reputation as
manufacturers of big bombers, progressing
through the Virginia to the Wellington and the
Valiant, first of the post-Second World War
jet V-bombers.

Vickers Virginia *Great Britain:* Designed as a
long-range replacement for the Vimy, the
Virginia was the Royal Air Force's standard
heavy night bomber for most of the inter-war
period. The prototype first flew on 24 November
1922, after which Virginias were built in several
versions up to the Mk X, the only model to have
an all-metal structure and Handley Page slots.

219

Mk Is entered service with two squadrons in 1924, those of No 7 Squadron being the first RAF bombers to be fitted with automatic pilots.

During the Virginia's production run, which totalled 126 aircraft, various improvements were made to the general design and armament. The Mk IX, for example, was the first version to have a rear gunner's tail cockpit, an improvement in defensive armament which was to become standard on bombers during the Second World War. During its early career with the RAF, the Virginia was an impressive sight and a formidable weapon, although its bomb load was only a little heavier than that of the Vimy and its speed virtually the same. The crew still sat in open cockpits, the two pilots being joined by a nose gunner and a dorsal gunner in a mid-position along the fuselage.

The Virginia was still the RAF's main heavy bomber in 1933, the year in which Winston Churchill gave the first warnings to the British Parliament about growing German air power. Remarkably, the last Virginias were not retired from their designed task for a further four years, after which they were used at Henlow for training parachutists.

Vickers Viscount *Great Britain:* The first prototype Vickers Viscount made its maiden flight, as a 32-passenger airliner, at Wisley, Surrey, on 16 July 1948. This was an important date in the history of commercial transportation, as it marked the first flight of a turboprop-powered airliner. The Viscount design centred around the use of four Rolls-Royce Dart engines, which made it slightly faster than US airliners like the Lockheed Constellation. However, its real benefits were its pressurized cabin (which allowed the airliner to fly at higher altitudes and so give the passengers a more comfortable journey), economy in oper-

ation because the engines burned cheaper kerosene instead of petrol, and its need for considerably less ground maintenance.

Three prototypes were built, the third becoming the prototype for the initial Series 700 production aircraft, with a lengthened fuselage for up to 48 passengers. This flew on 19 April 1950. On 28 July of the same year the original prototype was awarded an airworthiness certificate. On the following day a Viscount was flown by BEA pilots from London to Paris, with all passenger seats filled, marking the first passenger service by a turboprop airliner. However, this should not be confused with BEA's first scheduled passenger service proper, for the prototype was only borrowed from Vickers on a four-week trial basis, to get passenger reaction to such a revolutionary type.

Reaction was very favourable, and BEA ordered 26 larger 53-passenger V.701s, with which it began scheduled passenger services on 18 April 1953 – the first turboprop services in the world. A special V.770D variant of the Viscount was produced for North American customers, with more powerful Rolls-Royce Dart engines

Top Vickers Virginia X being used for paratroop training, hence the instructor and trainee on the outer wing. Note the cameraman in the nose of the aircraft.

Above Vickers Wellington Mk VIII

220

Voisin 'Chicken coop' bomber Type V LA.S, powered by a 150 hp Salmson-Canton-Unné engine

Vought F4U-1A Corsairs in the Pacific theatre of war, each carrying a single underfuselage bomb to attack Japanese ground positions

and other changes. By the close of production, 287 Series 700 Viscounts had been built.

In July 1956 a new version made its maiden flight as the Series 800. It was followed in December 1957 by the Series 810, with Dart 525 engines of 1990 ehp each and structural changes to accommodate between 52 and 75 passengers. A total of 151 Series 800 and 810 Viscounts was produced, production ending completely in 1964. Many Viscounts were exported, including several to China.

Vickers Wellington *Great Britain:* The Wellington medium bomber (known affectionately as the 'Wimpey') was the second aircraft built around the geodetic (lattice-work) constructional method devised by Barnes Wallis. The first had been the Vickers Wellesley general-purpose monoplane bomber, which served with the Royal Air Force from 1937 to 1941, latterly as a reconnaissance aircraft in the Middle East theatre of war. The geodetic framework gave great strength to the Wellington and enabled it to absorb tremendous damage from enemy action and still remain in the air.

The prototype Wellington first flew on 15 June 1936, powered by two Pegasus X engines of 850 hp each. The first production model, the Mk I, had Pegasus XVIII engines of 1000 hp each and was delivered to the RAF in the autumn of 1938. It was followed by Mks IA and IC. Wellingtons quickly went into action after war had been declared in September 1939, initially to attack German shipping at Wilhelmshaven.

Bombing German shipping by daylight had caused unacceptable losses, the raid of 18 December 1939 alone resulting in nearly half the Wellington force of 24 aircraft being destroyed. Thereafter, bombing was carried out at night. The RAF gradually despatched more and more aircraft, and by May 1940 raids on the Ruhr involved as many as 93 Wellingtons and Whitleys. The first 4000 lb 'block-buster' bomb was dropped from a Wellington during a raid on Emden on the night of 31 March/1 April 1941, and Wellingtons remained Bomber Command's main strategic aircraft until the arrival of the larger Stirlings, Halifaxes and Lancasters from 1941 onwards. After that, they continued to play important roles in the war at sea.

From the start of the war, Germany had tried to defeat Britain by sinking the merchant ships bringing essential food and supplies from overseas. Disastrous early losses were inflicted by secret mines, first dropped from aircraft around the British coast in November 1939. One retrieved intact showed scientists that they were magnetic, detonated by the passing of a metal hull. Various methods of exploding them harmlessly were tried, including putting a 14.6 m (48 ft) diameter degaussing ring around Wellingtons and flying them low over the water to trigger off the mines.

Vickers Wellington IC

Vickers Vimy taking off from Newfoundland

Later, Wellingtons were used for long-range maritime reconnaissance (some with a row of radar antennae along the upper fuselage) and as torpedo-bomber aircraft with Coastal Command, as troop and general transports and trainers for radar operators. Production eventually totalled 11 461 aircraft, of which the Mk X of 1943 was the last and most produced bomber version.

Voisin bomber *France:* 'Chicken coop' was the nickname given to the Voisin bomber which, although it served throughout the First World War as a day and night bomber, and as a ground-attack aircraft, looked more like one of the 'stick and string' aircraft flown by the early

pioneers than a tough combat aeroplane. Yet, despite its appearance, it proved both strong in construction and reliable in service with French, British, Russian, Italian and Belgian units.

From the outbreak of war in 1914 until the latter part of 1916, Salmson-Canton-Unné pusher engines were fitted to the Voisin bomber types III to VI. The last of these could achieve the unremarkable speed of 119 km/h (74 mph) when carrying a crew of two and bomb load. The first Voisins carried about 60 kg (130 lb) of bombs, which the observer threw over the side, but later models had proper racks for bombs or containers of steel darts called flechettes on the outside of the cockpit nacelle. Others mounted

Vickers Viscount 813 of
British Midland Airways

Vought A-7 Corsair II *USA:* The A-7 Corsair II is an attack aircraft which was used during the Vietnam War and was able to carry and drop large weights of bombs in conditions unfavourable to supersonic jet aircraft. Yet it was itself developed from an earlier aircraft of nearly twice the A-7's speed, and has never replaced completely the aircraft it was intended to supersede.

Its story can be said to date from 1957, when the US Navy began to receive F-8 Crusader airsuperiority fighters from the manufacturer, Vought. These were the first jet fighters with variable-incidence wings. In 1963 a design competition was held in the United States for a carrier-based attack aircraft to replace the Douglas Skyhawk, the basic requirements being subsonic performance and the ability to carry more than 4500 kg (10 000 lb) of weapons externally. To meet this need, Vought proposed a modified version of the F-8, and this was chosen for development as the A-7 in the following year.

The first of 199 A-7As were delivered to the US Navy in October 1966, and later versions have brought the Navy total to nearly 1000 aircraft, some of which have been converted into trainers. In addition, the United States Air Force has purchased over 400 A-7Ds, and 60 A-7Hs were built for Greece.

machine-guns or cannon, and it was a Voisin crew that shot down the first German airplane (a two-seat Aviatik) destroyed over France, on 5 October 1914.

By 1916, fighter aircraft were flying at well over 160 km/h (100 mph), so Peugeot and Renault engines were fitted which made possible 135 km/h (84 mph) and the carriage of a much heavier weight of bombs.

Such was the continued importance of the aircraft that no fewer than 26 squadrons were soon equipped with Voisin VIIIs and Xs, powered by the new engines.

Vought F4U Corsair *USA:* The name Corsair has been applied to a succession of United States Navy aircraft through many decades, but none has been more devastating to an enemy than the F4U Corsair, a distinctive 'cranked wing' monoplane fighter.

Development of the F4U began in 1938, when the US Navy ordered a new carrier-based fighter. The prototype first flew in May 1940, and by February 1943 the aircraft was operational with the US Marine Corps against the Japanese in the Pacific area, flying initially from land bases as the US Navy considered it too fast for carrier operations. This was proved wrong when Corsairs delivered to the Royal Navy were flown from carriers with great success from April 1944.

To the Japanese the Corsair was a terrifying sight, and they soon gave it the nickname 'whistling death', partly because of the engine sound. In all, about 12 600 Corsairs were built in many versions ranging from F4U-1 to F4U-6 (AU-1), up to 1952, many as fighter-bombers, or night fighters. Corsairs actually destroyed over 2000 enemy airplanes.

After the war, Corsairs continued flying with several air forces, and became the final piston-engined fighters built in the United States. When the Korean War started in 1950, Corsairs were again used by the US Marines for ground attack; others supplied to the French Navy remained in service until the early 1960s. Not until the mid-seventies did the last South American country finally withdraw the type from service.

Vought A-7D Corsair II
attack aircraft of the USAF

Wallis autogyros *Great Britain:* The series of small autogyros built by Wing Commander K. Wallis represent not only Britain's top designs but probably the finest of their type in the world. As a result, Wallis autogyros hold virtually all the world records for altitude, speed and distance flown in a straight line and in a closed circuit.

Autogyro design dates back to the 1920s, and the production of small modern autogyros for private and club flying was under way by the 1950s, with types like the US Bensen Gyro-Copters available in do-it-yourself form. But Wallis's first design, flown in 1961, introduced many notable refinements. Designated WA-116, it could be flown with hands and feet off the controls, and was fitted with a drive-shaft enabling the rotor to be turned like that of a helicopter until take-off, when it was disengaged from the engine and autorotated.

Unlike a helicopter, an autogyro has a rotor which is not powered in flight. Instead, an engine mounted behind the pilot of a Wallis aircraft drives a pusher propeller. This causes the autogyro to travel forward at sufficient speed for the slipstream to turn the free-mounted rotor like the sails of a windmill as it goes through the air. The rotor gives enough lift to keep the aircraft in the air, leaving the engine free to use all its power to drive the autogyro forward.

Although Wing Commander Wallis does not offer his designs for home construction or sale, examples have been used for many unusual tasks. One was armed and used in a James Bond film; others have had special equipment fitted for detecting from the air anything buried, such as the bodies of murder victims.

Westland Lysander *Great Britain:* The Lysander was a strongly-built and well-liked aircraft, of which the first prototype made its initial flight on 15 June 1936. Production Mk Is were operational with the Royal Air Force by the end of 1938, and were given the nickname 'Lizzie' by the British forces with which they served.

Only eight days after the Germans had launched their attack on Poland, and five days after war had been declared by Britain, five squadrons of Lysanders (together with Hurricanes and Blenheims) were flown to France as part of the British Expeditionary Force, thus joining the squadrons of Fairey Battles that had left for France on 2 September. The Lysanders were widely operated in France until the British withdrawal, and also in North Africa, not only for observation but for carrying supplies where needed, and perform-

ing light strikes against ground forces with the six small bombs that could be mounted on the undercarriage stub-wings. However, army co-operation duties in North Africa were generally taken over by the US Curtiss Tomahawk from 1941.

After that Lysanders operated mainly on air-sea rescue, target-towing and glider-towing duties – but their most famous wartime task was also the most secret. In August 1940, Winston Churchill gave the order that a special RAF Flight should be formed to carry British intelligence agents into occupied Europe, together with volunteers, to set up and then to work with underground resistance groups. Following the delivery of a Whitley bomber, several Lysander IIIs were handed over to the Flight. Agent dropping operations at night began in November 1940, and soon a special version of the Lysander had been evolved as the Mk IIIA, which relied on its STOL performance to land or pick up agents surreptitiously in Europe. This version had a special auxiliary fuel tank to extend its range. Although designed to accommodate only one passenger, sometimes as many as four agents at a time were picked up when escaping in emergencies. As these missions grew in number and importance, the Special Air Services received more Lysanders as well as other types of aircraft.

The faithful 'Lizzie' was finally withdrawn from service in 1944. Production totalled well over 1500 aircraft, including 447 IIIAs and 225 Lysanders built in Canada.

Westland Wapiti *Great Britain:* Air control was the term applied to the policing activities carried out by the Royal Air Force during the 1920s and 1930s in India, Iraq, the Sudan, Palestine and elsewhere. Its purpose was to keep under control marauding tribesmen who traditionally threatened order in these areas. Its importance stemmed from the fact that operations against leaders like the 'Mad Mullah' in Somaliland kept the RAF alive and independent during a period of drastic defence economies.

Initially, the policing tasks were carried out mainly by de Havilland D.H.9As of wartime vintage. The mere presence of an airplane buzzing overhead frightened rebellious tribesmen; but some soon realized that a volley of carefully aimed rifle fire could bring down an airplane, particularly by holing the radiator or fuel tanks. And, it was anything but healthy for a downed crew if caught by the natives. Soon RAF aircraft were unable to fly safely below 915 m (3000 ft), and only went lower when actually attacking native forces.

As time passed the old D.H.9As needed replacing – so a competition was held in Britain for a plane incorporating as many D.H.9A components as possible to save costs. The winner was the Westland Wapiti, which had better all-round performance than the earlier type. No 84 Squadron RAF, stationed in Iraq,

Westland Wapiti Mk IIA of No 30 Squadron RAF, based in Iraq during the 1930s

was the first to receive Wapitis, in 1928, but most of the 500 or so that were built were stationed in India or at home. Those based abroad often carried long underfuselage hooks with which to pick up messages from ground forces without having to land. They could operate on wheels, floats or skis, often carried extra fuel and spare wheels, and packed water and survival rations for the crew in case of an emergency landing in hostile terrain. The Indian-based Wapitis served right up to the Second World War, but those at home were superseded by newer types from 1937 onwards, when they were transferred to Auxiliary Air Force squadrons. Other Wapitis served with the air forces of several British Commonwealth countries and China.

Westland Wessex *Great Britain:* The Sikorsky S-55 appeared soon after the end of the Second World War. For the first time the engine had been positioned in a way that left the main cabin completely free, allowing the carriage of ten troops, six stretchers, freight or rescue equipment. S-55s were used during the Korean War, the first conflict in which helicopters were operated widely.

From the S-55 was developed the larger S-58, as an anti-submarine helicopter for the US Navy. The prototype made its maiden flight on 8 March 1954. From then until 1970, some 1821 S-58s were built as general-purpose helicopters, in both civil and military guises. In 1956 Westland Helicopters of Great Britain received a licence from Sikorsky to build a turbine-powered version of the S-58, which Westland named the Wessex. To aid the development programme, Westland received a Sikorsky-built S-58, which was re-engined with an 1100 shp Gazelle turboshaft engine. Flight testing began in the middle of May 1957.

In 1960 Westland began delivering Wessex HAS Mk 1 anti-submarine helicopters to the Royal Navy, with 1450 shp Gazelle 161 engines. Variants included an assault transport for carriage by HMS *Albion* and the more powerful HAS Mk 3. Meanwhile, a Wessex had flown with two coupled Gnome engines, and this variant went into production for the Royal Air Force as the HC Mk 2, of which two were converted into Queen's Flight HCC Mk 4s. From the Mk 2 was developed the naval

The famous Wright Flyer at Kill Devil Hill in 1903

commando assault HU Mk 5, with provision for carrying air-to-surface missiles, guns, torpedoes or rockets, in addition to troops. Other Wessex helicopters were exported to several countries.

Westlands also produced Wessex 60s for commercial use, and a number of these are flying in support of offshore oil exploration.

Wright Flyer *USA:* Most renowned of all aviation pioneers were the American Wright brothers, Orville and Wilbur. It is difficult to say what started these men in aviation – what is known is that they followed with interest the activities of men like the German hang-gliding pioneer Otto Lilienthal, who built and flew most successfully a series of small gliders from 1891 until his death following a flying accident five years later.

Owners of a small bicycle repair shop, the Wrights had the necessary facilities to enable them to start their own experiments. These began in 1899 when they constructed and flew a 1.52 m (5 ft) kite-type biplane to investigate their warping wing control theory. After a successful design had been developed, they built their first man-carrying glider, a 5.18 m (17 ft) span biplane which could be flown as a glider or kite, with the pilot lying on the lower wing. Realizing that the wing span was far too small, the Wrights built their glider No 2 in 1901, using published information on wing angles and aerofoils. Unfortunately, the published material had been drastically wrong and No 2 was unsuccessful. From that time the Wrights stopped using the results and calculations of others and set up a wind tunnel to test a great many model wings of varying aerofoil shapes to obtain more accurate data.

The No 3 glider of 1902 was constructed to embody their test results, and proved highly successful. The time had come to build a powered version and this appeared in 1903 as the Wright Flyer, powered by a single engine of Wright design and manufacture. Based at Kill Devil Hill, Kitty Hawk, North Carolina, the Wrights started up the engine on 14 December 1903 but Wilbur failed to achieve a flight. Three days later, Orville attempted a flight and managed to become airborne for 12 seconds, covering about 36 m (120 ft). This was history's first piloted, sustained, controlled and powered airplane flight. The same day three other flights were made, the longest lasting nearly a minute.

Remarkably, the newspapers were not interested in the Kitty Hawk experiments, and it was some years before Press and public were convinced that flights had been made. From that moment the Wrights achieved international fame, and it was not until 1909 that other pioneer aircraft could match the performance of the Wright Flyers. It was also a Wright Flyer that became the first airplane purchased for military use in August 1909.

Wallis WA-116/F autogyro

Westland Lysander III army co-operation aircraft

Royal Navy Westland Wessex 3

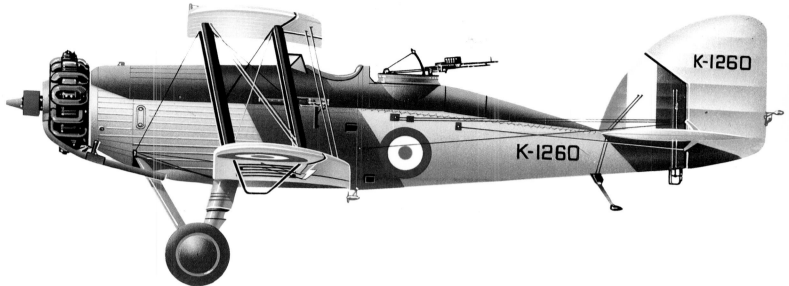

Westland Wapiti IIA of the
RAF

K-1260

K-1260

Y

Yakovlev Yak-9 *USSR:* Together with the Lavochkin La-5 fighter, the Yak-9 made its operational debut in October 1942 during the grim Battle of Stalingrad, where it faced the latest versions of the Luftwaffe's Messerschmitt Bf 109. Up to then the Red Air Force had been having a bad time. Its original fighters had been virtually wiped out by the Germans in earlier battles, and for a time it had depended on the British and American fighters sent to bridge the gap.

With the Yak-9, Soviet pilots could at last meet the Germans on equal terms. If they succeeded in manoeuvring their prey down to a

Yakovlev Yak-9D fighters

height that gave the Yak an edge in performance, the Luftwaffe pilots could only call on their greater experience to get them out of trouble. As production continued, so the number of variants increased, and later Yak-9s proved more than a match for any German opponent. Increased tankage in the Yak-9D allowed the fighters to support Soviet bomber forces as they began to smash past the enemy defences and fly on over the border into Germany itself. Some Yak-9Ts were fitted with large-bore cannon and were used with reasonable success as 'tank-busters' and anti-shipping fighters.

Production of the family of Yakovlev piston-engined fighters, including the Yak-1, -3, -7 and -9, totalled over 36 000, and the Yak-9s continued in service with the Red Air Force until the introduction of the first jets. Elsewhere they served even longer, and a fairly large number made up the fighter force of North Korea in 1950.

Yakovlev Yak-36 (Forger) *USSR:* The name 'Forger' is the NATO reporting name given to a new vertical take-off and landing (VTOL) aircraft which was first seen on board the Soviet Navy's first operational aircraft carrier, *Kiev*, in July 1976, and which is designated Yak-36.

Western intelligence had known for some time that the Soviet Navy was building aircraft carriers, not only for obvious combat usefulness but to enable the Soviet Union to show a military presence in certain areas. Small and rather crude VTOL aircraft suitable for shipboard operation had been under test in the Soviet Union since 1967, and had undergone deck-landing trials on board a helicopter carrier.

It caused no surprise, therefore, when reconnaissance photographs taken by Royal Air Force Nimrods and Canberras showed a more developed VTOL aircraft on the deck of the *Kiev* when it entered the Mediterranean on 19

July 1976. It transpired that the *Kiev* had accommodation for about 36 aircraft, including a large number of Kamov Ka-25 ('Hormone') helicopters. The remaining aircraft were probably all Forgers. *Kiev* also differs from US carriers in having a large number of guns and missiles for attacking surface targets and for its own defence.

Forger is a single-seater for combat roles, and two-seater for operational training. Larger than the British Harrier, it appears to lack that aircraft's short take-off capability, as a means of increasing its fuel/weapon load. Vertical take-off is performed by means of two vertically-mounted 'lift-jets' housed in the fuselage aft of the cockpit, which work in conjunction with the two rotating exhaust nozzles of the main propulsion engine. With a maximum speed of around Mach 1.2 at height, it is probably intended for tactical support, area defence, anti-submarine and anti-shipping duties.

At least one other Soviet aircraft carrier is operational, the *Minsk*, with two more in the pipeline – Forger will probably be seen on all of these, as well as at land bases in Eastern Europe.

Yokosuka Ohka *Japan:* Perhaps exceeded only by the atomic bomb and German V2 rocket as the most awesome weapon of the Second World War, the Japanese suicide plane was the terror of the US Navy in the Pacific.

By 1944, the war was going badly for Japan. The great sea battles between the carrier forces of the United States and Japan, in 1942, had turned the tide of war in America's favour and had demonstrated that the Japanese were not invincible. Subsequently, it had become the accepted policy of the Allies that the defeat of Japan should follow the defeat of Germany. The US Navy's carrier forces were becoming more of a threat to the Japanese homeland every day, as further victories were won over Japanese land, air and sea forces, bringing the 'island-hopping' Americans ever nearer.

In a last-ditch effort to counter the Allied warships, the Japanese formed special suicide air squadrons in the autumn of 1944. Named the Kamikaze (Divine Wind) Corps, they originally flew Zero-Sen fighters armed with large bombs. The Kamikazes struck their first successful blow on 25 October, when two aircraft dived into, and sank, the US escort carrier *St Lo* off the Philippines. The wooden decks of the US carriers proved very susceptible to such attack. In contrast, no Royal Navy carrier hit by Kamikazes was out of action for more than 24 hours, because these vessels had steel decks.

Meanwhile, the Japanese Yokosuka company had been flight testing a prototype rocket-powered suicide aircraft named the Ohka, specially designed for the task. This was intended to be air-launched and then to fly some 80 km (50 miles) before igniting its main engines and diving into its target, the warhead being carried in the nose of the aircraft. No defensive

armament was carried. By March 1945 about 750 Ohkas (Cherry Blossoms) had been built and production continued. There was also a glider version for training pilots.

Many historians state that all Japanese suicide pilots were volunteers. This appears to be true of the early Zero-Sen pilots, who considered it an honour to be selected for the duty. However, with the mass conversion and production of suicide aircraft, some pilots are said to have been chosen against their will.

According to Japanese records, the last suicide attack was made on 15 August 1945, by which time 2257 suicide attacks had been carried out in the Philippines, Formosa and Okinawa areas. Over 1320 Japanese aircraft pressed home suicide attacks and a further 900 returned, the latter presumably being modified fighter types rather than the short-range Ohkas. In just ten months, those that attacked accounted for 48% of all US warships damaged and 21% of those sunk in the whole 44-month Pacific War.

Top Yakovlev Yak-36 VTOL attack aircraft, known to NATO as 'Forger-A', on board the new Soviet aircraft carrier *Kiev*

Above Yokosuka Ohka suicide aircraft discovered by British forces after the Japanese surrender in 1945

Tables of Technical Data

Name (Country of Origin)	Version	Engine/s	Wing Span	Length	Maximum Weight	Maximum Speed	Range	Accommodation/ Armament
Aeritalia G91 (Italy)	G91Y	Two General Electric J85-GE-13A turbojets (each 1235kg; 2720lb st)	9.01m 29ft 6½in	11.67m 38ft 3½in	8700kg 19180lb	Mach 0.95	Combat radius 600km 372 miles	Crew of one. Two fixed 30mm DEFA cannon, plus attachments for four 1000lb bombs, napalm, rocket packs or missiles.
Aermacchi MB326 (Italy)	MB 326GB	One Rolls-Royce Bristol Viper 20 Mk 540 turbojet (1547kg; 3410lb st)	10.85m 35ft 7in	10.64m 34ft 11in	5216kg 11500lb	867km/h 539mph	1850km 1150 miles	Crew of two. Up to 1816kg (4000lb) of bombs, 80mm SURA rockets or other rocket packs, two AS.12 missiles, 12.7mm gun pod, 30mm Aden gun packs or camera pack.
Aero L-39 (Czechoslovakia)	—	One Walter Titan turbofan (1720kg; 3792lb st)	9.46m 31ft 0½in	12.32m 40ft 5in	4535kg 9998lb	Mach 0.8	910km 565 miles	Crew of two. Bombs, rocket pods, air-to-air missiles etc.
Aero Spacelines Guppy (USA)	Guppy-201	Four Allison 501-D22C turboprops (each 4912eshp)	47.62m 156ft 3in	43.84m 143ft 10in	77110kg 170000lb	Cruising 409km/h 254mph	813km 505 miles	Crew of four, plus large-section freight.
Aérospatiale Alouette II and III (France)	SA 319B Alouette III Astazou	One 870shp Turboméca Astazou XIV turboshaft (derated to 600shp)	Rotor diam. 11.02m 36ft 1¾in	10.03m 32ft 10¾in	2250kg 4960lb	220km/h 136mph	605km 375 miles	Pilot, plus six passengers, freight or two stretchers and two medical attendants. Armament carried on some military Alouette IIIs.
Aérospatiale SE 210 Caravelle (France)	Carav-elle 12	Two Pratt and Whitney JT8D-9 turbofans (each 6577kg; 14500lb st)	34.30m 112ft 6in	36.24m 118ft 10½in	58000kg 127870lb	825km/h 512mph	2540km 1580 miles	Crew of two/four, plus between 104 and 139 passengers.
Aérospatiale Super Frelon (France)	—	Three Turboméca Turmo IIIC6 turboshafts (each 1550shp)	Rotor diam. 18.90m 62ft 0in	19.40m 63ft 7¾in	13000kg 28660lb	Cruising 249km/h 155mph	820km 509 miles	Crew of two. Freight and passenger accommodation (see entry).
Aérospatiale/ Westland Gazelle (France/GB)	—	One Turboméca Astazou IIIA turboshaft (590shp)	Rotor diam. 10.50m 34ft 5½in	9.53m 31ft 3¼in	1800kg 3970lb	310km/h 192mph	670km 415 miles	Crew of one or two, plus three passengers, freight or two stretchers. Armament can include AS.11, AS.12, TOW or Hot air-to-surface missiles, rocket pods or guns.
Aérospatiale/ Westland Puma (France/GB)	SA 330B	Two Turboméca Turmo IIIC4 turboshafts (each 1328shp)	Rotor diam. 15.00m 49ft 2½in	14.06m 46ft 1½in	6400kg 14110lb	281km/h 174mph	620km 390 miles	Crew of two, plus up to 20 passengers or six stretchers, etc. Armament can include air-to-surface missiles, 20mm cannon and 7.62mm machine-guns.

229

Tables of Technical Data

Name (Country of Origin)	Version	Engine/s	Wing Span	Length	Maximum Weight	Maximum Speed	Range	Accommodation/ Armament
Aichi D3A (Japan)	D3A1	One Mitsubishi Kinsei 43 radial (1000hp)	14.37m 47ft 2in	10.19m 33ft 5½in	3650kg 8047lb	386km/h 240mph	1475km 915 miles	Crew of two. Two fixed 7.7mm Type 97 machine-guns, plus one 250kg (551lb) bomb and two 60kg (132lb) bombs.
Airbus Industrie A300 (France/West Germany/GB/the Netherlands/ Spain)	A300B2	Two General Electric CF6-50C turbofans (each 23130kg; 51000lb st)	44.84m 147ft 1in	53.62m 175ft 11in	142000kg 313055lb	668km/h 415mph	4261km 2648 miles	Crew of three, plus between 220 and 336 passengers.
Albatros D.I-D.V (Germany)	D.V	One Mercedes D.IIIa piston engine (180hp)	9.04m 29ft 8in	7.33m 24ft 0½in	937kg 2066lb	186km/h 116mph	Endur- ance 2 hours	Crew of one. Two forward-firing Spandau machine-guns.
Amiot 143M (France)	M4	Two Gnome Rhône 'Mistral Major' 14kirs/kjrs radials (each 870hp)	26.45m 79ft 6in	18.24m 59ft 10½in	8630kg 19030lb	295km/h 183.5mph	—	Crew of four for night bombing, five for daylight. Three or four 7.5mm machine-guns in nose, dorsal and ventral positions. Up to 900kg (1984lb) of bombs internally, 800kg (1765lb) under wings.
Antoinette (France)	VII	One Levavasseur Antoinette piston engine (50hp)	12.80m 42ft 0in	11.51m 37ft 9in	590kg 1300lb	70km/h 43½mph	—	Crew of one
Antonov An-2 (USSR)	Polish An-2P	One Shvetsov ASz-62IR piston engine (1000hp)	Upper 18.18m 59ft 8½in	12.74m 41ft 9½in	5500kg 12125lb	258km/h 160mph	900km 560 miles	Crew of two, plus twelve adults and two children.
Arado Ar 234 Blitz (Germany)	Ar 234B-2	Two Junkers Jumo 004B turbojets (each 900kg; 1980lb st)	14.11m 46ft 3½in	12.64m 41ft 5½in	9850kg 21715lb	692–742 km/h 430–461 mph	up to 1630km 1015 miles	Crew of one. Two fixed rear-firing 20mm MG 151 cannon, plus up to 1500kg (3300lb) of bombs.
Armstrong Whitworth Argosy biplane (GB)	Mk I	Three Armstrong Siddeley Jaguar III piston engines (each 385hp)	27.43m 90ft 0in	19.66m 64ft 6in	8165kg 18000lb	Cruising 153km/h 95mph	531km 330 miles	Crew of two, plus twenty passengers.
Armstrong Whitworth Whitley (GB)	Mk V	Two Rolls-Royce Merlin X piston engines (each 1075hp)	25.60m 84ft 0in	22.10m 72ft 6in	12790kg 28200lb	367km/h 228mph	2414km 1500 miles	Crew of five. Five 0.303in machine-guns, plus up to 3175kg (7000lb) of bombs.
Avro 504 (GB)	504B	One Gnome rotary piston engine (80hp)	10.97m 36ft 0in	8.97m 29ft 5in	714kg 1575lb	132km/h 82mph	—	Two seats in tandem.
Avro Lancaster (GB)	Mk I	Four Rolls-Royce Merlin 20 or 22 piston engines (each 1460hp)	31.09m 102ft 0in	21.13m 69ft 6in	30844kg 68000lb	462km/h 287mph	2670km 1660 miles	Crew of seven. Up to ten 0.303in Browning machine-guns, plus normal bomb load of 6350kg (14000lb).
Avro Vulcan (GB)	B. Mk 2	Four Rolls-Royce Bristol Olympus 301 turbojets (each 9070kg; 20000lb st)	33.83m 111ft 0in	30.45m 99ft 11in	81650kg 180000lb	Mach 0.98	Combat radius 2735–4630 km 1700–2870 miles	Twenty-one 454kg (1000lb) or free fall nuclear bombs.

Name (Country of Origin)	Version	Engine/s	Wing Span	Length	Maximum Weight	Maximum Speed	Range	Accommodation/ Armament
BAC One-Eleven (GB)	Series 500	Two Rolls-Royce Spey Mk 512 DW turbofans (each 5692kg; 12550lb st)	28.50m 93ft 6in	32.61m 107ft 0in	47400kg 104500lb	871km/h 541mph	3484km 2165 miles	Crew of two, plus up to 119 passengers.
BAC Strikemaster (GB)	—	One Rolls-Royce Bristol Viper Mk 535 turbojet (1424kg; 3140lb st)	11.23m 36ft 10in	10.27m 33ft 8½in	5215kg 11500lb	760km/h 472mph	2224km 1382 miles	Crew of two. Two 7.62mm FN machine-guns, plus up to 1360kg (3000lb) of bombs, napalm, rockets, etc.
BAC/ Aérospatiale Concorde (France/GB)	—	Four Rolls-Royce/ SNECMA Olympus 593 Mk 610 turbojets (each 17260kg; 38050lb st with afterburning)	25.56m 83ft 10in	62.10m 203ft 9in	181065kg 408000lb	Cruising Mach 2.04	6580km 4090 miles	Crew of three, plus between 128 and 144 passengers.
Bede BD-5 Micro (USA)	BD-5G	One Xenoah piston engine (70hp)	5.18m 17ft 0in	4.05m 13ft 3½in	385kg 850lb	370km/h 230 miles	1818km 1130 miles	Crew of one.
Bell HueyCobra (USA)	AH-1G	One Lycoming T53-L-13 turboshaft (derated to 1100shp)	Rotor diam. 13.41m 44ft 0in	13.59m 44ft 7in	4309kg 9500lb	352km/h 219mph	574km 357 miles	Crew of two. One XM-197 three-barrel 20mm cannon in undernose turret, plus four underwing points for gun pods, rockets, grenade launchers or TOW missiles.
Bell Iroquois (USA)	Model 205 (UH-1H)	One Lycoming T53-L-13 turboshaft (1400shp)	Rotor diam. 14.63m 48ft 0in	12.77m 41ft 10¾in	4309kg 9500lb	204km/h 127mph	511km 318 miles	Pilot, plus up to 14 troops, six stretchers and an attendant, or internal or external freight.
Bell JetRanger (USA)	Jet-Ranger II	One Allison 250-C20 turboshaft (400shp)	Rotor diam. 10.16m 33ft 4in	9.50m 31ft 2in	1451kg 3200lb	225km/h 140mph	624km 388 miles	Pilot, plus four passengers, stretchers, or internal or external freight.
Bell Model 47 (USA)	Model 47G-3B-2A	One Lycoming TVO-435-F1A piston engine (280hp)	Rotor diam. 11.32m 37ft 1½in	9.63m 31ft 7in	1338kg 2950lb	Cruising 135km/h 84mph	397km 247 miles	Pilot, plus two passengers, externally-carried stretchers or freight.
Bell X-1 (USA)	—	One Reaction Motors E6000-C4 rocket motor (2723kg; 6000lb st)	8.53m 28ft 0in	9.45m 31ft 0in	6078kg 13400lb	1540km/h 957mph	—	Crew of one.
Blériot XI monoplane (France)	—	One Anzani piston engine (25hp)	7.80m 25ft 7in	8.00m 26ft 3in	300kg 660lb	75km/h 47mph	—	Crew of one.
Boeing 707 (USA)	707–320	Four Pratt and Whitney JT3D-7 turbofans (each 8620kg; 19000lb st)	44.42m 145ft 9in	46.61m 152ft 11in	151315kg 333600lb	1010km/h 627mph	6920km 4300 miles	Crew of three/five, plus up to 219 passengers.
Boeing 727 (USA)	727–200	Three Pratt and Whitney JT8D-9 turbofans (each 6577kg; 14500lb st), or optionally JT8D-11, -15 or -17 engines	32.92m 108ft 0in	46.69m 153ft 2in	95027kg 209500lb	1017km/h 632mph	4635km 2880 miles	Crew of three, plus up to 189 passengers.

Tables of Technical Data

Name (Country of Origin)	Version	Engine/s	Wing Span	Length	Maximum Weight	Maximum Speed	Range	Accommodation/ Armament
Boeing 747 (USA)	747–200B	Four Pratt and Whitney JT9D-7AW turbofans (each 22030kg; 48570lb st), or other engines	59.64m 195ft 8in	70.51m 231ft 4in	356070kg 785000lb	978km/h 608mph	10424km 6477 miles	Crew of three/four, plus up to 500 passengers.
Boeing B-17 Flying Fortress (USA)	B-17G	Four Wright GR-1820-97 Cyclone radials (each 1200hp)	31.64m 103ft 9½in	22.66m 74ft 4in	24950kg 55000lb	483km/h 300mph	2977km 1850 miles	Crew of ten. Thirteen 0.50in machine-guns. plus up to 7983kg (17600lb) of bombs.
Boeing B-29 Superfortress (USA)	B-29	Four Wright R-3350-23 Cyclone radials (each 2200hp)	43.05m 141ft 3in	30.18m 99ft 0in	56245kg 124000lb	574km/h 357mph	over 6437km 4000 miles	Crew of ten/fourteen. Twelve 0.50in machine-guns, plus normally 5443kg (12000lb) of bombs.
Boeing B-52 Stratofortress (USA)	B-52H	Eight Pratt and Whitney TF33-P-3 turbofans (each 7718kg; 17000lb st)	56.42m 185ft 0in	47.55m 156ft 0in	221350kg 488000lb	1040km/h 650mph	20125km 12500 miles	Crew of six. One rear-firing 20mm cannon, plus twenty SRAM nuclear missiles, conventional bombs and diversionary rocket packs.
Boeing E-3A AWACS/Tupolev Tu-126 (USA/USSR)	Tu-126	Four Kuznetsov NK-12MV turboprops (each 14795shp)	51.10m 167ft 8in	57.30m 188ft 0in	—	870km/h 540mph	about 8950km 5550 miles	No armament. Large rotating early warning radar above fuselage.
Boeing Model 247 (USA)	247D	Two Pratt and Whitney R-1340-S1H1G radials (each 550hp)	22.56m 74ft 0in	15.72m 51ft 7in	6193kg 13650lb	304km/h 189mph	1200km 745 miles	Crew of two, plus ten passengers and mail or freight.
Boeing P-12 (USA)	F4B-1	One Pratt and Whitney R-1340B Wasp piston engine (450hp)	9.14m 30ft 0in	6.29m 20ft 7½in	1235kg 2724lb	267km/h 166mph	837km 520 miles	Crew of one. Two forward-firing machine-guns, plus one 227kg (500lb) bomb.
Boeing Stratocruiser (USA)	—	Four Pratt and Whitney R-4360 Double Wasp piston engines (each 3500hp)	43.05m 141ft 3in	33.63m 110ft 4in	67130kg 148000lb	604km/h 375mph	6759km 4200 miles	Crew of five, plus up to 100 passengers.
Breguet 14 and 19 (France)	19B-2	One Lorraine piston engine (450hp) or similar Lorraine, Hispano-Suiza or Renault engine from 375–800hp	14.83m 48ft 8in	9.51m 31ft 2½in	2200kg 4850lb	227km/h 141mph	797km 495 miles	Crew of two (Breguet 14B-1, pilot only). Machine-guns and bombs.
Bristol 170 Freighter (GB)	Mk 32	Two Bristol Hercules 734 piston engines (each 1980hp)	32.92m 108ft 0in	22.35m 73ft 4in	19958kg 44000lb	362km/h 225mph	1320km 820 miles	Crew of three. Two or three cars and 23 passengers.
Bristol Beaufighter (GB)	Mk X	Two Bristol Hercules XVII radials (each 1770hp)	17.63m 57ft 10in	12.70m 41ft 8in	11520kg 25400lb	515km/h 320mph	2365km 1470 miles	Crew of two. Four Hispano 20mm cannon, six 0.303in Browning machine-guns, one Vickers machine-gun, plus up to a 965kg (2127lb) torpedo, eight rocket projectiles or two 113kg (250lb) bombs.

Name (Country of Origin)	Version	Engine/s	Wing Span	Length	Maximum Weight	Maximum Speed	Range	Accommodation/ Armament
Bristol Blenheim (GB)	Mk IV	Two Bristol Mercury XV radials (each 905hp)	17.17m 56ft 4in	12.98m 42ft 7in	6123kg 13500lb	428km/h 266mph	2350km 1460 miles	Crew of three. Five 0.303in Browning machine-guns, plus up to 454kg (1000lb) of bombs.
Bristol Boxkite (GB)	—	One Gnome, ENV or Renault piston engine (50hp)	10.52m 34ft 6in	11.73m 38ft 6in	476kg 1050lb	64.5km/h 40mph	—	Pilot and passenger seated side by side.
Bristol Bulldog (GB)	Mk IIA	One Bristol Jupiter VIIF or VIIFP radial (490hp)	10.32m 33ft 10in	7.67m 25ft 2in	1660kg 3660lb	280km/h 174mph	—	Crew of one. Two forward-firing Vickers machine-guns, plus optional 9kg (20lb) bombs.
Bristol F.2 Fighter (GB)	F.2B	One Rolls-Royce Falcon II or III piston engine (190–220hp), or similar type of engine	11.96m 39ft 3in	7.87m 25ft 10in	1292kg 2848lb	201km/h 125mph	Endurance 3 hours	Crew of two. One forward-firing Vickers machine-gun and one or two rear-mounted Lewis guns. Up to 109kg (240lb) of bombs.
Britten Norman Islander/ Trislander/ Defender (GB)	BN-2A Islander	Two Lycoming O-540-E4C5 piston engines (each 260hp), or IO-540-K1B5s (each 300hp)	14.94m 49ft 0in	10.86m 35ft 7¾in	2993kg 6600lb	273–290 km/h 170–180 mph	1400km 870 miles	Crew of one plus up to nine passengers, or freight.
CANT Z.1007bis Alcione (Italy)	—	Three Piaggio P.IX RC.40 piston engines (each 1000hp)	24.80m 81ft 4in	18.47m 60ft 8¼in	13621kg 30030lb	456km/h 283mph	over 2000km 1243 miles	Crew of five. Two 12.7mm Scotti or Breda and two 7.7mm SAFAT machine-guns, plus up to 2000kg (4409lb) of bombs or two 454kg (1000lb) torpedoes.
Caproni 1914–18 bombers (Italy)	Ca46	Three Fiat A.12*bis* piston engines (each 300hp), or similar engines	23.39m 76ft 9in	12.61m 41ft 4½in	5302kg 11690lb	153km/h 95mph	Endurance 4 hours	Two Revelli machine-gun positions on nose and aft of wings, plus 540kg (1190lb) of bombs.
Caproni Ca 101 (Italy)	—	Three Alfa Romeo D.2 piston engines (each 235hp)	19.68m 64ft 6¾in	14.38m 47ft 2in	4100kg 9020lb	208km/h 129mph	2000km 1243 miles	Crew of four. Three machine-guns in dorsal and ventral positions, plus freight, stretchers or four light bombs.
Cessna Model 172 (USA)	Sky-hawk land-plane	One Lycoming O-320-E2D piston engine (150hp)	10.92m 35ft 10in	8.20m 26ft 11in	1043kg 2300lb	232km/h 144mph	1185km 737 miles	Pilot and three passengers, plus optional family seat or baggage.
Cierva Autogiros (Spain)	C-6A	One Clerget rotary piston engine (130hp)	Rotor diam. 10.97m 36ft 0in	10.46m 34ft 4in	676kg 1490lb	—	—	Crew of one.
Cody's British Army Aeroplane No 1 (GB)	—	One Antoinette piston engine (50hp)	15.85m 52ft 0in	about 13.41m 44ft 0in	1152kg 2540lb	64km/h 40mph	—	Pilot and one passenger.
Consolidated B-24 Liberator (USA)	B-24J	Four Pratt and Whitney R-1830-65 Twin Wasp radials (each 1200hp)	33.53m 110ft 0in	20.47m 67ft 2in	25400kg 56000lb	483km/h 300mph	3380km 2100 miles	Crew of twelve. Ten 0.50in machine-guns, plus up to 5800kg (12800lb) of bombs.

Name (Country of Origin)	Version	Engine/s	Wing Span	Length	Maximum Weight	Maximum Speed	Range	Accommodation/ Armament
Consolidated PBY Catalina (USA)	PBY-5A	Two Pratt and Whitney R-1830-92 Twin Wasp radials (each 1200hp)	31.70m 104ft 0in	19.46m 63ft 10in	15410kg 33970lb	288km/h 179mph	4989km 3100 miles	Crew of eight. Five 0.30in. machine-guns, plus about 2030kg (4480lb) of bombs or torpedoes.
Convair B-58 Hustler (USA)	B-58A	Four Pratt and Whitney J79 turbojets	17.32m 56ft 10in	29.49m 96ft 9in	72575kg 160000lb	over Mach 2	3862km 2400 miles	Crew of three. One 20mm Vulcan cannon in tail, plus a nuclear bomb.
Convair F-106 Delta Dart (USA)	F-106A	One Pratt and Whitney J75-P-17 turbojet (11125kg; 24500lb st with afterburning)	11.67m 38ft 3½in	21.56m 70ft 8¾in	15875kg 35000lb	Mach 2.3	1850km 1150 miles	Crew of one. One M-61 20mm cannon in some aircraft, plus four Super Falcon air-to-air missiles and one Genie or Super Genie rocket.
Cornu helicopter (France)	—	One Antoinette piston engine (24hp)	Rotor diam. (each) 5.99m 19ft 8in	—	260kg 573lb	—	—	Crew of one.
Curtiss F9C Sparrowhawk (USA)	—	One Wright R-975-22 Whirlwind radial (420hp)	7.77m 25ft 6in	6.12m 20ft 1in	1310kg 2888lb	285km/h 177mph	590km 366 miles	Crew of one. Two forward-firing machine-guns.
Curtiss JN Jenny (USA)	JN-4D	One Curtiss OX-5 piston engine (90hp)	13.30m 43ft 7½in	8.33m 27ft 4in	966kg 2130lb	121km/h 75mph	Endurance 2¼ hours	Crew of two.
Curtiss P-40 Warhawk (USA)	P-40N	One Allison V-1710-99 piston engine (1200hp)	11.38m 37ft 4in	10.16m 33ft 4in	3787kg 8350lb	563km/h 350mph	over 1207km 750 miles	Crew of one. Six 0.50in Browning machine-guns, plus optional 680kg (1500lb) of bombs.
Curtiss pusher biplane (USA)	—	One Curtiss four-cylinder engine (30hp)	8.00m 26ft 3in	10.21m 33ft 6in	226kg 500lb	72.5km/h 45mph	—	Crew of one.
Dassault Mirage III (France)	III-E	One SNECMA Atar 9C turbojet (6200kg; 13670lb st with afterburning)	8.22m 26ft 11½in	15.03m 49ft 3½in	13500kg 29760lb	Mach 2.2	1200km 745 miles	Crew of one. Two 30mm DEFA cannon, plus one Matra R-530 and two Sidewinder air-to-air missiles, bombs, air-to-surface missiles or rockets.
Dassault Mirage IV-A (France)	—	Two SNECMA Atar 09K turbojets (each 6985kg; 15400lb st)	11.85m 38ft 10½in	23.50m 77ft 1in	33475kg 73800lb	Mach 2.2	Combat radius 1240km 770 miles	Crew of two. Nuclear bomb or sixteen 454kg (1000lb) conventional bombs, or Martel air-to-surface missiles.
De Havilland Comet (GB)	Comet 4	Four Rolls-Royce Avon 525 turbojets (each 4760kg; 10500lb st)	32.87m 107ft 10in	35.97m 118ft 0in	71665kg 158000lb	846km/h 526mph	over 5000km 3100 miles	Crew of four, plus up to 101 passengers.
De Havilland D.H.2 (GB)	Early D.H.2s	One Gnome Monosoupape rotary (100hp)	8.61m 28ft 3in	7.68m 25ft 2½in	654kg 1441lb	150km/h 93mph	Endurance 2¾ hours	Crew of one. One forward-firing Lewis machine-gun.

Name (Country of Origin)	Version	Engine/s	Wing Span	Length	Maximum Weight	Maximum Speed	Range	Accommodation/ Armament
De Havilland D.H.4 (GB)	—	One Rolls-Royce Eagle VIII piston engine (375hp)	12.90m 42ft 4½in	9.19m 30ft 2in	1575kg 3472lb	230km/h 143mph	700km 435 miles	Crew of two. Forward-firing Vickers and rear-mounted Lewis machine-guns, plus up to 208kg (460lb) of bombs, etc.
De Havilland D.H.9A (GB)	—	One Liberty 12 piston engine (400hp)	14.00m 45ft 11in	9.22m 30ft 3in	2107kg 4645lb	198km/h 123mph	1000km 621 miles	Crew of two. One forward-firing Vickers and one or two rear-mounted Lewis machine-guns, plus up to 300kg (660lb) of bombs.
De Havilland Mosquito (GB)	NF Mk XIX	Two Rolls-Royce Merlin 25 piston engines (each 1635hp)	16.51m 54ft 2in	12.78m 41ft 11in	8890kg 19600lb	608km/h 378mph	2945km 1830 miles	Crew of two. Four 20mm Hispano cannon.
De Havilland Moth (GB)	Cirrus Moth	One Cirrus piston engine (60hp)	8.84m 29ft 0in	7.17m 23ft 6in	567kg 1250lb	145km/h 90mph	—	Two seats.
De Havilland Vampire (GB)	FB Mk 9	One de Havilland Goblin DGn3 turbojet (1520kg; 3350lb st)	11.58m 38ft 0in	9.37m 30ft 9in	5620kg 12390lb	882km/h 548mph	1963km 1220 miles	Crew of one. Four 20mm cannon.
De Havilland Canada DHC-2 Beaver (Canada)	Turbo-Beaver	One Pratt and Whitney Aircraft of Canada PT6A turboprop (578ehp)	14.63m 48ft 0in	10.74m 35ft 3in	2436kg 5370lb	Cruising 253km/h 157mph	over 1086km 675 miles	Pilot and ten passengers or freight.
De Havilland Canada Twin Otter and Otter (Canada)	Twin Otter	Two Pratt and Whitney Aircraft of Canada PT6A-27 turboprops (each 652ehp)	19.81m 65ft 0in	15.77m 51ft 9in	5670kg 12500lb	Max. cruising 338km/h 210mph	1277km 794 miles	Crew of one or two, plus up to 20 passengers or freight.
Dewoitine D 520 (France)	D 520S	One Hispano-Suiza 12Y-45 piston engine (910hp)	10.20m 33ft 5½in	8.75m 28ft 8½in	2780kg 6129lb	550km/h 342mph	1247km 775 miles	Crew of one. Four 7.5mm machine-guns plus one 20mm cannon.
Dornier Do 17 (Germany)	Do 17Z	Two Bramo 323P radials (each 1000hp)	18.00m 59ft 1in	15.85m 52ft 0in	8541kg 18830lb	423km/h 263mph	2993km 1860 miles	Crew of up to five. Six machine-guns, plus up to 1000kg (2200lb) of bombs.
Dornier Do 24 (Germany)	—	Three Bramo 323R radials (each 1000hp)	27.00m 88ft 7in	22.00m 72ft 2in	18400kg 40560lb	306–340km/h 190–211mph	4747km 2950 miles	Crew of five. Two machine-guns and one 20mm cannon, plus 600kg (1320lb) of bombs, etc.
Dornier Do X (Germany)	—	Twelve Curtiss Conqueror piston engines (each 600hp)	48.00m 157ft 5in	40.05m 131ft 4in	56000kg 123458lb	216km/h 134mph	—	Crew of ten, plus 150 passengers.
Douglas DC-1/2/3 (USA)	DC-3	Two Pratt and Whitney R-1830-90 piston engines (each 1200hp)	28.96m 95ft 0in	19.63m 64ft 5in	12700kg 28000lb	Cruising 312km/h 194mph	2430km 1510 miles	Crew of three, plus 36 passengers or freight.

Tables of Technical Data

Name (Country of Origin)	Version	Engine/s	Wing Span	Length	Maximum Weight	Maximum Speed	Range	Accommodation/Armament
Douglas Dauntless (USA)	SBD-5	One Wright R-1820–60 Cyclone radial (1200hp)	12.64m 41ft 6in	10.06m 33ft 0in	4241kg 9350lb	406km/h 252mph	1794km 1115 miles	Crew of two. Four machine-guns, plus up to 454kg (1000lb) of bombs, depth charges, rocket projectiles, etc.
Douglas World Cruiser (USA)	—	One Liberty piston engine (420hp)	15.24m 50ft 0in	10.82m 35ft 6in	up to 3710kg 8180lb	166km/h 103mph	3540km 2200 miles	Crew of two.
English Electric Canberra (GB)	B 6	Two Rolls-Royce Avon 109 turbojets (each 3360kg; 7400lb st)	19.51m 63ft 11½in	19.96m 65ft 6in	24950kg 55000lb	933km/h 580mph	6100km 3790 miles	Crew of three. 2721kg (6000lb) of bombs internally, plus 907kg (2000lb) of weapons under wings on some aircraft, including bombs, missiles or rockets.
English Electric Lightning (GB)	F Mk6	Two Rolls-Royce Avon 301 turbojets (each 7420kg; 16360lb st with afterburning)	10.61m 34ft 10in	16.84m 55ft 3in	22680kg 50000lb	over Mach 2	—	Crew of one. Two Firestreak or Red Top air-to-air missiles and optional twin 30mm Aden gun pack. Two packs of 24 air-to-air rockets optional instead of missiles.
Fairchild A-10A (now named Thunderbolt II) (USA)	—	Two General Electric TF34-GE-100 turbofans (each 4112kg; 9065lb st)	17.53m 57ft 6in	16.26m 53ft 4in	21148kg 46625lb	729km/h 453mph	1000km 620 miles	Crew of one. One GAU-8/A 30mm multi-barrel cannon, plus up to 7257kg (16000lb) of bombs, dispenser weapons, Maverick missiles, gun pods, etc.
Fairey IIID (GB)	—	One Napier Lion piston engine (450hp)	14.06m 46ft 1¼in	10.97m 36ft 0in	2290kg 5050lb	193km/h 120mph	764km 475 miles	Crew of three. One forward-firing Vickers machine-gun and one rear-mounted Lewis machine-gun.
Fairey Battle (GB)	—	One Rolls-Royce Merlin piston engine (1030hp)	16.46m 54ft 0in	15.90m 52ft 2in	4895kg 10790lb	388km/h 241mph	1690km 1050 miles	Crew of three. One forward-firing and one rear-mounted gun, plus up to 454kg (1000lb) of bombs.
Fairey Flycatcher (GB)	—	One Armstrong Siddeley Jaguar IV piston engine (400hp)	8.84m 29ft 0in	7.01m 23ft 0in	1329kg 2930lb	216km/h 134mph	499km 310 miles	Crew of one. Two forward-firing Vickers machine-guns, plus optional small bombs.
Fairey Fox (GB)	Fox Mk I	One Curtiss D.12 piston engine (480hp)	11.58m 38ft 0in	9.50m 31ft 2in	1867kg 4117lb	251km/h 156mph	805km 500 miles	Crew of two. One forward-firing Vickers machine-gun and one rear-mounted Lewis machine-gun, plus up to 209kg (460lb) of bombs.
Fairey Rotodyne (GB)	Rotodyne Y	Two Napier Eland N.E.L.3 turboprops (each 3000ehp), plus tipjets	Rotor diam. 27.43m 90ft 0in	17.83m 58ft 8in	14968kg 33000lb	298km/h 185mph	up to 724km 450 miles	Crew of two, plus up to 40 passengers.

Name (Country of Origin)	Version	Engine/s	Wing Span	Length	Maximum Weight	Maximum Speed	Range	Accommodation/ Armament
Fairey Swordfish (GB)	Mk I	One Bristol Pegasus III M3 radial (690hp)	13.87m 45ft 6in	10.87m 35ft 8in	3406kg 7510lb	222km/h 138mph	877km 545 miles	Crew of two or three. Two 0.303in. machine-guns, plus one 727kg (1610lb) torpedo, one mine or bombs. Mk II version could carry eight 27kg (60lb) rocket projectiles.
Farman Goliath (France)	F.60	Two Salmson CM.9 radials (each 260hp)	26.50m 86ft 10in	14.33m 47ft 0in	4770kg 10515lb	Cruising 120km/h 75mph	400km 248 miles	Crew of two, plus 12 to 25 passengers.
Felixstowe F.2A (GB)	—	Two Rolls-Royce Eagle piston engines (each 345hp)	29.13m 95ft 7½in	14.09m 46ft 3in	4535kg 10980lb	153km/h 95mph	Endurance 6 hours	Four to seven Lewis machine-guns, plus two 103kg (230lb) bombs.
Fiat C.R.42 Falco (Italy)	—	One Fiat A.74 RC38 radial (840hp)	9.70m 31ft 9¾in	8.27m 27ft 1½in	2290kg 5049lb	430km/h 267mph	772km 480 miles	Crew of one. Two 12.7mm Breda-SAFAT machine-guns, plus optional two 99kg (220lb) bombs.
Fieseler Fi 103 (V1) (Germany)	—	One Argus As 014 pulse jet engine (330kg; 728lb st)	5.30m 17ft 4½in	7.90m 25ft 11in	2180kg 4806lb	656km/h 408mph	330km 205 miles	No crew, except in specially adapted piloted version. Warhead of 850kg (1874lb).
Fieseler Fi 156 Storch (Germany)	C-3	One Argus As 10C piston engine (240hp)	14.25m 46ft 9in	9.91m 32ft 6in	1320kg 2910lb	175km/h 109mph	380km 236 miles	Crew of two. One 7.9mm MG 15 machine-gun.
Focke-Wulf Fw 190 (Germany)	Fw 190-A8	One BMW 801D-2 radial (2100hp)	10.50m 34ft 5½in	8.84m 29ft 0in	4422kg 9750lb	656km/h 408mph	805km 500 miles	Crew of one. Four 20mm cannon and two 13mm machine-guns.
Focke-Wulf Fw 200 Condor (Germany)	Fw 200C	Four Bramo 323R-2 radials (each 1200hp)	33.00m 108ft 3in	23.85m 78ft 3in	22680kg 50000lb	386km/h 240mph	6357km 3950 miles	Crew of six to eight. Five machine-guns and one cannon, plus up to 2095kg (4620lb) of bombs.
Fokker D.VII (Germany)		One BMW IIIa piston engine (185hp) or Mercedes D.III (160hp)	8.90m 29ft 2¼in	6.95m 22ft 9¾in	904kg 1993lb	200km/h 124mph	Endurance 1½ hours	Crew of one. Two forward-firing Spandau machine-guns.
Fokker Dr.1 Triplane (Germany)	—	One Oberursel or Thulin-produced French Le Rhône piston engine (110hp)	7.20m 23ft 7½in	5.77m 18ft 11in	585kg 1290lb	166km/h 103mph	Endurance 1½ hours	Crew of one. Two forward-firing Spandau machine-guns.
Fokker Eindecker (Germany)	E.III	One Oberursel U.I rotary (100hp)	9.52m 31ft 3in	7.30m 23ft 11¼in	635kg 1400lb	141km/h 87mph	—	Crew of one. One 7.9mm Spandau (LMG. 08 Maxim) forward-firing machine-gun.
Fokker F.VII (The Netherlands)	F.VIIA/ 3m	Three Wright Whirlwind radials (each 220hp)	19.30m 63ft 4in	14.60m 47ft 10¾in	4000kg 8818lb	190km/h 118mph	—	Crew of two, plus up to ten passengers or freight.
Fokker F.27 Friendship (The Netherlands)	Mk 400	Two Rolls-Royce Dart Mk 532-7R turboprops (each 2140shp)	29.00m 95ft 2in	23.56m 77ft 3½in	20410kg 45000lb	Cruising 480km/h 298mph	about 1935km 1203 miles	Crew of two or three, plus up to 40 passengers and freight.

Tables of Technical Data

Name (Country of Origin)	Version	Engine/s	Wing Span	Length	Maximum Weight	Maximum Speed	Range	Accommodation/ Armament
Ford Trimotor (USA)	4-AT-E	Three Wright J6 Whirlwind radials (each 300hp)	22.56m 74ft 0in	15.19m 49ft 10in	4595kg 10130lb	209km/h 130mph	1835km 1140 miles	Crew of two; four carried on Antarctic flight.
General Dynamics F-16 (and McDonnell Douglas F-18) (USA)	F-16	One Pratt and Whitney F100-PW-100(3) turbofan (about 11340kg; 25000lb st with afterburning)	9.45m 31ft 0in	14.52m 47ft 7½in	14968kg 33000lb	over Mach 2	Combat radius 925km 575 miles	Crew of one. One M-61A-1 20mm cannon, plus two or more AIM-9J/L Sidewinder missiles and up to 6895kg (15200lb) of stores on six underwing and one underfuselage point.
General Dynamics F-111 and FB-111 (USA)	F-111F	Two Pratt and Whitney TF30-P-100 turbofans (each 11385kg; 25100lb st with afterburning)	Swept 9.74m 31ft 11½in	22.40m 73ft 6in	45359kg 100000lb	Mach 2.5	over 4707km 2925 miles	Crew of two side by side. One 20mm M-61 cannon, plus two B43 bombs in bay and six underwing points for missiles, napalm, bombs, etc. FB-111A can carry 6 SRAM attack missiles or 14288kg (31500lb) of conventional bombs.
Gloster E.28/39 (GB)	—	One Power Jets W.1 turbojet (390kg; 860lb st)	8.84m 29ft 0in	7.72m 25ft 3¾in	1678kg 3700lb	544km/h 338mph	—	Crew of one.
Gloster Gladiator (GB)	Mk I	One Bristol Mercury IX radial (840hp)	9.83m 32ft 3in	8.35m 27ft 5in	2155kg 4750lb	407km/h 253mph	660km 410 miles	Crew of one. Four 0.303in. Browning machine-guns.
Gloster Meteor (GB)	Mk III	Two Rolls-Royce Derwent 1 turbojets (each 907kg; 2000lb st)	13.11m 43ft 0in	12.57m 41ft 3in	3996kg 8810lb	793km/h 493mph	2156km 1340 miles	Crew of one. Four 20mm Hispano cannon.
Gotha G series (Germany)	G.V	Two Mercedes D.IVa piston engines (each 260hp)	23.72m 77ft 10in	12.37m 40ft 7in	3900kg 8600lb	114km/h 71mph	491km 305 miles	Two Parabellum machine-guns, plus up to 499kg (1100lb) of bombs.
Grumman A-6 Intruder (USA)	A-6E	Two Pratt and Whitney J52-P-8A turbojets (each 4218kg; 9300lb st)	16.15m 53ft 0in	16.64m 54ft 7in	27397kg 60400lb	1035km/h 643mph	3096km 1924 miles	Crew of two. Thirty 227kg (500lb) bombs, or three 907kg (2000lb) bombs and two drop-tanks, or other stores.
Grumman E-2 Hawkeye (USA)	—	Two Allison T56-A-422/425 turboprops (each 4591shp)	24.56m 80ft 7in	17.55m 57ft 7in	23391kg 51570lb	602km/h 374mph	up to 2583km 1605 miles	Crew of five. Early warning radar carried above fuselage.
Grumman F4F Wildcat (USA)	F4F-3	One Pratt and Whitney R-1830-76 Twin Wasp radial (1200hp)	11.58m 38ft 0in	8.79m 28ft 10in	3175kg 7000lb	528km/h 328mph	1850km 1150 miles	Crew of one. Four 0.50in machine-guns, plus optional two 45kg (100lb) bombs.
Grumman F-14A Tomcat (USA)	F-14A	Two Pratt and Whitney TF30-P-412A turbofans (each 9480kg; 20900lb st with afterburning)	Swept 11.65m 38ft 2½in	18.89m 61ft 11¾in	33724kg 74348lb	Mach 2.34	—	Crew of two. One 20mm M61A-1 Vulcan gun, plus up to 6577kg (14500lb) of Phoenix, Sidewinder or Sparrow missiles, bombs, etc.

Name (Country of Origin)	Version	Engine/s	Wing Span	Length	Maximum Weight	Maximum Speed	Range	Accommodation/ Armament
Grumman FF-1 (USA)	—	One Wright R-1820-78 piston engine (750hp)	10.51m 34ft 6in	7.47m 24ft 6in	2177kg 4800lb	347km/h 216mph	1046km 650 miles	Crew of two. One or two forward-firing and two rear-mounted Browning machine-guns.
Grumman TBF Avenger (USA)	TBF-1	One Wright R-2600-8 Double Cyclone radial (1850hp)	16.51m 54ft 2in	12.19m 40ft 0in	7212kg 15900lb	436km/h 271mph	about 1931km 1200 miles	Crew of three. Five machine-guns, plus up to 907kg (2000lb) of weapons including a torpedo, bombs, mines, etc.
Handley Page H.P.42 (GB)	—	Four Bristol Jupiter XFBM or XIF radials (each 550hp)	39.62m 130ft 0in	27.36m 89ft 9in	13380kg 29500lb	204km/h 127mph	193km 120 miles	Crew of three, plus 24 or 38 passenger seats (E and W versions respectively), mail and baggage.
Handley Page Halifax (GB)	Mk III	Four Bristol Hercules XVI radials (each 1615hp)	31.75m 104ft 2in	21.36m 70ft 1in	24675kg 54400lb	454km/h 282mph	1657km 1030 miles	Crew of seven. Nine 0.303in Browning machine-guns, plus 5896kg (13000lb) of bombs.
Handley Page Hampden (GB)	—	Two Bristol Pegasus XVIII radials (each 965hp)	21.08m 69ft 2in	16.33m 53ft 7in	8507kg 18755lb	410km/h 255mph	1931– 3202km 1200– 1990 miles	Crew of four. Four to six machine-guns, plus up to 1814kg (4000lb) of bombs.
Handley Page O/400 (GB)	—	Two Rolls-Royce Eagle VIII piston engines (each 360hp), or other similar engines	30.48m 100ft 0in	19.16m 62ft 10¼in	6060kg 13360lb	156km/h 97mph	Endur- ance 8 hours	Crew of four. Three to five Lewis machine-guns, plus up to 907kg (2000lb) of bombs.
Handley Page Victor (GB)	K Mk 2	Four Rolls-Royce Conway R. Co.17 Mk 201 turbojets (each 9345kg; 20600lb st)	36.58m 120ft 0in	35.03m 114ft 11in	77110kg 170000lb	Mach 0.92	7400km 4600 miles	Crew of five, plus fuel.
Hawker Fury (GB)	Fury I	One Rolls-Royce Kestrel IIS piston engine (525hp)	9.14m 30ft 0in	8.02m 26ft 3¾in	1520kg 3350lb	333km/h 207mph	—	Crew of one. Two forward-firing Vickers machine-guns.
Hawker Hart (GB)	—	One Rolls-Royce Kestrel IB piston engine (525hp)	11.35m 37ft 3in	8.79m 28ft 10in	2102kg 4635lb	296km/h 184mph	756km 470 miles	Crew of two. One forward-firing Vickers machine-gun and one rear-mounted Lewis machine-gun, plus up to 227kg (500lb) of bombs.
Hawker Hunter (GB)	FGA Mk 9	One Rolls-Royce Avon 207 turbojet (4540kg; 10000lb st)	10.26m 33ft 8in	13.98m 45ft 10½in	10885kg 24000lb	Mach 0.92	up to 2965km 1840 miles	Crew of one. Four 30mm cannon, plus up to two 454kg (1000lb) bombs or rockets.
Hawker Hurricane (GB)	Mk IIB	One Rolls-Royce Merlin XX piston engine (1280hp)	12.19m 40ft 0in	9.83m 32ft 3in	3742kg 8250lb	545km/h 339mph	756– 1480km 470–920 miles	Crew of one. Twelve 0.303in. Browning machine-guns, plus bombs or rocket projectiles. *See entry.*
Hawker Typhoon (GB)	Mk IB	One Napier Sabre IIA piston engine (2200hp)	12.67m 41ft 7in	9.73m 31ft 11in	6010kg 13250lb	671km/h 417mph	with auxiliary fuel 1577km 980 miles	Crew of one. Four 20mm Hispano cannon, plus up to 907kg (2000lb) of bombs or eight 3in rocket projectiles.

Tables of Technical Data

Name (Country of Origin)	Version	Engine/s	Wing Span	Length	Maximum Weight	Maximum Speed	Range	Accommodation/ Armament
Hawker Siddeley Buccaneer (GB)	S Mk 2A/B	Two Rolls-Royce RB.168-1A Spey Mk 101 turbofans (each 5035kg; 11100lb st)	13.41m 44ft 0in	19.33m 63ft 5in	28123kg 62000lb	Mach 0.85	3700km 2300 miles	Crew of two. Internally and externally carried nuclear or conventional bombs, Bullpup or Martel missiles or rocket packs, up to 7257kg (16000lb) weight.
Hawker Siddeley Harrier (GB)	GR Mk 3	One Rolls-Royce Bristol Pegasus Mk 103 vectored-thrust turbofan (9750kg; 21500lb st)	7.70m 25ft 3in	13.87m 45ft 6in	over 11340kg 25000lb	above 1186km/h 737mph	with one refuelling 5560km 3455 miles	Crew of one (two in training version). Underfuselage and underwing hardpoints for guns, missiles, bombs, rockets, etc., up to about 2270kg (5000lb) weight. *See entry.*
Hawker Siddeley Hawk (GB)	—	One Rolls-Royce/ Turboméca RT.172-06-11 Adour 151 turbojet (2420kg; 5340lb st)	9.39m 30ft 9¾in	11.17m 36ft 7¾in	7375kg 16260lb	955km/h 595mph	—	Two seats in tandem. One 30mm Aden gun, plus up to 2270kg (5000lb) of stores.
Hawker Siddeley Nimrod (GB)	MR Mk 1	Four Rolls-Royce 168-20 Spey Mk 250 turbofans (each 5506kg; 12140lb st)	35.00m 114ft 10in	38.63m 126ft 9in	87090kg 192000lb	926km/h 575mph	Typical endurance 12 hours	Normal crew of 12. Nine torpedoes, depth charges, mines, bombs, air-to-surface missiles, rockets, cannon pods etc.
Hawker Siddeley Trident (GB)	3B	Three Rolls-Royce RB.163-25 Mk 512-5W turbofans (each 5425kg; 11960lb st), plus one RB.162.86 turbojet (2380kg; 5250lb st) in tail	29.87m 98ft 0in	39.98m 131ft 2in	68040kg 150000lb	967km/h 601mph	3798km 2360 miles	Crew of three, plus 122 to 180 passengers.
Heinkel He 111 (Germany)	H-6	Two Junkers Jumo 211F-2 piston engines (each 1340hp)	22.59m 74ft 1½in	16.60m 54ft 5½in	11340kg 25000lb	415km/h 258mph	2800km 1740 miles	Crew of five. One 20mm cannon, six machine-guns, plus up to 2500kg (5510lb) of bombs.
Heinkel He 177 Greif (Germany)	—	Two Daimler-Benz DB610A coupled piston engines (each 2950hp)	31.45m 103ft 2in	21.95m 72ft 0in	31070kg 68500lb	475km/h 295mph	3556km 2260 miles	Crew of six. Two 20mm MG 151 cannon, four to six machine-guns, plus up to 6000kg (13220lb) of bombs.
Henschel Hs123 (Germany)	A-1	One BMW 132Dc radial (880hp)	Upper 10.50m 34ft 5¼in	8.33m 27ft 4in	normal 2217kg 4888lb	341km/h 212mph	859km 534 miles	Crew of one. Two 7.9mm MG 17 machine-guns, plus four 110lb bombs, 92 small anti-personnel bombs in each of two containers, or two 20mm cannon.
IAI Kfir (Lion Cub) (Israel)	Kfir-C2	One General Electric J79 (modified GE-17) turbojet (8120kg: 17900lb st with afterburning)	8.22m 26ft 11½in	15.55m 51ft 0¼in	14600kg 32188lb	over Mach 2.2	Combat radius 1300km 807 miles	Crew of one. Two 30mm DEFA cannon, plus underwing pylons for Rafael Shafrir air-to-air missiles. Ground attack version can carry air-to-surface missiles, bombs and rocket pods.

Name (Country of Origin)	Version	Engine/s	Wing Span	Length	Maximum Weight	Maximum Speed	Range	Accommodation/ Armament
Ilyushin Il-2 (USSR)	—	One Mikulin AM-38 piston engine (1300hp)	14.58m 47ft 10in	11.60m 38ft 1in	5556kg 12250lb	434km/h 270mph	—	Crew of one or two. Two 20mm cannon, two 7.62mm and one 12.7mm machine-guns, plus up to 400kg (881lb) of bombs or rocket projectiles.
Junkers F13 (Germany)	—	One BMW IIIa piston engine (185hp)	17.75m 58ft 3in	9.60m 31ft 6in	1730kg 3815lb	Cruising 140km/h 87mph	—	Crew of two, plus four passengers.
Junkers G38 (Germany)	—	Eventually four Junkers Jumo 204 diesel engines (each 750hp)	44.00m 144ft 4in	23.20m 76ft 1½in	24000kg 52910lb	208km/h 129mph	—	Crew of seven, plus 34 passengers.
Junkers Ju 52 (Germany)	Ju 52/3m	Three BMW 132A radials (each 575hp)	29.21m 95ft 10in	18.90m 62ft 0in	10977kg 24200lb	266km/h 165mph	1287km 800 miles	Crew of two or three, plus up to 18 passengers. One 13mm MG 131 and two 7.9mm MG 15 machine-guns, plus bombs (carried during latter 1930s).
Junkers Ju 87 (Germany)	Ju 87D-1	One Junkers Jumo 211J-1 piston engine (1400hp)	13.80m 45ft 3½in	11.50m 37ft 8¾in	6577kg 14500lb	410km/h 255mph	1000km 621 miles	Crew of two. Two 7.9mm MG 81 and two MG 17 machine-guns, plus up to 1796kg (3960lb) of bombs, or anti-tank cannon.
Junkers Ju 88 (Germany)	Ju 88A-4	Two Junkers Jumo 211J-1 piston engines (each 1400hp)	20.08m 65ft 10½in	14.36m 47ft 1¼in	12122kg 26725lb	471km/h 293mph	normal 2500km 1550 miles	Crew of four. Four to five machine-guns and 20mm cannon, plus up to 1796kg (3960lb) of bombs.
Kamov Ka-25 (USSR)	—	Two Glushenkov GTD-3 turboshaft engines (each 1400hp)	Rotor diam. 15.74m 51ft 8in	9.75m 32ft 0in	7300kg 16100lb	220km/h 137mph	650km 405 miles	Crew of two, plus 12 passengers, freight or anti-submarine weapons, including torpedoes and nuclear depth charges.
Leduc 0.10 (France)	—	One Athodyd or ramjet engine (6500kg; 14330lb st)	11.60m 38ft 1in	12.50m 41ft 0in	6000kg 13225lb	Mach 0.87	—	Crew of one.
Lockheed C-5A Galaxy (USA)	—	Four General Electric TF39-GE-1 turbofans (each 18600kg; 41000lb st)	67.88m 222ft 8½in	75.54m 247ft 10in	348810kg 769000lb	919km/h 571mph	10505km 6529 miles	Crew of five (with rest area for 15 other crew members), plus about 100228kg (220967lb) of freight.
Lockheed C-130 Hercules (USA)	C-130H	Four Allison T56-A-15 turboprops (each 4508ehp)	40.41m 132ft 7in	29.78m 97ft 9in	70310kg 155000lb	Cruising 621km/h 386mph	up to 8264km 5135 miles	Crew of four, plus up to 19872kg (43810lb) of freight.
Lockheed F-80 Shooting Star (USA)	T-33	One Allison J33-A-35 turbojet (2360kg; 5200lb st)	11.86m 38ft 10½in	11.44m 37ft 6in	7643kg 16850lb	nearly 965km/h 600mph	nearly 2180km 1355 miles	Crew of two. Six 0.50in. machine-guns, plus optional 454kg (1000lb) of bombs.

Tables of Technical Data

Name (Country of Origin)	Version	Engine/s	Wing Span	Length	Maximum Weight	Maximum Speed	Range	Accommodation/ Armament
Lockheed SR-71A (USA)	—	Two Pratt and Whitney JT11D-20B turbojets (each 14740kg; 32500lb st with afterburning)	16.95m 55ft 7in	32.74m 107ft 5in	77110kg 170000lb	3717km/h 2310mph	4800km 2980 miles	Crew of two.
Lockheed F-104 Starfighter (USA)	F-104S	One General Electric J79-GE-19 turbojet (8120kg; 17900lb st with afterburning)	6.68m 21ft 11in	16.69m 54ft 9in	14060kg 31000lb	Mach 2.2	Combat radius 1247km 775 miles	Crew of one. One 20mm M61 cannon, plus two Sparrow III missiles and up to four Sidewinder missiles, rocket packs or bombs.
Lockheed TriStar (and McDonnell Douglas DC-10) (USA)	L-1011-1 TriStar	Three Rolls-Royce RB.211-22B turbofans (each 19050kg; 42000lb st)	47.34m 155ft 4in	54.17m 177ft 8½in	195045kg 430000lb	Cruising 964km/h 599mph	5760km 3580 miles	Crew of thirteen (including service staff), plus 256 to 400 passengers.
Lockheed U-2 (USA)	—	One Pratt and Whitney J57C or J75-P-13 turbojet (4990kg; 11000lb st)	24.38m 80ft 0in	15.11m 49ft 7in	7832kg 17270lb	795km/h 494mph	4185km 2600 miles	Crew of one. No armament. Two-seat trainer in service.
Lockheed Vega (USA)	—	One Wright Whirlwind J-5 radial (220hp)	12.49m 41ft 0in	8.38m 27ft 6in	1370kg 3200lb	217km/h 135mph	890km 550 miles	Pilot and six passengers.
Martin Marietta X-24 (USA)	X-24B	One Thiokol XLR11 turbo-rocket engine (3625kg; 8000lb st)	Width 5.84m 19ft 2in	11.43m 37ft 6in	5895kg 13000lb	1863km/h 1158mph	—	Crew of one.
McDonnell XF-85 Goblin (USA)	—	One Westinghouse 24C turbojet (1361kg; 3000lb st)	6.47m 21ft 2¾in	4.53m 14ft 10½in	2193kg 4835lb	837km/h 520mph	—	Crew of one.
McDonnell Douglas A-4 Skyhawk (USA)	A-4M	One Pratt and Whitney J52-P-408 turbojet (5080kg; 11200lb st)	8.38m 27ft 6in	12.29m 40ft 4in	11113kg 24500lb	1040km/h 646mph	3225km 2000 miles	Crew of one. Two 20mm Mk 12 cannon, plus up to 4535kg (10000lb) of stores including Sidewinder and Bullpup missiles, torpedoes, nuclear or conventional bombs, rocket packs and gun pods, etc.
McDonnell Douglas DC-9 (USA)	Series 30	Two Pratt and Whitney JT8D-7 turbofans (each 6350kg; 14000lb st) or other P and W engines	28.47m 93ft 5in	36.37m 119ft 3½in	54884kg 121000lb	Cruising 909km/h 565mph	2775km 1725 miles	Crew of two, plus 105 to 115 passengers.
McDonnell Douglas F-4 Phantom II (USA)	F-4E	Two General Electric J79-GE-17A turbojets (each 8120kg; 17900lb st with afterburning)	11.77m 38ft 7in	19.20m 63ft 0in	24765kg 54600lb	over Mach 2	Combat radius 1266km 786 miles	Crew of two. Four Falcon, Sparrow, Shrike, Sidewinder or other missiles or up to 7250kg (16000lb) of bombs, etc.
McDonnell Douglas YC-15 (and Boeing YC-14) (USA)	YC-15 Second prototype	Four Pratt and Whitney JT8D-17 turbofans (each 7257kg; 16000lb st)	33.63m 110ft 4in	37.87m 124ft 3in	98284kg 216680lb	805km/h 500mph	Ferry 4818km 2994 miles	Crew of two, plus originally 150 troops or 28122kg (62000lb) freight.

Name (Country of Origin)	Version	Engine/s	Wing Span	Length	Maximum Weight	Maximum Speed	Range	Accommodation/ Armament
McDonnell Douglas F-15 Eagle (USA)	F-15A	Two Pratt and Whitney F100-PW-100 turbofans (each 11340kg; 25000lb st)	13.05m 42ft 9¾in	19.43m 63ft 9in	25401kg 56000lb	over Mach 2.5	normal ferry 4631km 2878 miles	Crew of one. One 20mm M-61A-1 cannon, four AIM-9L Sidewinder missiles, four AIM-7F Sparrow missiles, or up to 7257kg (16000lb) of other stores and ECM equipment.
Messerschmitt Bf 109 (Germany)	Bf 109G	One Daimler-Benz DB 605D piston engine (1800hp)	9.97m 32ft 8½in	8.94m 29ft 4in	3493kg 7700lb	689km/h 428mph	563km 350 miles	Crew of one. One 30mm Mk 108 cannon and two 13mm MG 131 machine-guns.
Messerschmitt Bf 110 (Germany)	Bf 110G-4	Two Daimler-Benz DB 605B piston engines (each 1475hp)	16.28m 53ft 4¾in	12.67m 41ft 6¾in	9888kg 21800lb	550km/h 342mph	2100km 1305 miles	Crew of three. Two 30mm MK 108 and two MG 151 20mm cannon (or four MG 151 cannon) and two MG 81 7.9mm machine-guns.
Messerschmitt Me 163 Komet (Germany)	Me 163B	One Walter HWK 109 rocket motor (1700kg; 3750lb st)	9.32m 30ft 7in	5.69m 18ft 8in	4310kg 9500lb	959km/h 596mph	—	Crew of one. Two 30mm Mk 108 cannon.
Messerschmitt Me 262 (Germany)	Me 262A1	Two Junkers Jumo 004B turbojets (each 898kg; 1980lb st)	12.48m 40ft 11½in	10.60m 34ft 9½in	6395kg 14100lb	869km/h 540mph	1046km 650 miles	Crew of one. Four 30mm Mk 108 cannon.
Mikoyan MiG-15 (USSR)	MiG-15*bis*	One Klimov VK-1 turbojet (2700kg; 5950lb st). One RD-45 in other versions	10.08m 33ft 0¾in	10.10m 33ft 1¾in	5786kg 12755lb	1076km/h 668mph	1860km 1155 miles	Crew of one. One 37mm N-37 and two 23mm NR-23 forward-firing cannons, plus up to 1000kg (2205lb) of bombs, rockets, etc.
Mikoyan MiG-19/Shenyang F-6 (USSR/China)	F-6	Two Chinese-built Klimov R-9B turbojets (each 3250kg; 7165lb st with afterburning)	9.00m 29ft 6½in	14.90m 48ft 10½in	8700kg 19180lb	1452km/h 902mph	2200km 1365 miles	Crew of one. Two or three 30mm NR-30 guns (not installed in MiG-19PF), plus missiles, air-to-air rockets or bombs.
Mikoyan MiG-21 (USSR)	Fishbed-J	One Tumansky R-13-300 turbojet (6600kg; 14550lb st with afterburning)	7.15m 23ft 5½in	15.76m 51ft 8½in	9400kg 20725lb	Mach 2.1	1100km 683 miles	Crew of one. One 23mm GSh-23 gun, plus two 'Atoll' and two 'Advanced Atoll' missiles or rocket packs. Air-to-surface missiles, rockets and bombs for ground attack role.
Mikoyan MiG-23/27 (USSR)	Flogger-B	One turbojet (9300kg; 20500lb st with afterburning)	Swept 8.17m 26ft 9½in	16.80m 55ft 1½in	15000kg 33050lb	Mach 2.3	Combat radius 960km 600 miles	Crew of one. One 23mm GSh-23 gun, plus five attachment points for 'Apex' and 'Aphid' missiles, or other stores.
Mikoyan MiG-25 (USSR)	Foxbat-A	Two Tumansky R-266 turbojets (each 11000kg; 24250lb st)	13.95m 45ft 9in	22.30m 73ft 2in	36200kg 79800lb	Mach 2.8–3.2	Combat radius 1300km 805 miles	Crew of one. Four air-to-air missiles of the 'Acrid' type, or other stores.
Mil Mi-1/2/4 (USSR)	Mi-2	Two Isotov GTD-350 turboshafts (each 450shp)	Rotor diam. 14.50m 47ft 6¾in	11.40m 37ft 4¾in	3700kg 8158lb	210km/h 130mph	170km 105 miles	Nine or ten persons. *See entry*

Name (Country of Origin)	Version	Engine/s	Wing Span	Length	Maximum Weight	Maximum Speed	Range	Accommodation/ Armament
Mil Mi-6/10 (USSR)	Mi-6	Two Soloviev D-25V turboshafts (each 5500shp)	Rotor diam. 35.00m 114ft 10in	33.18m 108ft 10½in	42500kg 93700lb	300km/h 186mph	1050km 652 miles	Crew of five, plus 65 passengers or other cargoes. *See entry*
Mil Mi-12 (V-12) (USSR)	—	Four Soloviev D-25VF turboshafts (each 6500shp)	Rotor diam. 35.00m 114ft 10in. each	37.00m 121ft 4½in.	105000kg 231500lb	260km/h 161mph	500km 310 miles	Crew of seven, plus 50 passengers and 25–30000kg (55–66000lb) of freight.
Mil Mi-24 (USSR)	Hind-A	Two Isotov TV2-117A turboshafts (each 1500shp)	Rotor diam. 17.00m 55ft 9in.	17.00m 55ft 9in.	10000kg 22000lb	Probably about 322km/h 200mph	—	Crew of two, plus eight troops. One 12.7mm machine-gun, plus four 'Swatter' anti-tank missiles and rocket pods or other stores.
Mitsubishi A5M (Japan)	A5M4	One Nakajima Kotobuki 41 radial (785hp)	11.00m 36ft 1¼in.	7.57m 24ft 10in.	1671kg 3684lb	435km/h 270mph	1200km 746 miles	Crew of one. Two 7.7mm Type 89 machine-guns, plus two 30kg (66lb) bombs.
Mitsubishi A6M Zero Sen (Japan)	A6M5	One Nakajima Sakae 21 radial (1130hp)	11.00m 36ft 1¼in.	9.12m 29ft 11in.	2742kg 6047lb	565km/h 351mph	1922km 1194 miles	Crew of one. Two 7.7mm Type 97 machine-guns and two 20mm Type 99 cannon, plus optional 317kg (700lb) of bombs.
Mitsubishi G3M/G4M (Japan)	G4M2	Two Mitsubishi Kasei 21 radials (each 1800hp). Later models had Kasei 25 or 27 radials	24.89m 81ft 8in.	19.63m 64ft 4¾in.	12500kg 27558lb	438km/h 272mph	up to 6060km 3765 miles	Crew of seven. Two 20mm Type 99 cannon and three 7.7mm Type 92 machine-guns, plus up to 1000kg (2205lb) of bombs or a 800kg (1760lb) torpedo.
Mitsubishi Ki-46 (Japan)	Ki-46-II	Two Mitsubishi Ha 102 radials (each 1080hp)	14.70m 48ft 2¾in.	11.00m 36ft 1in.	5800kg 12787lb	604km/h 375mph	2474km 1537 miles	Crew of two. One 7.7mm Type 89 rear-firing gun. Ki-46-III Kai (Type 100) fighter variant had one 37mm and 20mm forward-firing cannon.
Mitsubishi T-2 (Japan)	T-2A	Two Rolls-Royce/ Turboméca Adour turbofans (each 3206kg; 7070lb st with afterburning)	7.88m 25ft 10¼in.	17.85m 58ft 6¾in.	clean 9805kg 21616lb	Mach 1.6	up to 2593km 1610m miles	Crew of two. One 20mm Vulcan JM-61 cannon, plus two air-to-air missiles, bombs or other stores.
Nakajima Ki-43 (Japan)	Ki-43-II	One Nakajima Ha 115 radial (1150hp)	10.84m 35ft 6¾in.	8.92m 29ft 3⅓in.	2925kg 6450lb	530km/h 329mph	1760km 1095m miles	Crew of one. Two 12.7mm Type 1 machine-guns, plus optional two 249kg (550lb) bombs.
Navy-Curtiss NC-4 (USA)	—	Four Liberty piston engines (each 400hp)	38.40m 126ft 0in.	20.85m 68ft 3½in.	12925kg 28500lb	146km/h 91mph	—	Crew of six.
North American B-25 Mitchell (USA)	B-25J	Two Wright R-2600-29 Cyclone radials (each 1850hp)	20.60m 67ft 7in.	16.13m 52ft 11in.	up to 15195kg 33500lb	442km/h 275mph	normal 2172km 1350 miles	Crew of six. Thirteen 0.50in. machine-guns, plus up to 1814kg (4000lb) of bombs.

Name (Country of Origin)	Version	Engine/s	Wing Span	Length	Maximum Weight	Maximum Speed	Range	Accommodation/ Armament
North American F-86 Sabre (USA)	F-86F	One General Electric J47-GE-27 turbojet (2708kg; 5970lb st)	11.91m 39ft 1in.	11.44m 37ft 6½in	9350kg 20610lb	1105km/h 687mph	1475km 920 miles	Crew of one. Six 0.50in. machine-guns, plus two Sidewinder missiles, eight rockets or two 454kg (1000lb) bombs.
North American P-51 Mustang (USA)	P-51D	One Packard-built Rolls-Royce Merlin V-1650-7 piston engine (1490hp)	11.28m 37ft 0in.	9.83m 32ft 3in.	5261kg 11600lb	703km/h 437mph	3347km 2080 miles	Crew of one. Four or six 0.50in. machine-guns, plus up to 907kg (2000lb) of bombs or rocket projectiles.
North American X-15 (USA)	X-15A-2	One Thiokol XLR99-RM.2 rocket motor (25855kg; 57000lb st)	6.70m 22ft 0in.	15.98m 52ft 5in.	23095kg 50914lb	Mach 6.72	—	Crew of one.
Northrop F-5 and Tiger II (USA)	F-5E	Two General Electric J85-GE-21A turbojets (each 2267kg; 5000lb st)	8.13m 26ft 8in.	14.68m 48ft 2in.	11192kg 24675lb	Mach 1.63	up to 2946km 1831 miles	Crew of one. Two 20mm M-39A2 cannon, plus two Sidewinder missiles and up to 3175kg (7000lb) of bombs, napalm and rocket packs, etc.
Panavia Tornado (West Germany/ Italy/GB)	—	Two Turbo Union RB.199-34R-2 turbofans (each 6577kg; 14500lb st with afterburning)	Swept 8.60m 28ft 2½in.	16.70m 54ft 9½in.	18145kg 40000lb	over Mach 2	—	Crew of two. Two 27mm IWKA-Mauser cannon, plus Sky Flash, Sidewinder, Sparrow and Aspide 1A air-to-air missiles, bombs, napalm, etc.
Piper Cub (USA)	PA-18 Super Cub 150	One Lycoming O-320 piston engine (150hp)	10.73m 35ft 2½in.	6.88m 22ft 7in.	794kg 1750lb	209km/h 130mph	735km 460 miles	Two persons, plus baggage.
Piper Pawnee (USA)	Pawnee-D	One Lycoming O-540-B2B5 piston engine (235hp)	11.02m 36ft 2in.	7.53m 24ft 8½in.	1315kg 2900lb	200km/h 124mph	434km 270 miles	Crew of one. Various items of spraying equipment.
Pitts Special (USA)	S-1S	One Lycoming IO-360-B4A piston engine (180hp) or other engines of 100–180hp	5.28m 17ft 4in.	4.72m 15ft 6in.	521kg 1150lb	285km/h 177mph	507km 315 miles	Crew of one.
Polikarpov I-15 (USSR)	I-15*bis*	One M-25V radial (750hp)	10.21m 33ft 6in.	6.32m 20ft 9in.	1737kg 3830lb	370km/h 230mph	about 805km 500 miles	Crew of one. Four forward-firing ShKAS machine-guns, plus optional bombs or rockets.
Polikarpov I-16 (USSR)	I-16-10	One M-25V radial (750hp). I-16-24 powered by one Shvetsov M-62 (1000hp) radial	9.00m 29ft 6½in.	6.07m 19ft 11in.	1716kg 3783lb	451km/h 280mph (I-16-24) 525km/h: 326mph)	about 805km 500 miles	Crew of one. Four forward-firing ShKAS machine-guns.
PZL P-7 and P-11 (Poland)	P-7	One Polish licence-built Bristol Jupiter VIIF radial (485hp)	10.30m 33ft 9½in.	7.16m 23ft 6in.	1382kg 3048lb	328km/h 204mph	700km 435 miles	Crew of one. Two 7.7mm forward-firing Vickers machine-guns.

Name (Country of Origin)	Version	Engine/s	Wing Span	Length	Maximum Weight	Maximum Speed	Range	Accommodation/ Armament
Republic P-47 Thunderbolt (USA)	P-47D	One Pratt and Whitney R-2800-59 Double Wasp radial (2535hp)	12.42m 40ft 9in.	11.00m 36ft 1in.	7938kg 17500lb	690km/h 429mph	normal 950km 590 miles	Crew of one. Six or eight 0.50in. machine-guns, plus up to 1134kg (2500lb) of bombs or rocket projectiles.
Rockwell International B-1 (USA)	—	Four General Electric YF101-GE-100 turbofans (each 13607kg; 30000lb st with afterburning)	Swept 23.84m 78ft 2½in.	45.78m 150ft 2½in.	179168kg 395000lb	over Mach 2	9815km 6100 miles	Crew of four. Originally intended to be armed with 24 SRAM nuclear attack missiles or up to 52160kg (115000lb) of bombs, ALCM or decoy missiles.
Royal Aircraft Factory B.E.2 (GB)	B.E.2c	One Royal Aircraft Factory 1a piston engine (90hp)	11.28m 37ft 0in.	8.31m 27ft 3in.	972kg 2142lb	116km/h 72mph	Endurance 3 hours	Crew of two. One forward-firing Vickers machine-gun and one Lewis machine-gun for observer.
Royal Aircraft Factory F.E.2b and d (GB)	F.E.2b	One Beardmore piston engine (160hp) or one 120hp engine	14.55m 47ft 9in	9.83m 32ft 3in	1377kg 3037lb	146km/h 91mph	399km 248 miles	Crew of two. Forward-firing and rear-mounted Lewis machine-guns, plus up to three 50kg (112lb) bombs.
Royal Aircraft Factory S.E.5/5a (GB)	S.E.5a (with 200hp Wolesley)	One Wolseley or Hispano-Suiza piston engine (200–240hp)	8.115m 26ft 7½in	6.38m 20ft 11in	902kg 1988lb	222km/h 138mph	547km 340 miles	Crew of one. One fixed Vickers and one Lewis machine-gun, latter movable on upper wing.
Ryan NYP Monoplane (USA)	NYP	One Wright J-5C Whirlwind radial (237hp)	14.02m 46ft 0in	8.43m 27ft 8in	2381kg 5250lb	200km/h 124mph	7483km 4650 miles	Crew of one.
Saab 37 Viggen (Sweden)	JA 37	One Volvo Flygmotor RM8B turbofan (12750kg; 28108lb st with afterburning)	10.60m 34ft 9¼in	16.40m 53ft 9¾in	17000kg 37478lb	Mach 2	Combat radius 1000km 620 miles	Crew of one. Three underfuselage and four underwing attachment points for various weapons. *See entry*
Santos-Dumont 14-*bis* (France/Brazil)	Rebuilt	One Antoinette piston engine (50hp)	11.20m 36ft 9in	9.70m 31ft 10in	300kg 661lb	40km/h 25mph	—	Crew of one.
Santos-Dumont Demoiselle (France/Brazil)	1909 model	One Darracq piston engine (30hp)	5.49m 18ft 0in	6.09m 20ft 0in	110kg 242lb	—		Crew of one.
Savoia-Marchetti S-55 (Italy)	S-55X	Two Isotta-Fraschini Asso piston engines (each 800hp)	24.36m 79ft 11in	16.51m 54ft 2in	normal 7700kg 16975lb	236km/h 147mph	3500km 2174 miles	Two pilots, plus gun crew, etc.
Savoia-Marchetti SM.79 Sparviero (Italy)	SM.79-II	Three Piaggio P.XI RC.40 radials (each 1000hp)	21.20m 69ft 6½in	16.20m 53ft 1¾in	11400kg 24912lb	435km/h 270mph	2000km 1243 miles	Crew of four. Three 12.7mm Breda-SAFAT and one 7.7mm machine-guns, plus up to 1250kg (2750lb) of bombs or two 450mm torpedoes.

Name (Country of Origin)	Version	Engine/s	Wing Span	Length	Maximum Weight	Maximum Speed	Range	Accommodation/ Armament
SEPECAT Jaguar (GB/France)	Jaguar S and A	Two Rolls-Royce/ Turboméca Adour Mk 102 turbofans (each 3313kg; 7305lb st with afterburning)	8.69m 28ft 6in	16.83m 55ft 2½in	15500kg 34000lb	Mach 1.5	Combat radius up to 1315km 818 miles	Crew of one (two in training versions). Two 30mm DEFA (A version) or Aden (S version) cannon, plus up to 4535kg (10000lb) of Martel anti-radar or Magic air-to-air missiles, AN52 tactical nuclear weapon (A version) or conventional bombs, rockets, napalm, etc.
Shin Meiwa PS-1 (Japan)	PS-1	Four Ishikawajima-built General Electric T64-IHI-10 turboprops (each 3060ehp), plus one T58-IHI-10 gas turbine (1400ehp) in upper fuselage	33.15m 108ft 9in	33.46m 109ft 9¼in	43000kg 94800lb	547km/h 340mph	normal 2168km 1347 miles	Crew of ten. Four homing torpedoes, four 149kg (330lb) anti-submarine bombs, six 5in. air-to-surface rockets, sonobuoys, etc.
Short C Class flying-boat (GB)	—	Four Bristol Pegasus radials (each 790hp)	34.77m 114ft 0in	26.84m 88ft 0in	18380kg 40500lb	322km/h 200mph	1245km 760 miles	Crew of three, plus 22 passengers and mail. Later, accommodation reduced to 17 passengers. Bunks provided for night flights.
Short Skyvan (GB)	Series 3	Two Garrett AiResearch TPE.331-201 turboprops (each 715shp)	19.79m 64ft 11in	12.21m 40ft 1in	5670kg 12500lb	Cruising 327km/h 203mph	1115km 694 miles	Crew of one or two, plus up to 19 passengers, 22 troops or 2086kg (4600lb) of freight.
Short Stirling (GB)	Mk I	Four Bristol Hercules XI radials (each 1590hp)	30.20m 99ft 1in	26.59m 87ft 3in	26943kg 59400lb	418km/h 260mph	950–3750km 590–2330 miles	Crew of seven or eight. Eight 0.303in. Browning machine-guns, plus up to 6350kg (14000lb) of bombs.
Short Sunderland (GB)	Mk V	Four Pratt and Whitney R-1830 Twin Wasp radials (each 1200hp)	34.39m 112ft 10in	26.00m 85ft 4in	27215kg 60000lb	343km/h 213mph	4796km 2980 miles	Crew of thirteen. Two 0.50in Vickers and eight or twelve 0.303in. Browning machine-guns, plus up to 907kg (2000lb) of bombs, depth charges, etc.
Sikorsky R-4 (USA)	R-4B	One Warner R-550-3 Super Scarab radial (200hp)	Rotor diam. 11.58m 38ft 0in	14.68m 48ft 2in	1150kg 2535lb	132km/h 82mph	210km 130 miles	Crew of two.
Sikorsky S-61 series (USA)	S-61N	Two General Electric CT58-140-2 turboshafts (each 1500shp)	Rotor diam. 18.90m 62ft 0in	22.20m 72ft 10in	9980kg 22000lb	235km/h 146mph	796km 495 miles	Crew of three, plus 28 passengers or freight. *See entry*
Sikorsky S-64 Skycrane (USA)	CH-54A	Two Pratt and Whitney T73-P-1 turboshafts (each 4500shp)	21.95m 72ft 0in	21.41m 70ft 3in	19050kg 42000lb	203km/h 126mph	370km 230 miles	Crew of three, plus over 9072kg (20000lb) payload.

Tables of Technical Data

Name (Country of Origin)	Version	Engine/s	Wing Span	Length	Maximum Weight	Maximum Speed	Range	Accommodation/ Armament
Sikorsky S-67 Blackhawk (USA)	Proto-type	Two General Electric T58-GE-5 turboshafts (each 1500shp)	Rotor diam. 18.90m 62ft 0in	19.74m 64ft 9in	10 002kg 22050lb	310km/h 193mph	Endur-ance 3 hours	Crew of two. Intended to have one TAT 140 gun turret for 20mm or 30mm cannon or 40mm grenade launcher, plus six TOW missiles, or eight rocket launchers.
Sikorsky VS-300 (USA)	early config-uration	One Lycoming piston engine (75hp)	Rotor diam. 9.14m 30ft 0in	8.48m 27ft 10in	585kg 1290lb	80km/h 50mph	120km 75 miles	Crew of one.
Sikorsky Le Grand/Ilya Mourometz (USSR)	Le Grand	Four Argus piston engines (each 100hp)	28.00m 91ft 11in	20.00m 65ft 8in	4080kg 9000lb	Cruising 88km/h 55mph	—	Crew of two, plus normal accommodation for four passengers.
Sopwith 1½-Strutter (GB)	—	One Clerget or Le Rhône rotary (110hp)	10.21m 33ft 6in	7.70m 25ft 3in	975kg 2150lb	171km/h 106mph	Endur-ance 4½ hours	Crew of one or two. One forward-firing Vickers and one rear-mounted Lewis machine-guns. 59–102kg (130–224lb) of bombs in bomber versions.
Sopwith Camel (GB)	130hp Clerget engine	One Clerget rotary (130hp), Le Rhône (110hp), Gnome Monosoupape (100hp), or Bentley B.R.1 (150hp)	8.53m 28ft 0in	5.72m 18ft 9in	659kg 1453lb	185km/h 115mph	Endur-ance 2½ hours	Crew of one. Two forward-firing Vickers machine-guns, plus optional four 11.3kg (25lb) bombs.
Sopwith Pup (GB)	Le Rhône	One Le Rhône rotary (80hp) or Gnome Monosoupape (100hp)	8.08m 26ft 6in	5.89m 19ft 3¾in	556kg 1225lb	179km/h 111mph	Endur-ance 3 hours	Crew of one. One Vickers or Lewis forward-firing machine-gun. Some could carry Le Prieur rockets.
SPAD XIII (France)	—	One Hispano-Suiza 8 Be piston engine (235hp)	8.20m 26ft 11in	8.74m 20ft 8in	820kg 1808lb	222km/h 138mph	Endur-ance 2 hours	Crew of one. Two Vickers forward-firing machine-guns.
Sukhoi Su-7 (USSR)	Su-7B	One Lyulka AL-7F-1 turbojet (10000kg; 22046lb st with afterburning)	8.93m 29ft 3½in	17.37m 57ft 0in	13500kg 29750lb	Mach 1.2–1.6	1450km 900 miles	Crew of one. Usually two 30mm NR-30 cannon, two 750kg (1653lb) and two 500kg (1102lb) bombs or rocket packs.
Supermarine Spitfire (GB)	Mk XIV	One Rolls-Royce Griffon 65 piston engine (2050hp)	11.23m 36ft 10in	9.96m 32ft 8in	3833kg 8450lb	721km/h 448mph	1368km 850 miles	Crew of one. Two 20mm cannon, four 0.303in machine-guns, plus optional 454kg (1000lb) of bombs.
Tupolev TB-3 (USSR)	1932 model	Four M-17F piston engines (each 730hp)	39.49m 129ft 7in	24.40m 80ft 0½in	17400kg 38360lb	200km/h 124mph	1350km 840 miles	Crew of six. Ten machine-guns, plus over 2200kg (4850lb) of bombs.
Tupolev Tu-16 (USSR)	—	Two Mikulin AM-3M turbojets (each 9500kg; 20950lb st)	33.50m 110ft 0in	36.50m 120ft 0in	normal 68000kg 150000lb	945km/h 587mph	6400km 3975 miles	Crew of seven. Seven 23mm cannon, plus 9000kg (19840lb) of bombs or air-to-surface missiles of the 'Kelt', 'Kipper' types.

Name (Country of Origin)	Version	Engine/s	Wing Span	Length	Maximum Weight	Maximum Speed	Range	Accommodation/ Armament
Tupolev Tu-22 (USSR)	Blinder-A	Two turbojets (each 12250kg; 27000lb st with afterburning)	27.70m 90ft 10in	40.53m 132ft 11½in	83900kg 185000lb	Mach 1.4	2250km 1400 miles	Crew of three. Free-fall bombs carried in weapons bay. Blinder-B carries 'Kitchen' air-to-surface missile. Radar-controlled tail-gun.
Tupolev Tu-26 (USSR)	Backfire-B	Probably two Kuznetsov NK-144 turbofans, uprated for military use from 20000kg (44090lb st)	Swept 26.21m 86ft 0in	40.23m 132ft 0in	approx. 122500kg 270000lb	Mach 2.25–2.5	approx. (standard) 5745km 3570 miles	Nuclear or conventional bombs, 'Kitchen' or AS-6 air-to-surface missiles, etc. May have one radar-controlled tail-gun.
Tupolev Tu-95 (USSR)	—	Four Kuznetsov NK-12MV turboprops (each 14795ehp)	48.50m 159ft 0in	47.50m 155ft 10in	154220kg 340000lb	805km/h 500mph	12550km 7800 miles	Up to six 23mm cannon, plus up to 11340kg (25000lb) of bombs or 'Kangaroo' air-to-surface long-range missile.
Tupolev Tu-104 (USSR)	Tu-104B	Two Mikulin AM-3M-500 turbojets (each 9700kg; 21385lb st)	34.54m 113ft 4in	40.06m 131ft 5in	76000kg 167550lb	Cruising 900km/h 560mph	2650km 1650 miles	Crew of three, plus 100 passengers.
Tupolev Tu-134 (USSR)	Tu-134A	Two Soloviev D-30 turbofans (each 6800kg;14990lb st)	29.01m 95ft 2in	37.05m 121ft 6½in	47000kg 103600lb	Cruising 885km/h 550mph	3500km 2175 miles	Crew of three, plus 80 passengers.
Tupolev Tu-144 (USSR)	—	Four Kuznetsov NK-144 turbofans (each 20000kg; 44090lb st with afterburning)	28.80m 94ft 6in	65.70m 215ft 6in	180000kg 396830lb	Cruising Mach 2.35	Designed up to 6500km 4030 miles	Crew of three or four, plus up to 140 passengers.
Vickers F.B.5 Gunbus (GB)	F.B.5	One Gnome Monosoupape rotary (100hp)	11.05m 36ft 6in	8.28m 27ft 2in	930kg 2050lb	113km/h 70mph	—	Crew of two. One forward-firing Lewis machine-gun.
Vickers Vernon, Victoria and Valentia (GB)	Victoria Mk V	Two Napier Lion X1 radials (each 570hp)	26.62m 87ft 4in	18.14m 59ft 6in	—	177km/h 110mph	1239km 770 miles	Crew of two, plus 22 troops, freight or bombs.
Vickers Vimy (GB)	Mk IV	Two Rolls-Royce Eagle VIII piston engines (each 360hp)	20.73m 68ft 0in	13.27m 43ft 6½in	5670kg 12500lb	166km/h 103mph	1344km 835 miles	Crew of three. Lewis machine-guns, plus up to 1123kg (2476lb) of bombs.
Vickers Virginia (GB)	Mk X	Two Napier Lion VB piston engines (each 580hp)	26.72m 87ft 8in	18.97m 62ft 3in	7983kg 17600lb	174km/h 108mph	1585km 985 miles	Crew of four. Three machine-guns, plus up to 1360kg (3000lb) of bombs.
Vickers Viscount (GB)	-700	Four Rolls-Royce Dart 504 turboprops (each 1400ehp)	28.65m 94ft 0in	24.74m 81ft 2in	26535kg 58500lb	Cruising 514km/h 321mph	—	Crew of three, plus up to 53 passengers or freight.
Vickers Wellington (GB)	Mk X	Two Bristol Hercules VI radials (each 1585hp)	26.26m 86ft 2in	19.69m 64ft 7in	14288kg 31500lb	410km/h 255mph	over 2132km 1325 miles	Crew of six. Six 0.303in. Browning machine-guns, plus 2722kg (6000lb) of bombs.
Voisin bomber (France)	Type X	One Renault RE 12 Fe piston engine (300hp)	17.93m 58ft 9¾in	10.35m 33ft 11½in	2200kg 4850lb	135km/h 84mph	499km 310 miles	Crew of two. One Hotchkiss gun, plus 300kg (661lb) of bombs.

Tables of Technical Data

Name (Country of Origin)	Version	Engine/s	Wing Span	Length	Maximum Weight	Maximum Speed	Range	Accommodation/ Armament
Vought A-7 Corsair II (USA)	A-7E	One Allison TF41-A-2 turbofan (6800kg; 15000lb st)	11.80m 38ft 9in	14.06m 46ft 1½in	19050kg 42000lb	1041km/h 647mph	5188km 3224 miles	Crew of one. One 20mm Vulcan cannon, plus up to 6805kg (15000lb) of missiles, bombs, rockets, guns, etc.
Vought F4U Corsair (USA)	—	One Pratt and Whitney R-2800-18W Double Wasp radial (2450hp)	12.47m 40ft 11in	10.26m 33ft 8in	5625kg 12400lb	718km/h 446mph	2510km 1560 miles	Crew of one. Six 0.50in. Browning machine-guns, plus up to 907kg (2000lb) of bombs or rocket projectiles.
Wallis autogyros (GB)	WA-116/Mc	One McCulloch 4318 piston engine (72hp)	Rotor diam. 6.20m 20ft 4in	3.38m 11ft 1in	250kg 550lb	185km/h 115mph	225km 140 miles	Crew of one. (World distance record by Wallis autogyro stands at over 874km; 543 miles.)
Westland Lysander (GB)	Mk IIIA	One Bristol Mercury 30 radial (870hp)	15.24m 50ft 0in	9.30m 30ft 6in	up to 4535kg 10000lb	341km/h 212mph	Endurance up to 8 hours	Crew of two. Two 0.303in Browning forward-firing and two rearward-firing machine-guns. Provision for six small bombs.
Westland Wapiti (GB)	Mk IIA	One Bristol Jupiter VIIIF radial (550hp)	14.15m 46ft 5in	9.91m 32ft 6in	2450kg 5400lb	225km/h 140mph	over 579km 360 miles	Crew of two. One forward-firing Vickers and one rear-mounted Lewis machine-gun, plus up to 227kg (500lb) of bombs.
Westland Wessex (GB)	HU Mk 5	One Rolls-Royce Gnome 112 and one Gnome 113 turboshafts (1550shp coupled)	17.07m 56ft 0in	14.74m 48ft 4½in	6120kg 13500lb	212km/h 132mph	770km 478 miles	Crew of one or two, plus 16 troops, seven stretchers or freight. Provision for armament, including AS-11 missiles.
Wright Flyer (USA)	—	One Wright piston engine (12hp)	12.29m 40ft 4in	6.43m 21ft 1in	340kg 750lb	48km/h 30mph	—	Crew of one, in prone position on lower wing.
Yakovlev Yak-9 (USSR)	Yak-9D	One VK-107 piston engine (1650hp)	10.00m 32ft 9¾in	8.55m 28ft 0in	3100kg 6835lb	578km/h 359mph	1419km 882 miles	Crew of one. Two 12.7mm forward-firing machine-guns and one cannon.
Yakovlev Yak-36 (USSR)	Forger-A	One turbojet engine (7710kg; 17000lb st) plus two lift-jets (each 2540kg; 5600lb)	7.00m 23ft 0in	15.00m 49ft 3in	10000kg 22050lb	1380km/h 860mph	—	Crew of one (two in trainer version). Four underwing pylons for rocket packs, gun pods, bombs, etc.
Yokosuka Ohka (Japan)	Mk 11	Three Type 4 Mk 1 Model 20 rocket motors (each 267kg; 588lb st)	5.00m 16ft 5in	6.00m 19ft 8½in	2140kg 4718lb	917km/h 570mph	about 88.5km 55 miles	Crew of one. 1200kg (2645lb) of high-explosive in nose.

Glossary

Aerofoil A specially-shaped structure which produces 'lift' when moving forward through the air (e.g. an aeroplane wing)

AI Airborne Interception radar (*see* de Havilland Mosquito)

Airplane A heavier-than-air aircraft which uses fixed or variable-geometry wings to provide 'lift'

Airship A navigable lighter-than-air aircraft, also known as a dirigible

Amphibian An aircraft that can be operated from land or water

ASW Anti-submarine warfare

Autogyro An aircraft which derives its 'lift' from unpowered, horizontally-rotating blades (aerofoils), driven round by their passage through the air (*see* Wallis autogyros)

AWACS Airborne Warning and Control System (*see* Boeing E-3A)

BAC British Aircraft Corporation

BAe British Aerospace

BEA British European Airways

Biplane An airplane with fixed upper and lower wings, normally superimposed

BOAC British Overseas Airways Corporation

CAAC Civil Aviation Administration of China

CAM (Catapult Aircraft Merchantman (*see* Hawker Hurricane)

Cantilever Projecting beam or structure which is supported at one end only, without external bracing struts or wires. (Cantilever wing, *see* Hawker Hurricane)

CASA Construcciones Aeronauticas SA

Chord The length of a straight line between the leading- and trailing-edges of a wing parallel with the fuselage axis

Drone A pilotless aircraft, controlled from the ground or from another aircraft. Also known as an RPV or remotely piloted vehicle

ECM Electronic countermeasures

ehp Equivalent horsepower

FAA Fleet Air Arm

FAI Fédération Aéronautique Internationale

Ferry range Longest range, within the bounds of safety, that an aircraft can fly without a payload

Flying-boat Airplane with a watertight hull or lower fuselage, which is used as the principal flotation surface in water

Helicopter An aircraft which derives 'lift' from powered horizontally-rotating blades (aerofoils)

Hardpoint Strengthened part of an aircraft enabling external weapons or equipment to be attached

IAI Israel Aircraft Industries

JASDF Japan Air Self-Defence Force

JATO Jet-assisted take-off (rocket-assisted)

JGSDF Japan Ground Self-Defence Force

JMSDF Japan Maritime Self-Defence Force

kg Kilograms (weight or thrust)

KLM Koninklijke Luchtvaart Maatschappij NV (Royal Dutch Airlines)

lb Pound (weight or thrust)

Mach Ratio of the speed of a body to the speed of sound

Monoplane Airplane with one set of wings

NACA National Advisory Committee for Aeronautics

NASA National Aeronautics and Space Administration

NATO North Atlantic Treaty Organisation

Parasite Used in the context of this Encyclopedia as an aircraft carried on/in/under a larger aircraft and launched while airborne (*see* McDonnell Goblin, Tupolev TB-3)

Pusher propeller A propeller mounted behind the engine (*see* de Havilland D.H.2)

Pylon A structure on which external loads are attached and carried by an aircraft

PZL Panstwove Zaklady Lotnicze

Radius (combat) Distance an aircraft can fly and return without intermediate landing

RAF Royal Air Force

RCAF Royal Canadian Air Force

RFC Royal Flying Corps

RNAS Royal Naval Air Service

RNZAF Royal New Zealand Air Force

SAS Scandinavian Airlines System

Seaplane An airplane which operates from water on floats

shp Shaft horsepower

st Static thrust

STOL Short take-off and landing

Subsonic Below the speed of sound

Supersonic Above the speed of sound

Tractor propeller Propeller mounted in front of the engine

Triplane A fixed wing airplane with three sets of wings, normally superimposed

Turbofan A gas-turbine engine in which air ducted from a large diameter cowled fan is mixed with the jet efflux

Turbojet A gas-turbine engine made up of a compressor, combustion chamber, turbine and nozzle, which produces jet efflux

Turboprop A gas-turbine engine in which the energy is mostly used to drive a propeller, via a reduction gearbox

Turboshaft A gas-turbine engine in which the energy is mostly used to drive a shaft, as on a helicopter

U-boat German submarine

USAF United States Air Force

USAAF United States Army Air Force

USMC United States Marine Corps

USN United States Navy

Variable-geometry wings 'Swing wings', spread for low-speed flying, landing and take-off, swept for high-speed flight

V/STOL Vertical/short take-off and landing

VTOL Vertical take-off and landing

Index

Numbers in italic refer to main text entries